Dangerous Democracy?

Dangerous Democracy?

The Battle over Ballot Initiatives in America

Edited by
Larry J. Sabato, Howard R. Ernst,
and Bruce A. Larson

ROWMAN & LITTLEFIELD PUBLISHERS, INC.
Lanham • Boulder • New York • Oxford

ROWMAN & LITTLEFIELD PUBLISHERS, INC.

Published in the United States of America
by Rowman & Littlefield Publishers, Inc.
4720 Boston Way, Lanham, Maryland 20706
www.rowmanlittlefield.com

12 Hid's Copse Road, Cumnor Hill, Oxford OX2 9JJ, England

British Library Cataloging in Publication Information Available

Library of Congress Cataloging-in-Publication Data

Dangerous democracy? : the battle over ballot initiatives in America / edited by
Larry J. Sabato, Howard R. Ernst, and Bruce A. Larson.
    p. cm.
    Includes bibliographical references and index.
    ISBN 0-7425-1041-7 (alk. paper)—ISBN 0-7425-1042-5 (pbk. : alk. paper)
    1. Referendum—United States. I. Sabato, Larry. II. Larson, Bruce A., 1960–
III. Ernst, Howard R., 1970–
JF494.D35   2001
328.273—dc21   00-066462

Printed in the United States of America

♾ ™ The paper used in this publication meets the minimum requirements of
American National Standard for Information Sciences—Permanence of Paper for
Printed Library Materials, ANSI/NISO Z39.48-1992.

Contents

Acknowledgments vii

Introduction ix
 Larry J. Sabato, Bruce A. Larson, and Howard R. Ernst

1 The Historical Role of Narrow-Material Interests in Initiative
 Politics 1
 Howard R. Ernst
 • Challenging Initiatives: More than Just Special-Interest
  Money, an Issue of Political Civility 26
  Sue Tupper
 • Initiative Politics: A Useful Blend of Vested Interests and
  Citizen Politics 30
  Douglas M. Guetzloe

2 The Populist Legacy: Initiatives and the Undermining of
 Representative Government 33
 Bruce E. Cain and Kenneth P. Miller
 • Time to Walk the Talk 62
  Mike Gravel
 • Dumber than Chimps? An Assessment of Direct
  Democracy Voters 66
  Arthur Lupia

3 Campaign Financing of Ballot Initiatives in the American
 States 71
 Daniel A. Smith
 • Regulations on the Ballot Initiative Process: Interfering
  with Political Liberty 90
  Paul Grant
 • The Initiative Process: Where People Count 94
  Paul Jacob

4 Political Consultants and the Initiative Industrial Complex   101
       Todd Donovan, Shaun Bowler, and David S. McCuan
       • The Initiative Campaign Business: A Consultant's
         Perspective   135
         Gale R. Kaufman
       • Observations of Initiative Elections   139
         Ron Faucheux

5 The Logic of Reform: Assessing Initiative Reform Strategies   143
       Elisabeth R. Gerber
       • Prospects of Reforming the Initiative Process   172
         M. Dane Waters
       • An Alligator in the Bathtub: Assessing Initiative Reform
         Proposals   175
         Peter Schrag

6 A Call for Change: Making the Best of Initiative Politics   179
       Larry J. Sabato, Howard R. Ernst, and Bruce A. Larson
       • Response to "A Call for Change"   190
         Kenneth Mulligan

Notes   195

Bibliography   203

Index   219

About the Contributors   229

Acknowledgments

The editors would like to thank our American government students, past and present, for serving as brave foot soldiers in our effort to bridge the gap between responsive and responsible government. We would also like to thank the professional and volunteer staff of the University of Virginia's Center for Governmental Studies for their commitment to this project. In particular, the leadership offered by the center's chief of staff, Alex Theodoridis, was central to the successful completion of this work. Moreover, the book benefited from the countless hours of organizational support offered by Melissa Northern, Ian R. Bolton, and Michael Greenwald. Tracey Ernst and Alice Carter also offered guidance and inspiration at various stages of the project. We would also like to thank the professional staff at Rowman & Littlefield, in particular, Brigitte Scott and Jennifer Knerr, for their editorial assistance. Lastly, this book would not have been possible without the generous support of four education associations—the National Education Association, the California Teachers Association, the Oregon Education Association, and the Washington Education Association. Perhaps no group is more intimately aware of the pitfalls and opportunities provided by direct democracy than the education community. We thank these groups for their support and their efforts to make the initiative process work for American education.

Introduction

Larry J. Sabato, Bruce A. Larson, and Howard R. Ernst

> Pure democracies have ever been spectacles of turbulence and conten-
> tion; have ever been found incompatible with personal security or the
> rights of property; and have in general been as short in their lives as
> they have been violent in their deaths.
>
> —James Madison, *Federalist 10*

The framers of the U.S. Constitution, it is fair to say, were not advocates
of direct democracy. In crafting the Constitution, the framers opted instead for a *representative* democracy—a democracy in which elected officials representing the interests of their constituents were to make laws.
The framers' preference in part reflected the nation's large size. They recognized that it would be physically impossible to bring large numbers of
people together to participate effectively in national governance. But the
framers also believed that citizen lawmaking would empower turbulent
and contentious majorities and trample the rights of political minorities.
Representative government, in contrast, would guard against these dangers. Elected officials would be responsive to constituents' interests but
remain insulated from the immediate and unrefined passions of popular
majorities. In the framers' view, representative—not direct—democracy
was the key to keeping the Republic.

Yet direct democracy is alive and well in the form of statewide ballot
initiatives. Twenty-four states presently allow individuals and groups to
propose laws on constitutional amendments for direct voter consideration, and election-day lawmaking is at an all-time high.[1] (Indeed, the Oregon ballot for 2000 included no fewer than twenty-five measures for voters to consider.) Many states, of course, also use some variant of the ballot
referendum—a process by which the state legislature submits a constitutional amendment or legislative measure to voters for approval.[2] But state

ballot referendums are a decidedly less pure form of direct democracy than are state ballot initiatives. Whereas ballot referendums begin with legislation crafted by the state legislature, ballot initiatives typically begin with proposals crafted by individuals or groups outside of the legislature. As the most direct of direct democracy institutions, ballot initiatives are the primary focus of this book.

Without question, ballot initiatives have had a profound influence on public policy. As a model of such influence, one need look no further than California's Proposition 13. Passed by California voters in 1978, Proposition 13 slashed local property taxes and restricted the ability of localities to impose future tax increases. By most accounts, the effect on California's fiscal policies and public sector was monumental.[3] In addition, Proposition 13's political impact reverberated across the United States, as state after state enacted tax and spending limitations based on the California model and national politicians began running (and winning) on the issue of tax relief.

Important as Proposition 13 and its progeny are, the policy effects of direct legislation have reached far beyond the realm of fiscal policy. In direct democracy states, ballot initiatives have brought about substantial policy changes in the areas of health care, gay marriage, euthanasia, immigration, land conservation, affirmative action, criminal sentencing, medical use of marijuana, and the legalization of gambling. Moreover, by ushering in legislative term limits and comprehensive campaign finance reform, ballot initiatives have fundamentally altered the political playing field in many states (Tolbert 1998). Finally, the ballot initiative process has had a substantial *indirect* influence on policymaking, as interest groups induce legislatures to respond favorably to group concerns by threatening to draft ballot measures for voter consideration (Gerber 1996).

Although the impact of state ballot initiatives on state public policy is beyond question, the propriety of passing laws in this manner has been fiercely debated. Proponents of the initiative process argue that ballot initiatives serve as an important tool of "last resort" when legislatures fail to act in the public interest. They also maintain that initiatives allow the popular will to be expressed directly without the "distortion" of representative politics or "special" interests. What's more, argue proponents, ballot initiatives encourage change, reduce citizen alienation, heighten voter awareness, and eliminate corruption endemic to the legislative process.

To counter these arguments, critics of the ballot initiative offer a litany of complaints about the conduct and propriety of the process. For example, many critics claim that political consultants and moneyed interests now exercise far too much influence in ballot campaigns, polluting a process originally intended to give citizens a greater voice in policymaking. Other critics claim that voters possess neither the knowledge nor the expertise to understand and evaluate the measures on which they are voting. Still other critics have blasted the ballot initiative process for producing poorly written laws and facilitating the passage of legislation that disregards minority rights. Finally, many critics of ballot initiatives lament the shrill, uncompromising, and manipulative discourse typically found in contemporary ballot initiative campaigns. Such discourse, they argue, is a poor substitute for the deliberation and compromise that accompany serious legislative debate.

Our goal in this book is to evaluate the ballot initiative process and recommend some sensible reforms. Our analysis is performed by both academics and practitioners, with academics writing the book's primary chapters, and journalists, academics, and campaign professionals contributing insightful responses. In our view, both the study and practice of politics benefit when academics and practitioners exchange ideas. It is our hope that these benefits are evident throughout this book.

THE CHAPTERS

An understanding of modern initiative politics must begin with an understanding of its foundations. Toward this end, Howard Ernst opens the book by outlining trends in American initiative politics. His chapter begins with an important observation about the persistent advancement of direct democracy in the United States: while many states have adopted the ballot initiative process, none have ever repealed it. Employing a useful typological scheme to categorize some sixteen hundred statewide initiatives considered between 1904 and 1995, Ernst provides a coherent overview of ballot initiative trends in the twentieth century. His analysis shows that while use of the ballot initiative has ebbed and flowed throughout the twentieth century, the types of interests using the process—as well as the passage rates within interest categories—have remained remarkably stable. Importantly, moreover, Ernst shows that narrow-material interests have always been—and continue to be—at an electoral disadvantage in initiative politics. By providing readers with a historical sketch of trends in direct democracy, Ernst's analysis sets the stage for an evaluation of contemporary ballot initiative politics in the United States.

In chapter 2, Bruce Cain and Kenneth Miller make an important distinction between Populist and Progressive conceptions of direct democracy and wage a broad assault on the former. Although turn-of-the-century Populists and Progressives share responsibility for introducing direct democracy mechanisms in the United States, argue the authors, these two movements had very different conceptions about the relationship that direct democracy would have with representative government. Whereas Progressives sought direct democracy mechanisms to *supplement* representative government, Populists wanted such mechanisms to *replace* representative government. Moreover, according to Cain and Miller, these competing impulses continue to inform the contemporary debate over direct democracy in the United States, with the Progressive conception of direct democracy favoring recall elections, referendums, and legislative constitutional amendments and the Populist conception favoring direct citizen initiatives. Yet the increasing numbers of Populist-inspired citizen initiatives found on state ballots of late suggest that the Populist conception of direct democracy is winning the day—a development that Cain and Miller find unfortunate. In their view, the initiative process relinquishes important benefits of the legislative process, including legislative fine-tuning, norms of fairness, safeguards against conflict of interest, and openness at the front end of the policy process. Worse yet, by sidestepping the traditional legislative process, the initiative process isolates the courts as the sole institutional check on the majority's will, increasing the likelihood of a dangerous public backlash against the judiciary.

In chapter 3, Daniel Smith argues that the so-called citizen initiative is—and always has been—polluted by the influence of big (mostly corporate) money. To be sure, research on the impact of interest-group spending in ballot campaigns has yielded inconsistent findings. But Smith points out that almost all studies support one important conclusion: that big spending by opponents significantly increases the likelihood that a ballot measure will go down to defeat. Moreover, he points out, although this conclusion has been used to illustrate the limits of interest-group money in the initiative process, it might just as easily be used to illustrate the power of group money. A group's interests are, after all, often just as well served by preserving the policy status quo as by changing it. Yet while big money's influence on ballot initiatives suggests a need for reform, the federal courts have erected what Smith sees as an unjustifiable roadblock. In an insightful discussion of ballot initiative campaign finance law, Smith makes the important point that the Supreme Court has unnecessarily applied different standards in reviewing state regulation of corporate campaign expenditures, depending on whether the regulations apply to candidate or ballot campaigns. Unfortunately, moreover, the Court has shown little inclination to reconcile these competing standards of review.

In chapter 4, Todd Donovan, Shaun Bowler, and David McCuan describe and respond to popular criticisms of the modern "initiative industrial complex." According to critics, the professionals who orchestrate ballot campaigns are mercenaries who care little about public policy, employ manipulative tactics to mislead voters, and generate business for themselves by pitching ballot measures to well-heeled interest groups who can bankroll them. While acknowledging the initiative industry's excesses, the authors suggest that many of these claims are overblown. For example, belying critics' claims about consultants' lack of policy principles, the authors' survey of initiative professionals shows that ideology plays a significant role in consultants' decisions about which ballot campaigns to sign on with. Similarly, in response to claims that voters are misled by disingenuous campaign ads, the authors point out that voters rely much more heavily on official ballot summaries and media coverage for information on ballot measures than they do on consultant-crafted campaign advertisements. Finally, Donovan, Bowler, and McCuan are particularly skeptical of the claim that profit-motivated consultants have enriched themselves by crafting ballot measures designed to attract funding from moneyed interest groups. With ballot initiative pass rates so low, the authors ask, why would any group care to invest in such schemes in the first place? "The assumption of huckster consultants," they conclude, "depends on the existence of a number of well-heeled dupes."

In chapter 5, Elisabeth Gerber explores the logic and pitfalls of reforming the ballot initiative process. Underlying Gerber's approach is the belief that any ballot initiative reform must be based on sound, empirical evidence that a problem actually exists. Without such evidence, cautions Gerber, reformers risk enacting solutions to problems that do not exist, neglecting problems that do exist, implementing reforms that fail to solve the problems they are intended to address, and creating new problems along the way. Particularly important, Gerber notes, is that reforms to specific parts of the initiative process be considered in light of their potential effect on the overall process. For example, whereas increasing the petition circulation time period may help to empower citizen groups, it will also likely lead to a greater number of initiatives on the ballot—which in turn will create greater informational demands on voters. Finally, Gerber reminds reformers that they will continue to be highly constrained by both state and federal courts, which have viewed with intense scrutiny state regulations that limit groups' First Amendment protections. With courts committed to shielding group activity in the initiative process, reforms to put economic and citizen groups on more equal footing must do so by increasing the influence of citizen interests rather than limiting the activities of economic interests.

In the concluding chapter, we assess the arguments and evidence marshaled by the authors, identify the components of the ballot initiative process we believe to be most in need of repair, and put forth some reform ideas that would considerably improve direct legislation processes. The reforms we suggest are based on the premise that election-day lawmaking would be most improved by increasing levels of voter information. Toward that end, strengthened campaign finance disclosure rules would provide the public with critical information on financial contributors to ballot campaigns (information which, as many studies show, can serve as a vital cue for voters). Limited public subsidies provided to qualified ballot campaigns would ensure that no ballot campaign's message is drowned out by well-financed opponents. Improved voter guides would also go a long way toward increasing voter information. For each initiative on a statewide ballot, voter guides should include a simple summary of the measure, an independent analysis of the measure's likely impact on the state's economy, a list of groups and political elites that endorse and oppose the measure, campaign finance information, and arguments for and against the measure written by competing campaigns. Finally, limiting the number of initiatives appearing on statewide ballots would make more manageable the informational demands placed on voters.

Dangerous Democracy?

1

The Historical Role of Narrow-Material Interests in Initiative Politics

Howard R. Ernst

THE ISSUE

Ballot measures, hailed in the Progressive Era as a popular safeguard against electoral bias, have more recently come under fire by academics and activists alike as having evolved into yet another weapon in the arsenal of influence of special interests (Shockley 1978; Lyndenberg 1981; Lowenstein 1982; Zisk 1987). The extent to which narrow-material interests (i.e., organized labor interests and corporate interests) have come to control initiative politics in this country is a central concern of the research presented in this chapter. Simply put, this chapter explores the historical record, analyzing if narrow-material interests have been able to buy the passage of initiatives and if the influence of these types of interests has substantially grown over the last hundred years.

For several reasons, understanding the historical role of narrow-material interests in initiative politics is a particularly interesting and important undertaking. Initiative campaigns, unlike candidate elections, are not directly influenced by electoral factors such as party identification, name recognition, or incumbency. Consequently, it is feared that initiative campaigns, unfettered by what have proven to be powerful voting determinants in candidate elections, may be particularly susceptible to the effects of campaign expenditures and, consequently, open to the influence of narrow-material interests. Moreover, lopsided spending in initiative politics is a regular occurrence, even more so than in candidate elections. It is not uncommon for a well-financed interest to spend millions of dollars in support of one side of an initiative, while the competing interest spends little or nothing on the opposing side. These unique circumstances underscore the importance of understanding the role of narrow-material interests in initiative elections.

HISTORICAL BACKGROUND OF DIRECT DEMOCRACY IN THE UNITED STATES

At the local and state levels, direct democracy has a rich and lengthy tradition in this country. Since the seventeenth century, citizens in New England villages have assembled to propose and pass local laws (Cronin 1989, 41). Massachusetts in 1778 became the first state to refer its constitution for popular approval (rejected at first, the Massachusetts Constitution was not approved by the required two-thirds majority until 1780). In 1898, South Dakota became the first state to grant its citizens the initiative process. It was Oregon, however, that in 1904 became the first state to actually conduct statewide initiatives. By the early 1920s, nineteen states had followed the lead of Oregon and South Dakota, adopting and implementing constitutional or legislative initiatives. In addition, by this time twenty-two states had also adopted the legislative referendum.

Since the turn of the century, statewide popular governance has grown substantially in the American states. Today in all states but one, Alabama, popular approval is required for the adoption of state constitutional amendments (Council of State Governments 2000, 209). The legal right of American citizens to participate in direct democracy has, in fact, never been greater than it is today (see figure 1.1). In just under half the American states (twenty-four), citizens currently have the authority to propose laws or amendments to their state constitutions. In another twenty-six states, citizens have gained the right to vote on legislation referred to them by their state assemblies. The number of states with recall measures has also grown substantially, to twenty (Council of State Governments 2000).

Perhaps the most telling figure regarding the growing prominence of direct politics at the state level is illustrated in figure 1.1. The maps illustrate that, in more states than not, some type of popular governing device is currently extended to the voters. Clearly the rise of direct politics is not merely a curious trend limited to peculiar Western states, as is often thought, but a wider phenomenon. In their 1994 work, *Referendums around the World*, Butler and Ranney go so far as to claim that the growing popularity of direct forms of democracy is, in fact, global in nature.

Figure 1.1   Direct Democracy in the United States

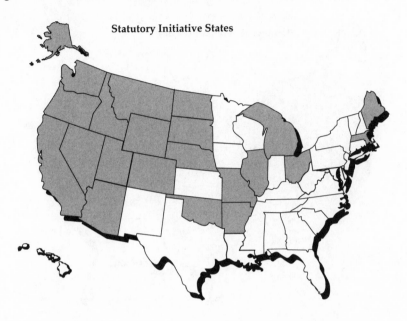

Statutory Initiative States

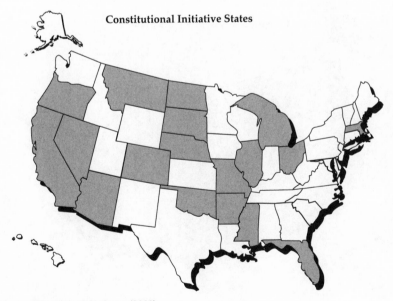

Constitutional Initiative States

Source: The Book of the States (2000).

Figure 1.1 (Continued)

Statutory Referendum States

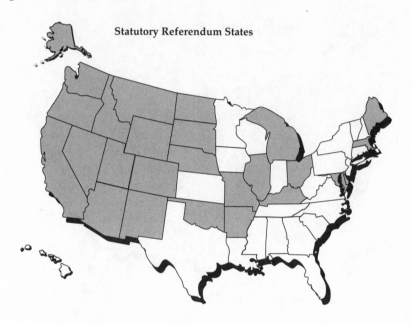

Constitutional Referendum States

Figure 1.1   (Continued)

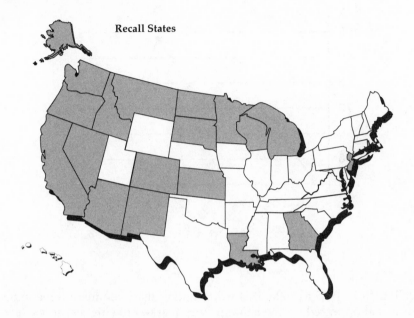

Recall States

When considering the number of states offering the devices of popular governance, it is important to note that no state that has awarded these political mechanisms to its citizens has ever revoked the devices (Schmidt 1989, 16–18). The history of initiative politics in this country suggests that the river of democracy flows in but one direction, toward the body politic. Moreover, it appears the process is expanding once again; in 1999 thirteen states formally considered establishing or strengthening their existing mechanisms for citizen governance (Initiative and Referendum Institute 1999).[1]

In recent years four states, Florida, Wyoming, Illinois, and Mississippi, approved statewide citizen initiatives. Wyoming and the District of Columbia adopted the legislative referendum. In the winter of 1977, the U.S. Senate went so far as to hold a series of hearings concerning the possibility of amending the U. S. Constitution to allow for national voter initiatives (see Graham 1978). Moreover, in the 2000 presidential election the Reform Party advocated a national initiative as part of their party platform.

Also important when considering the growing significance of direct politics in this country is to be aware of the increased frequency in which direct mechanisms are being implemented. Figure 1.2 plots the number of initiatives (statutory and constitutional) that appeared on statewide

Figure 1.2   Initiative Usage, 1985–2000

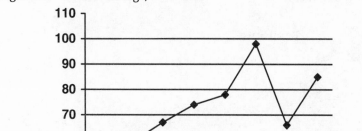

ballots from 1985 to 2000. It is worth noting that the ninety-three initiatives that appeared on the ballot in 1996 marked the highest single election-period usage of the initiative process in American history. Moreover, the 1996 election does not appear to be an anomaly, but merely a recent example of a general upward trend (discussed in detail below).

Historically, many of the nation's most controversial and important political battles were fought first in the public arena. Table 1.1 presents a summary of some of the more noteworthy issues that citizens in this country have voted on through the initiative process. Not intended to represent a comprehensive list, the table provides a summary illustration of the enduring and substantial impact of ballot measures at the state level.

During the Progressive Era, for example, profound reforms were implemented as a result of citizen initiatives. Women's suffrage, population-based representation, creation of presidential primaries, direct election of U.S. senators, banning of poll taxes, restrictions on child labor, and many other important measures were first proposed and implemented by popular means during this period. More recently, nuclear-freeze legislation, tax cuts, term limits, campaign finance regulations, and other consequential measures have been proposed through the initiative process. Issues perhaps too controversial to be decided through ordinary legislative means continue to find their way onto the ballot. Political bombshells such as gay rights, anti-affirmative action, legalization of certain controlled drugs, the "right to die," and school vouchers are only a few of the more controversial issues currently being decided by citizens in various states.

Table 1.1   Historical Sketch of Important Statewide Initiatives

Date	Description
1912	Citizens in Arizona and Oregon voted in favor of initiatives that extended suffrage to women (nine years before the national suffrage amendment).
	Citizens in Arizona voted in favor of an initiative that required reapportionment of the lower house of the state legislature based on population (more than fifty years prior to the U.S. Supreme Court ruling in favor of this method).
	Citizens in Arkansas, Maine, Montana, Oregon, and South Dakota voted in favor of initiatives that established candidate nominations through primary elections.
	Citizens in Montana and Oregon voted in favor of initiatives that required presidential primaries.
	Citizens in Montana and Oklahoma voted in favor of initiatives that called for the direct election of U.S. senators.
	Citizens in California, Oregon, and Washington voted in favor of initiatives that banned poll taxes.
1924	Citizens in Arkansas voted in favor of an initiative that restricted child labor.
By 1930	Citizens in twelve states voted in favor of initiatives intended to prohibit the sale of liquor.
1947–1954	Citizens in three states voted in favor of "right to work legislation," while similar legislation was rejected in five other states.
1948–1960	Citizens in Arizona, Utah, and Washington voted in favor of initiatives that required expansion and reform of the civil service systems.
1952–1962	Citizens in Arkansas, Colorado, Oregon, and Washington voted in favor of initiatives that required reapportionment.
1970–1980	Citizens in nine states made a statement by voting in favor of initiatives that called for a freeze on the production of nuclear weapons in the United States and the Soviet Union.
1970–1984	Citizens in twenty-three states considered ballot measures intended to ensure "equal rights" or "equal protection" for women.
1978–1990	Following the lead of California's Proposition 13, which called for a major reduction in taxes, citizens from across the country considered tax relief at the polls in the 1980s.
1990s	Citizens across the country voted in favor of initiatives proposing term limits on elected officials.
1994	Citizens in California voted in favor of an initiative that prohibited illegal aliens from receiving public services.
1996	Citizens in Arizona and California started a wave of "medical marijuana" initiatives by voting in favor of legalizing certain controlled drugs for medicinal purposes.
1998	Citizens in Maine and Arizona voted in favor of comprehensive campaign finance reform.

Sources: Graham 1978; McGuigan 1985; Schmidt 1989; Public Affairs Research Institute of New Jersey 1992, 1996.

BEYOND THE SURFACE: ASSESSING THE HISTORICAL ROLE OF NARROW-MATERIAL INTERESTS IN INITIATIVE POLITICS

The following discussion divides the history of initiative politics into three general time periods: the early period (1898–1940), the middle period (1941–1976), and the recent period (1977–1996). Each of these is a distinct period in the usage of the initiative process. The early period was an extremely active time for initiative politics, while the middle period saw usage drop considerably. In the most recent period, initiative politics has risen to unprecedented rates of usage.

Having divided initiative politics into three time periods, the analysis then gauges if typological changes correspond with usage fluctuations. In other words, the study investigates whether the influence of certain types of initiatives, namely initiatives aimed at securing narrow-material rewards, has grown over the years. If there have been substantial typological fluctuations in initiative politics over time, it makes sense that these substantive changes would be most evident at times when the process underwent other fluctuations (i.e., fluctuations in usage rates). Hence, the three time periods selected for this section should provide evidence of substantive typological transformations, if such changes did in fact take place.

To gauge general typological shifts in the initiative process, statewide initiative campaigns occurring in the United States from 1898 to 1995 were categorized by type.[2] If a campaign had a clear and direct material interest at stake in an initiative's outcome, the campaign was categorized as a narrow-material campaign (see table 1.2). Campaigns classified as narrow-material attempted to secure or protect material rewards for select groups in society (i.e., corporate or labor interests). These types of interests appeared on both the "yes" and "no" side of ballot measures. For example, an initiative that proposes casino gambling in a state would be classified as a narrow-material "yes" campaign. An example of a "no" side narrow-material campaign would be a campaign that opposes restrictions on the sale of tobacco products. Initiative campaigns without identifiable narrow-material interests at stake were placed into the study's default category as "other." See Bowler, Donovan, and McCuan (1997) for a recent initiative study that incorporates a similar typological schema.[3]

From these campaign classifications it is possible to classify each statewide ballot measure by the general interests at stake on each side. As table 1.2 illustrates, there are four possible types of initiatives that arise from this straightforward categorization schema. Dividing the initiatives this way enables the analysis to gauge whether certain types of groups appear more regularly on the "yes" or "no" side of initiatives, as well as

Table 1.2   Initiative Categories Defined

"Yes" Side v. "No" Side	*Definition*	*Examples*
Narrow-Material v. Narrow-Material	An initiative election in which a labor or corporate interest proposes legislation that is opposed by another labor or corporate interest.	a. Initiatives that restrict a worker's right to strike. b. Insurance companies proposing tort reform that is opposed by trial lawyers. c. Labor interests proposing a minimum-wage increase.
Narrow-Material v. Other	An initiative election in which a labor or corporate interest proposes legislation that is not opposed by another labor or corporate interest.	a. Gambling industry attempting to legalize gambling in a state. b. Liquor interests attempting to deregulate liquor industry. c. Mining industry attempting to reduce environmental regulations.
Other v. Narrow-Material	An initiative election in which an interest that does not represent a labor or corporate interest proposes legislation that is opposed by a labor or corporate interest.	a. Attempts to increase environmental regulations of a specific industry. b. Attempts to impose regulation on the liquor industries. c. Attempts to place taxes on the tobacco industry.
Other v. Other	An election in which neither side represents a labor or corporate interest.	a. Initiatives that aimed to extend suffrage rights to women. b. Campaign finance reform initiatives. c. Term limits initiatives.

the comparative success rates by initiative type on both sides of initiatives. In doing so, it can be determined if narrow-material interests have historically enjoyed a general advantage or disadvantage in initiative politics and the extent to which the process has been implemented against narrow-material interests.

While far from perfect, the simple categorizing schema described here is sufficient for the purposes at hand. First, the categories are clear and broad enough to allow all the diverse ballot measures under consideration to be exclusively assigned to one of the two typological categories.[4] Second, the broad and general nature of the categories frees the researcher from having to make difficult and potentially subjective decisions that follow from more specified categorizing schemas, assuring more consistent classification and less measurement error than would otherwise be possible. Third, the available descriptive information regarding initiatives is often scant, making assignment to highly differentiated categories impossible in many cases. Last, there is no reason to believe that the categorizing schema used here should bias the findings of the research. The categories, though broad, allow us to meaningfully gauge whether the initiative process has changed qualitatively over the years. That is, using these categories, we can judge in general terms whether the influence that narrow-material interests wield in the initiative process has likely increased or decreased over the last century.

The Early Period (1898–1940): Frequency of Usage

At the turn of the century, initiative politics exploded onto the political scene. From 1898 until 1918, nineteen states adopted the initiative process. Twenty-two states adopted the legislative referendum (see table 1.3). It is worth noting that states in every geographical region were beginning to experiment with direct democracy at this time. Northeastern states, such as Maine and Massachusetts, were acting in tandem with their southern counterparts, such as Missouri and Arkansas. Leading the movement toward statewide democratic politics were the western states. It was here that states adopted the initiative and referendum earlier and in greater numbers than in any other region of the country.

Not only were a large number of states adopting the mechanisms of direct democracy in the early period, but initiative states were also using the mechanisms of direct democracy at high rates. By 1915, some 222 separate initiative measures had been voted on in the eighteen states using the initiative process. The state of Oregon alone, during its first five years with the initiative process, used the device a total of forty-eight times. California and Colorado made use of the initiative process during their five-year inaugural periods twenty-four and thirty-six times, respectively.

Table 1.3　State Adoption of Initiative and Referendum, 1898–1940

State Adoption of Constitutional or Legislative Initiative	State Adoption of Legislative Referendum
1) South Dakota (1898)	1) South Dakota (1898)
2) Utah (1900)	2) Utah (1900)
3) Oregon (1902)	3) Oregon (1902)
4) Montana (1906)	4) Nevada (1904)
5) Oklahoma (1907)	5) Montana (1906)
6) Maine (1908)	6) Oklahoma (1907)
7) Missouri (1908)	7) Maine (1908)
8) Arkansas (1910)	8) Missouri (1908)
9) Colorado (1910)	9) Arkansas (1910)
10) Arizona (1911)	10) Colorado (1910)
11) California (1911)	11) Arizona (1911)
12) Idaho (1912)	12) California (1911)
13) Nebraska (1912)	13) New Mexico (1911)
14) Nevada (1912)	14) Idaho (1912)
15) Ohio (1912)	15) Nebraska (1912)
16) Washington (1912)	16) Ohio (1912)
17) Michigan (1913)	17) Washington (1912)
18) North Dakota (1914)	18) Michigan (1913)
19) Massachusetts (1918)	19) North Dakota (1914)
	20) Kentucky (1915)
	21) Maryland (1915)
	22) Massachusetts (1918)

Sources: Cronin 1989; Schmidt 1989; Council of State Governments 2000.

By the end of the initial forty-two-year period, 777 initiatives had been voted on by citizens in the nineteen states with the initiative process (see figure 1.3). During this period, the average initiative usage rate was 77.7 per four-year presidential election cycle.

Another useful way to gauge the rate of initiative usage is to divide the number of initiatives that occurred during a given period by the number of states that allowed for the initiative process at the same time. By doing this, we control for increases in the number of states that adopted the initiative process and isolate increases or decreases in usage among initiative states. This technique is necessary because the sustained high frequency of initiative usage, evident in figure 1.3, might simply be the result of a greater number of states adopting the initiative process, not a result of sustained high usage by initiative states.

Figure 1.4 allows us to put these concerns to rest. This figure does not simply illustrate that initiative usage was high during this period in general: when we control for increases in the number of states with the

Figure 1.3   Rate of Initiative Usage: The Early Period (1898–1940)

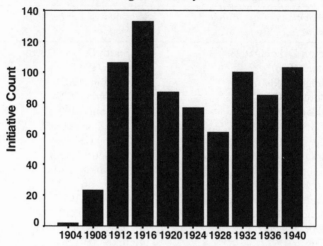

Sources: Graham 1978; Schmidt 1989.

Figure 1.4   Initiative Usage (Controlling for Increases in the Number of Initiative States): The Early Period (1898–1940)

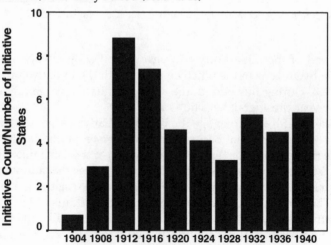

Sources: Compiled by author from Graham 1978; Schmidt 1989.

process, the findings experience little change. While usage rates in initiative states experienced a drop-off following the exuberant usage seen in the earliest years, usage rates leveled off from 1920 to 1940. From these two figures we can safely conclude that the high frequency of initiative usage displayed in figure 1.3 was not merely the consequence of an increased number of states adopting the initiative process. Initiative usage, in fact, remained relatively high in initiative states throughout this period. On average, initiative states used the initiative process 4.7 times per four-year presidential election cycle during this forty-year period. As we will see when comparing these figures to the middle period (1941–1976), this was a high usage period for the initiative process.

The Early Period (1898–1940): Type of Usage

The early years of the initiative process saw this new political tool being used in a wide array of causes. Issues ranging from prohibiting the teaching of evolution in public schools to establishing worker's compensation were debated and voted on through the statewide initiative process. To provide a general idea of the scope of measures being considered during this period, table 1.4 lists the twenty that appeared on a single statewide ballot during the early period of initiative usage—Colorado's 1912 ballot.

Although meaningful generalizations cannot really be drawn from it, the 1912 Colorado ballot does provide an interesting prelude for our analysis of initiative types in the early period. In many ways the 1912 Colorado ballot is indicative of the large number and wide array of issues that appeared on ballots during the earliest period of the process's history. Generally speaking, the early ballots, like the Colorado ballot, were labor-friendly, reform-minded efforts that simultaneously moved to increase the role of government in society and increase the general public's control over government.

However, not even in the earliest period of initiative politics did progressive issues monopolize the initiative process. Narrow-material interests pursued their objectives through the initiative process even in the early period. For instance, during this period gambling interests proposed ten ballot measures that sought to legalize gambling in various states. The liquor industry proposed thirteen initiatives that aimed to secure its material interests against the forces of prohibition. More generally, narrow-material interests placed numerous tax limits and tax reduction proposals on the ballot during the early period.

A more systemic inquiry into the types of issues appearing on the ballot during the early period offers further insights into the nature of initiative politics at this time. Using the schema outlined in table 1.2, table 1.5 divides the initiatives that appeared on statewide ballots from 1898–1940

Table 1.4   Colorado Ballot Issues (1912)

Statewide prohibition
Special funds for the state immigration bureau
Home rule for cities and towns
Recall of elected officials
Amending the initiative process
Defining contempt of court
Creating a public utilities court to fix reasonable utility rates
Increasing local control of schools
Overruling Supreme Court decisions by a vote of the people
Highway bonds
Eight-hour workday for women
Regulation of public service corporations
Establishing a state fair
Subsidizing printing materials for initiative and referendum campaigns
Amending election laws
Aid to dependent and neglected children
Civil service reform
Eight-hour workday in underground mines, smelters, mills, and coke ovens
Giving the state highway commission control of certain funds
Tunnel construction through James Peak

Source: Graham 1978.

by type. According to this classification schema, the least common type of initiative election during the early period was the narrow-material versus other category. In less than 10.2 percent of all initiatives did narrow-material interests propose measures against interests that were not narrow and material. Also important to note, only 26 percent of the cases in this category were approved by the voters—for a total of only 19 approved narrow-material versus not narrow and material initiatives out of the 777 total initiatives in the early period. The passage rate for initiatives in which narrow-material interests proposed legislation against an interest that was not narrow and material was the lowest passage rate of the four categories. From these findings it appears that, at least during the early years of initiative usage, narrow-material interests were at a general disadvantage in initiative politics.

Table 1.5 reveals several other trends that should not go unmentioned. First, there may be a general bias against the "yes" side in initiative elections. For all categories, the "yes" side was successful less often than the "no" side, with only 36.2 percent of the classified initiatives passing during the initial forty-year period. Second, the apparent bias against narrow-material interests seems to disappear when interests that are not narrow and material propose initiatives against narrow-material opponents.

Table 1.5 Frequency and Success Rates of Initiative Campaigns by Type: The Early Period (1898–1940)

Category		% of All Initiatives in Time Period[a]	Passage Rate within Type
"Yes" Side v.	"No" Side		
Narrow-Material	Narrow-Material	35.4% ($N = 254$)	33.1% ($N = 84$)
Narrow-Material	Other	10.2% ($N = 73$)	26.0% ($N = 19$)
Other	Narrow-Material	10.5% ($N = 75$)	36.0% ($N = 27$)
Other	Other	44.0% ($N = 316$)	41.1% ($N = 130$)
Total		100.0% ($N = 718$)	36.2% ($N = 260$)

Sources: Categorized by author from initiative descriptions in Graham 1978; Schmidt 1989.
Note: 7.6 percent ($N = 59$) of the initiative descriptions during this time period lacked sufficient information for classification and were consequently omitted from the analysis.
[a]Percent totals in this column do not equal 100% because of rounding.

The success rate for interests that are not narrow and material in these cases is only 36.0 percent, nearly identical to the average success rate for all initiatives during this time period—36.2 percent. Lastly, it should be pointed out that the other versus other category made up the bulk of the initiatives during the early period; 44.0 percent of all initiatives fell into this category. Not only did these initiatives appear more regularly during the early period than any other initiative type, but they also had the highest passage rate—41.1 percent.

The Middle Period (1941–1976): Frequency of Usage

The explosive impact of initiatives at the turn of the century began to fizzle out around midcentury. During 1941–1976 only four additional states adopted the initiative process—Alaska, Florida, Wyoming, and Illinois. Only two states, Alaska and Wyoming, adopted the legislative referendum (see table 1.6). It is important to note, however, that while additional states were not adopting the initiative process in large numbers, no

Table 1.6 State Adoption of Initiative or Referendum (1941–1976)

State Adoption of Constitutional or Legislative Initiative	State Adoption of Legislative Referendum
Alaska (1956)	Alaska (1959)
Florida (1968)	Wyoming (1968)
Wyoming (1968)	
Illinois (1970)	

Sources: Adapted from Schmidt 1989; Cronin 1989.

states went so far as to withdraw the process from their citizens. As will be shown, the middle years were more a dormant period for initiative politics in this country than an outwardly hostile era.

Comparing the usage rates of the middle period to those of the early period affords further insights into the changes that were taking place. While an average of nearly seventy-eight initiatives per presidential election cycle occurred nationwide in the early period, the middle period averaged only forty-seven initiatives per presidential cycle—a 40 percent decrease in usage. Figure 1.5 graphically illustrates the drop-off in usage that occurred in the middle period.

When controlling for the number of states adopting the initiative process, the decline in usage becomes even more pronounced. As I did when discussing the early period, I control for the increase in the number of states adopting the process by dividing the number of states with the initiative process by the number of initiatives that occurred nationwide during a given time period. The average state usage per presidential cycle for the middle period was 2.0 initiatives per initiative state, while the average during the early years was 4.7 initiatives per initiative state—a substantial drop of 57 percent.

From figures 1.5 and 1.6 it is clear that the initiative process had undergone a substantial change in usage rates from the early period (1898–1940) to the middle period (1941–1976). What remains for us to explore,

Figure 1.5 Initiative Usage: The Early Period (1898–1940) through the Middle Period (1941–1976)

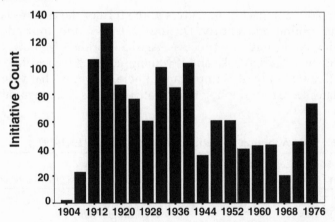

Sources: Graham 1978; Schmidt 1989.

Figure 1.6   Initiative Usage (Controlling for Increases in the Number of Initiative States): The Early Period (1898–1940) through the Middle Period (1941–1976)

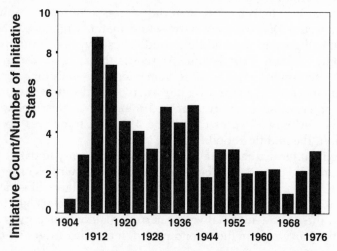

Sources: Graham 1978; Schmidt 1989.

however, is whether this change in usage corresponded with a change in the types of issues that were being addressed during the middle period. In other words, did a change in kind correspond with the change in frequency?

The Middle Period (1941–1976): Type of Usage

We begin this period's discussion of initiative types as we did with the earlier period, by looking at the issues appearing on one specific ballot during this time period—in this case, the 1956 Arkansas ballot issues (table 1.7). As with the 1912 Colorado ballot issues discussed above, the Arkansas ballot issues serve as a useful introduction to the types of issues being debated in initiative politics during this period, but should be given limited weight in our overall analysis.

The Arkansas ballot is indicative of the period in general in that a wide range of issues continued to appear on the ballot and no one type of issue dominated the process. Political reform measures are situated side –by side with attempts to legalize gambling and to increase worker's compensation. A systematic analysis of the types of issues appearing on ballot measures during the middle period (table 1.8) confirms what the Arkansas ballot suggests, that this period was not qualitatively different from the earlier period.

Initiatives in which narrow-material interests launched campaigns against interests that were not narrow and material remained the least common category in the middle period. These types of initiatives occurred only 10.2 percent of the time. Moreover, the success rate of narrow-material interests in these rare cases remained low—only 26.2 percent of these initiatives were enacted by the voters. Stated differently, narrow-material interests successfully proposed initiatives against unlike typed opponents in only 11 cases out of the 413 total initiatives occurring throughout the middle period.

Figure 1.7 offers a direct comparison between the early initiative period and the middle period. In this figure, the occurrence rates of initiative types are compared for the two time periods. As the figure illustrates, the similarities between the two time periods are remarkable. Only the first category, the narrow-material verses narrow-material category, saw any substantial movement in the second period, increasing from 35.4 percent

Table 1.7   Arkansas Ballot Issues (1956)

Setting salaries for judges
Opposing desegregation
Preserving state senatorial apportionment
Legalizing pari-mutuel wagering on horse racing
Increasing workers' compensation
School reform

Source: Graham 1978.

Table 1.8   Frequency and Success Rates of Initiative Campaigns by Type: The Middle Period (1941–1976)

Category		% of All Initiatives in Time Period	Passage Rate within Type
"Yes" Side v. "No" Side			
Narrow-Material	Narrow-Material	44.6% (N = 184)	34.8% (N = 64)
Narrow-Material	Other	10.2% (N = 42)	26.2% (N = 11)
Other	Narrow-Material	12.0% (N = 49)	22.4% (N = 11)
Other	Other	33.4% (N = 138)	53.6% (N = 74)
Total		100.2% (N = 413)	38.7% (N = 160)

Sources: Graham 1978; Schmidt 1989.
Note: 1.9 percent (N = 8) of the initiative descriptions during this time period lacked sufficient information for classification and were consequently omitted from the analysis.

Figure 1.7 Comparison of Usage Rates for the Early Period (1898–1940) and the Middle Period (1941–1976) by Initiative Type

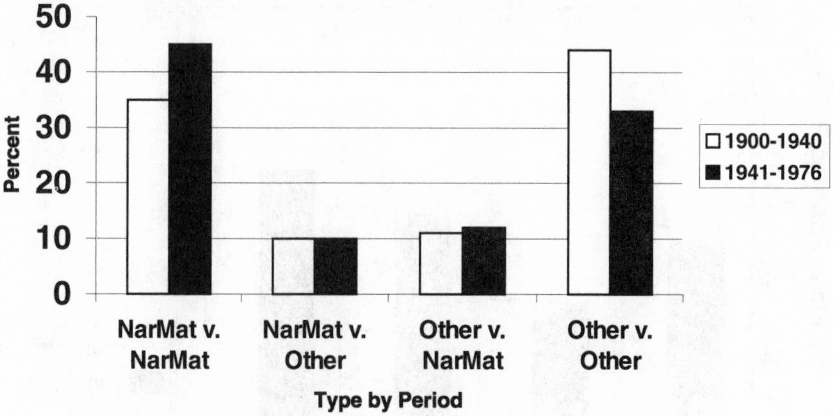

Sources: Graham 1978; Schmidt 1989.

of the cases in the early period to 44.6 percent of the cases in the middle period. This movement provides limited evidence to suggest that narrow-material interests were beginning to make use of the initiative process more regularly during the middle period, at least against other narrow-material interests. However, the overall findings presented in figure 1.7 suggest that substantial typological movement had not taken place in the middle period.

If figure 1.7 suggests that narrow-material interests were beginning to use the initiative process more regularly in the middle period, figure 1.8 illustrates that they were not using the process more effectively. In this figure, the mean passage rates of the different categories are compared for the two time periods. The average success rate for narrow-material interests proposing initiatives remains stable and low for the two periods. This suggests that while narrow-material interests were introducing a slightly higher percentage of initiatives in the middle period, they were not winning at a substantially higher rate than they had in the earlier period.

Taken together, figures 1.7 and 1.8 paint a clear picture. The drop-off in initiative usage from the first period to the second period did not correspond with a substantial change in the types of interests being pursued during the two periods, nor in a substantial change in the passage rates of the different interest types. Generally speaking, the two periods had remarkably similar types of initiatives appearing on the ballot and equally similar passage rates.

Figure 1.8   Comparison of Passage Rates for the Early Period (1898–1940) and the Middle Period (1941–1976) by Initiative Type

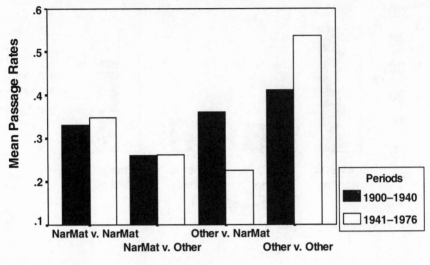

Initiative Type by Period

Sources: Graham 1978; Schmidt 1989.

Moreover, the general bias against the "yes" side of issues remained in the middle period, with only 39 percent of all initiatives passing. As in the early period, the bias against narrow-material interests disappeared when other interests proposed measures against narrow-material opponents during the middle period. Lastly, the other versus other category for both time periods had the highest passage rates of any category.

The Recent Period (1977–1996): Frequency of Usage

In the recent period (1977–1996) initiative politics underwent a rebirth in the United States.[5] While only one additional state adopted the process (Mississippi in 1992), several other states formally considered enacting or strengthening their existing mechanisms of citizen governance (Initiative and Referendum Institute 1999). The actual increase experienced in the recent period is most evident when one looks at the frequency of usage among initiative states during this period. Figures 1.9 and 1.10 track the fluctuations in initiative usage throughout the three time periods.

Comparing the usage rates of the recent period to those of the middle and early periods, figure 1.9 gives us a clear perspective on the tremendous growth in usage that has occurred in the recent period. While the middle period only averaged 47 initiatives nationwide per presidential

Figure 1.9 Initiative Usage: The Early Period (1898–1940), the Middle Period (1941–1976), and the Recent Period (1977–1996)

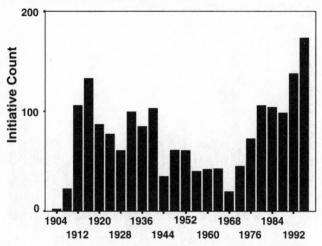

Four-Year Periods Ending in Presidential Election Years

Sources: Graham 1978; Schmidt 1989; Public Affairs Research Institute of New Jersey 1992, 1996.

cycle, and the earlier period averaged 78, the recent period averaged over 124 initiatives nationwide for its four-year presidential cycles. This represents a remarkable 164 percent increase in total usage from the middle period to the recent period.

When controlling for the number of states with the initiative process over the entire history of initiative politics, we see similar results. The recent period has not only experienced an increase in usage over the middle period, but it has actually achieved an average per-initiative state usage rate that exceeds even the earliest period. As discussed earlier, the study controls for the increase in the number of states adopting the process by dividing the number of states with the initiative process by the number of initiatives that occurred during a given period. The per-initiative state usage per presidential cycle is graphed in figure 1.10. For the middle period, the state average was 2.0 initiatives per presidential election cycle. In comparison, the recent period attained a state average of 5.7 initiatives per cycle, while the earliest period's state average per cycle was less at 4.7 initiatives.

The findings make clear that the usage of the initiative process has experienced three distinct periods over the course of its history in the United States. The early period (1898–1940) was a high-usage period for

Figure 1.10   Initiative Usage (Controlling for Increases in the Number of Initiative States): The Early Period (1898–1940), the Middle Period (1941–1976), and the Recent Period (1977–1996)

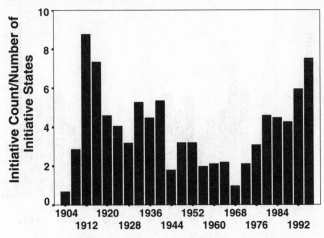

Four-Year Periods Ending in Presidential Election Years

Sources: Graham 1978; Schmidt 1989; Public Affairs Research Institute of New Jersey 1992, 1996.

initiative politics, while the middle period (1941–1976) saw a considerable drop-off in initiative usage, and the recent period (1977–1996) experienced a tremendous upsurge in usage. But the more important question remains to be addressed. Did the change in usage that occurred in the recent period have a corresponding change in initiative types? In other words, as the process transformed, did certain types of initiatives, namely narrow-material interests, become better able to compete in initiative politics than other types, or has the evolution in initiative politics, as evidenced in the two earlier periods, been primarily limited to fluctuations in usage rates?

The Recent Period (1977–1996): Type of Usage

As for the previous periods, I begin the discussion of the recent period's[6] initiative types by exploring the issues that appeared on one state ballot—Oregon in 1994 (table 1.9).

The 1994 Oregon ballot, as with ballots generally appearing during the recent period, witnessed an incredible variety of issues. Attempts to limit taxes appear alongside such issues as prison reform and antidiscrimination

Table 1.9   Oregon Ballot Issues (1994)

Tax reduction
Restrictions on political contributions
Antidiscrimination legislation
Against expanding legal protection based on sexual orientation
Public employee pensions
Mandatory sentencing
Repealing the wage-rate requirement for workers on public works
Increased regulation of the chemical mining process
School funding
Allowing terminally ill adults to obtain lethal drugs
Requiring state prison inmates to work full time
Banning certain techniques for hunting bears
Limiting free speech for obscene materials
Restructuring the state tax codes

Source: Public Affairs Research Institute of New Jersey 1996.

measures. One reform-oriented issue that appeared regularly during this period was the issue of term limits. But neither the Oregon example nor a general survey of the issues occurring at this time gives us reason to believe that the types of issues appearing during this period changed substantially.

In fact, table 1.10 provides solid evidence that the recent period was very much like the earlier periods in regard to the appearance and success rates of the various issue types. As in the earlier periods, the initiative

Table 1.10   Frequency and Success Rates of Initiative Campaigns by Type: The Recent Period (1981–1995)

Category		% of All Initiatives in Time Period	Passage Rate within Type
"Yes" Side v. "No" Side			
Narrow-Material	Narrow-Material	36.4% ($N = 149$)	34.9% ($N = 52$)
Narrow-Material	Other	7.8% ($N = 32$)	28.1% ($N = 9$)
Other	Narrow-Material	12.2% ($N = 50$)	30.0% ($N = 15$)
Other	Other	43.5% ($N = 178$)	60.7% ($N = 108$)
Total		100.0% ($N = 409$)	45.0% ($N = 184$)

Sources: Public Affairs Research Institute of New Jersey 1992, 1996.

Note: 2.9 percent ($N = 12$) of the initiative descriptions lacked sufficient information for classification and were consequently omitted from the analysis. Initiative descriptions are currently unavailable for the years 1978–1980, and these years were omitted from this part of the research.

category in which narrow-material interests launched campaigns against other interest types remained the least common type of initiative in recent years, occurring only 7.8 percent of the time. Moreover, the success rate of narrow-material interests in these cases remained remarkably low— only 28.1 percent of these initiatives were approved by the voters. All told, narrow-material interests proposing initiatives opposed by other typed interests were successful in only 9 cases, out of 409 total initiatives categorized for the recent period.

Our first direct typological comparison between the three periods, figure 1.11, illustrates the striking similarities among the three time periods. For each of the periods, typological occurrence rates show minimal fluctuation. Moreover, figure 1.11 reveals no apparent upward or downward trends among the categories. In other words, it does not appear that the initiative types under consideration are becoming more or less common as the process matures. In addition, the election type that is of the greatest concern to this study, the narrow-material versus other category, never made up more than 11 percent of the cases in any of the three time periods.

When we look at the comparative passage rates (figure 1.12), a similar picture unfolds for the three time periods. The passage rates for narrow-material versus other interests remain low in all the time periods. In fact, for all three time periods, when narrow-material interests proposed initiatives against other typed interests, the narrow-material side never won

Figure 1.11   Comparison of Usage Rates: The Early Period (1898–1940), The Middle Period (1941–1976), and the Recent Period (1981–1995) by Initiative Type

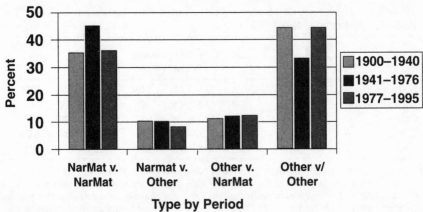

Sources: Graham 1978; Schmidt 1989; Public Affairs Research Institute of New Jersey 1992, 1996.

Figure 1.12   Comparison of Passage Rates: The Early Period (1898–1940), the Middle Period (1941–1976), and the Recent Period (1981–1995) by Initiative Type

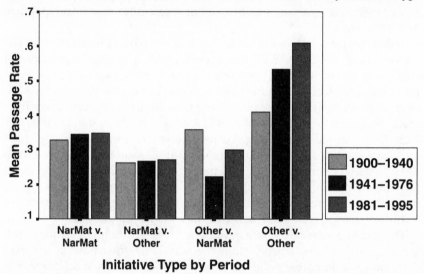

Sources: Graham 1978; Schmidt 1989; Public Affairs Research Institute of New Jersey 1992, 1996.

in more than 30 percent of the cases. Also important to note, the passage rate for other versus other interests was highest for each time period.

Figure 1.12 reveals at least one general trend in the data. The initiative elections classified as other verses other appear to be passing at greater and greater rates over time. It is important not to make too much out of this phenomenon. One simple explanation for the recent upward movement is related to term limits. Term limit initiatives, classified in this study as other versus other, have been extremely popular in initiative politics in recent years and account for a large part of the high success rate for this category in the recent period. As this issue fades, it is possible that the upward trend seen in the other versus other category will level off.

CONCLUSION

The analysis and historical sketch offered here is revealing in a number of ways. First, this chapter outlines the enduring impact of ballot measures in the arena of state politics in this country. The early part of this chapter provides evidence that the flow toward citizen politics is continuous and irreversible. As more and more states adopt the devices of direct politics, and those states that currently allow for direct citizen involvement continue to grow more comfortable with the procedures, direct citizen participation promises to become an even more significant political tool in the future.

Today, many scholars and activists fear that direct legislation in the United States no longer reflects the public will. The idealized notion of citizen-lawmakers moving the political system ever closer to true egalitarian democracy has been seriously challenged in recent years. A new vision of direct politics has evolved, one that depicts corporate executives manipulating public sentiment at will for their own material benefit. It is feared that, armed with political consultants, direct-mail firms, and paid signature gatherers, and waging exorbitant television campaigns, well-healed special interests manipulate the seemingly disinterested and uninformed voters. The absence of party identification, name recognition, and other common voting heuristics found in candidate elections is thought to further exasperate the influence of these moneyed interests.

The findings presented here, however, reveal a different picture of initiative politics. They suggest that the fear of narrow-material interest domination in initiative politics has been overstated. While differences in type appear to matter in initiative politics, the preliminary evidence presented here suggests that interest type has historically worked against narrow-material interests, despite whatever resource advantages these interests may enjoy. Narrow-material interests historically and currently operate at a severe electoral disadvantage in initiative politics.

Challenging Initiatives: More than Just Special-Interest Money, an Issue of Political Civility

Sue Tupper

The initiative process has been a big part of my professional life. I have worked as a campaign manager and grassroots organizer on both sides of initiatives. My attitudes, therefore, have been formed as a practitioner, not as a theoretician. My views are based on direct experience and observation, not extensive data analysis. I began my career in the mid-1970s as a community organizer and later applied skills I learned in that capacity to campaign work. I have committed a good deal of time and study to finding ways to motivate people to act—whether by expressing a particular point of view, uniting with others of a like mind to influence change, or simply taking the time to cast a vote. My work has been guided by a deep personal belief that our democracy is better served by more, not less, citizen involvement.

Contrary to what might seem a natural extension of my personal and professional commitment to making laws via direct democracy, I think the initiative process is a flawed vehicle for decision making. My primary reasons for arriving at this conclusion are that the initiative process is all but immune to amendment or refinement, that the only real citizen involvement in initiative politics is a forced vote that occurs on election day, and that the issues addressed through initiative politics often have consequences that are hidden to voters. Rather than grassroots democracy in action, initiatives are more like the political equivalent of a drive-by shooting.

LOOKING BEYOND WHO IS BEHIND THE CURTAIN

As Ernst points out, it is in vogue today to claim that the initiative process has become nothing more than a playground for special interests with the money to afford the toys. I am familiar with the role of money in issue campaigns. For example, I directed the campaign to build a new football stadium in Seattle, an effort funded by Paul Allen, a local billionaire of Microsoft wealth. Allen had agreed to purchase the Seahawks, keeping the NFL team in Seattle, if, and only if, the public shared in the cost of constructing a new stadium. That campaign is often mislabeled as an initiative; in fact, it was a punt to the people by a legislature that did not want to take the heat for a very controversial decision. It was the most expensive issue campaign in state history. So I know firsthand the role money plays in the process.

I am also familiar with the role of special interests (which Ernst refers to as "narrow-material" interests) in initiative elections. Ernst's analysis shows that special-interest involvement is not a new phenomenon. As long as the process has been a guaranteed right, special interests have attempted to use the tool. Narrowly defined interests of the past produced initiatives on issues such as prohibition, lowering property taxes, limiting the right to strike, or expanding pensions. In today's world, the subjects of our initiatives have changed, but special-interest involvement has not.

As Professor Ernst documents, it is too simplistic to say that money, or "narrow-material" interests more generally, is at the root of all evils associated with today's initiatives. I am familiar with many examples of special interests with financial strength going down in defeat. Likewise, there are many examples of successful initiative efforts being dramatically outspent. In Washington State, some of the most far-reaching and, in fact, most *harmful* laws passed by initiative have been sponsored by campaigns with meager funds but a powerful message.

For example, in 1993 an initiative became law that will forever limit state spending, indexing increases in spending to population growth and inflation. The sponsor was Linda Smith, at the time a self-avowed Christian conservative legislator with the goal to dismantle government. Smith led the campaign with no money but a powerful Populist message: "If our families have to live within budgets, balancing checkbooks, shouldn't our state government have to do the same?" Despite the fact that a state's budget is much more complicated than a family's, being subjected to ever-fluctuating demands of a growing and changing population, Smith's sound bite resonated in a powerful way. Now, eight years later, the state's public schools are bursting with students, transportation demands have seriously outstripped a decaying infrastructure of roads, bridges, and public transportation, and our elected officials have a very limited capacity to respond to these financial pressures.

Another 1993 ballot measure called "Three Strikes, You're Out" became law in Washington State, passing with a 75 percent majority. This statewide measure, while short on cash, was long on Populist appeal. The lead spokesperson, John Carlson, a radio talk-show host (and unsuccessful Republican candidate for governor in 2000), was expert in the use of the sound bite. His message was simple, clean, and powerful: "If you commit the crime, you should do the time." Amid the increasing perception that felons were lurking in every corner and that victims' rights were being trampled, the public didn't have to think very long or hard about supporting a measure that would put a three-time convicted felon behind bars— permanently. It doesn't matter that such mandatory sentencing measures may have consequences that erode the foundations of our judicial system. Voters don't care that "Three Strikes, You're Out" means that judges play virtually no role in considering any extenuating circumstances in passing sentence. Putting a criminal sentencing law to a popular vote had predictable results. If voters are asked if a criminal should be punished, are they going to say no? Now, in Washington State, if you are convicted of the crimes, you will do the time.

Another example occurred during the 1999 election cycle. In 1999 the voters of Washington State gave themselves a big tax break, limiting the state's motor vehicle excise tax to $30 per year per vehicle. The previous fee was much higher, ranging from $1,000 for expensive vehicles to a more moderate amount for cheaper and older cars. The measure included an additional provision that would subject all future tax and fee increases in any jurisdiction to a popular vote—a clause that would put direct democracy on steroids. The measure in question was placed on the ballot through a low-budget, almost exclusively volunteer effort and collected a record number of signatures—almost 500,000, more than double the number needed to qualify for the ballot. When the campaign took shape, the opponents of the effort outspent the backers almost five to one. Again, the money did not matter, the message did. For every voter with a car the vote was a simple pocketbook issue: "vote yes, and pay only $30 per year for your car license tags." In light of the fact that most households were destined to save hundreds of dollars on an unpopular tax, it was no big surprise that the effort enjoyed vast support. The measure passed overwhelmingly, with almost 60 percent of the voters saying "yes."

As evidenced by issues adopted in Washington State, some of the most onerous laws passed by initiative need only be championed by an individual with an ax to grind or a passion for Populism. While Ernst focuses on an important issue, the potential abuse of the system by moneyed interests, he perhaps misses the most damning impact of laws set by initiative. By its very design, the process ensures that concerns held by a minority—any minority—will be subjected to the will of the majority. It is not by accident that the founders of our nation considered and rejected this means of governance. Believing that government based solely on the unfiltered and unrefined views of the majority opens the door to tyranny, the founders based our republic upon the notion that lawmaking should be in the hands of those we elect.

Unlike the governing process debated and accepted by our founders, citizen lawmaking lacks the deliberation, refinement, and real citizen involvement that is essential for enlightened governance. Moreover, the hidden consequences of many ballot measures make it difficult for voters to accurately assess the many complex issues being addressed through ballot measures. It is for these reasons, not the common misconception that moneyed special interests dominate the system, that we should reassess the initiative process.

Initiative Politics: A Useful Blend of Vested Interests and Citizen Politics

Douglas M. Guetzloe

Professor Ernst successfully outlines the hundred-year history of the initiative process. From his chapter, we see that the initiative was a popular and effective tool for the emerging Populist and Progressive movements of the late nineteenth and early twentieth centuries. Moreover, we see that today these relics have been revitalized by an aggressive and influential, sometimes eclectic, group of special interests, both financially vested and popularly based.

The vested special interests, referred to by Ernst and others as "narrow-material interests," consist of those entities that are able and willing to put huge sums of money on the line to create a financial advantage for themselves or their industry. On the other hand, the popular special interests led by issue-oriented groups such as environmental rights, public safety, health, gun rights, and political groups are not as interested in financial advantage as they are in creating public policy and changing public law. I have actively participated in issues being promoted by both types of interest groups.

As a petition-gathering consultant retained in 1994 by the gaming giant, Bally, Inc., my company worked on behalf of a campaign that Professor Ernst identified as a "narrow-material" interest. In this campaign, I was the first consultant in the state of Florida to design and implement a direct-mail petition-gathering effort. I also watched the price of individual petition signatures escalate to $5.00 per signature by the end of the drive. Thanks in no small part to the financial wherewithal of Bally, we were able to collect more than 670,000 signatures in a fifty-day period, a Florida record unmatched today. Despite Bally's ability to dominate spending in the election, their measure was resoundingly defeated on election day.

In 1992, I was retained by another group that falls squarely within Professor Ernst's narrow-material category—the Organized Fishermen of Florida (OFF). OFF represents the political interests of Florida's commercial fishing industry. My company was hired to slow down and ultimately oppose an effort to ban net fishing in Florida.

The situation in December 1992 was not positive for OFF. By this time, the Save Our Sea-life Committee (SOS), the pro-ban side, had collected more than 350,000 signatures. The commercial fishermen needed to slow down the SOS effort or prevent it from reaching its goal. Over two years, we organized counterefforts that included direct intervention with petition gathering, radio advertising, and editorial board meetings. After a two-year effort the SOS petition finally qualified for the ballot by submitting slightly more than 430,000 required signatures. We had been successful in slowing it down, but failed to prevent ballot placement and eventual passage of the initiative.

Not all our clients, however, represent material interests. In the spring of 2000 we were retained by the Republican Party of Florida to establish a countereffort against a thinly disguised effort to take reapportionment out of the hands of the GOP legislature and governor. We organized a direct intervention effort in half a dozen congressional districts and prevented the immediate collection of nearly 10,000 signatures during Florida's March 14 Presidential Preference Primary.

Other direct democracy efforts, similar to our popular "Ax-the-Tax" effort, promote strictly nonprofit public policy goals. Ax-the-Tax has successfully led eleven antitax efforts, most of which were referendum efforts, helping to save taxpayers more than $5.3 billion. These efforts make Ax-the-Tax one of the most successful political committees of its kind in the United States.

From issue-oriented petition gathering to counterpetition efforts during the critical time periods, it is essential to hire competent, experienced consultants capable of assembling armies of workers in a relatively short time. The importance of positive relations with the veterans of petition battles must not be understated. Moreover, the financial ability of the petition sponsors is ascertained and clearly established prior to beginning any effort. The continuing financial health of every petition sponsor is carefully monitored to ensure that the vast army of workers is paid on a timely basis. In Napoleon's time, an army traveled on its stomach. Today, a petition-gathering army works and travels on a steady diet of financial disbursements, distributed in a fair and timely manner.

This is not to say money undermines the integrity of the initiative process. On the contrary, the health of the Republic is in good hands, with many states opening up the process by allowing referendum, initiative, and recall. The triad of Progressive Era weapons remains as the last best hope for citizens to redress their grievances with an otherwise distant government. While vested special interests remain a force in this arena, the opportunity exists for citizen and voter action, and it should remain so. Every state in the union should allow referendum, initiative, and recall and make specific rules to guide their implementation. To withdraw or make more restrictive these weapons of the people would be an unfortunate mistake.

Our forefathers strongly believed in a fluid constitutional republic fed by the wishes of an informed citizenry dedicated to the furtherance of community action and well-being. Efforts to limit or abolish direct democracy should be opposed at every turn, and the free flow of ideas should be forever encouraged through these tools of direct democracy.

2

The Populist Legacy: Initiatives and the Undermining of Representative Government

Bruce E. Cain and Kenneth P. Miller

The recall, referendum, and initiative are most commonly characterized as Progressive reforms because of the era in which they were introduced in the states. To be sure, members of the Progressive movement should be credited with helping to win acceptance for direct democracy mechanisms,[1] but so should the Populists who first recognized the potential of these mechanisms and agitated for their adoption. Even when the Populists' role in promoting direct democracy is openly acknowledged, the differences between their motives for doing so and those of the Progressives are rarely examined in any depth. It is our contention that these original differences matter, because they underlie the modern debate over whether the popular initiative has been misused, and whether it should be reformed.

In this chapter, we first draw distinctions between the Populist and Progressive conceptions of the initiative process and relate them to contemporary debates regarding initiative reform. Second, we argue that the Populist conception of the initiative process has prevailed over the Progressive conception, and we discuss the ways in which the Populist conception of direct democracy undermines representative government. We discuss how, ironically, direct democracy can actually be less democratic than representative democracy in that it fails to maximize democratic opportunities for refinement, informed deliberation, consensus building and compromise, and violates democratic norms of openness, accountability, competence, and fairness. Third, we analyze the ways in which the process of Populist-oriented initiative lawmaking affects policy out-

33

comes, especially in the areas of government reform and minority rights. Fourth, we review the role of courts in the initiative process. Because the Populist approach to initiative lawmaking has prevailed over the Progressive vision, the resulting structural shift has placed enormous responsibilities on state and federal courts. Indeed, more often than not, voter-approved initiatives are challenged in court, and thus courts have become a regular player in initiative lawmaking as the institutional check of first and last resort. In performing this role, courts have been reliable in overturning initiatives that infringe on basic rights, but they have been less aggressive in checking other problems that initiatives cause. Overall, courts have invalidated initiatives at a high rate, which irritates Populists and increases the danger of a backlash against the courts. Given these pressures, it is unrealistic to expect courts to play a larger role in checking initiatives than they already do. In the end, we argue for initiative reform that is more consistent with Progressive than Populist principles. But the big unanswered question is whether that prospect is politically feasible. Once the Populist genie is out of the bottle, there may be no forces strong enough to put it back.

DUELING LEGACIES

Populists and Progressives

For purposes of our discussion, it is important to define what we mean by the terms "Populist" and "Progressive." These words have dual meanings. On the one hand, they refer to political movements in specific historical moments (just before and just after the turn of the last century, respectively). On the other hand, they describe longer term, crucial, and often competing impulses within American political culture.

The historical political movement called "Populism" emerged in the last decades of the nineteenth century. It was a protest movement of political outsiders (mostly farmers, but also laborers, miners, ranchers, and debtors of all types, mainly in the Midwest and West and in pockets of the rural South) who had been dealt a series of blows by the industrial revolution, the commercialization of agriculture, and the concentration of capital. Populists sought relief from the government (through banking reform, currency inflation, regulation of railroads, etc.), but their petitions seemed to fall on deaf ears. In their view, this was because the existing political structures (i.e., parties and legislatures) were controlled by monied interests and were unresponsive or outright hostile to the needs of the common person. For a time, these outsiders sought to organize advocacy organizations (such as the nonpartisan Farmers' Alliance) and work for change within the existing party systems. Frustrated in these efforts, however, Populists founded a third party, the People's Party, drafted a series of platforms, and began fielding candidates for office.[2]

Populists were a factious group but agreed on two fundamental points: (1) the government must restrain the selfish, grasping tendencies of those who profit at the expense of the common person and (2) the "people" (not the monied elite) must control the government. The latter principle led them to advocate, almost obsessively, direct legislation by the people. For many Populists, adoption of the mechanisms of direct democracy overshadowed nearly every other issue (Hicks 1931, 406–407). Populist candidates enjoyed a measure of success in the elections of 1892 and 1894, capturing numerous state and local offices, seats in Congress, and electoral votes for the presidency. In 1896, however, when Populists endorsed the ill-fated candidacy of the Democratic presidential nominee, William Jennings Bryan, the party's fault lines emerged and it quickly disintegrated as an independent party and coherent political movement.

Populism's flowering as a political movement in the late nineteenth century was relatively short-lived, but the Populist impulse is perennial. It has existed in various manifestations throughout American history, from Shay's Rebellion to the Anti-Federalist movement, to Jacksonian democracy, to the late-nineteenth-century People's Party, to the latter-day taxpayers' revolt and crusade for term limits—and in many other times and places. Through various manifestations (of both left and right), Populism has maintained some consistent characteristics. First, it is essentially individualistic, which is to say that Populism is driven by individual self-interest, by the common person's aspiration for political equality and social and economic opportunity. Second, Populism assumes that common people are trustworthy and competent—given a chance, they will make wise choices. Third, and most important, Populism distrusts concentration of power in the hands of elites—either in the private sector or in government. In some periods (including the late nineteenth century), Populists have targeted concentrations of economic power, but more consistently they have set their sights on the institutions of government, where they believe concentrated and corrupt power thwarts the common people's will.

Progressivism as a political movement followed closely on the heels of the Populist revolt, and flourished during the first two decades of the twentieth century. The Progressive movement gathered together under a big tent of earnest reformers of all stripes—prohibitionists, trust-busters, muckrakers, conservationists, activists for social justice, and advocates of women's suffrage. The movement embraced eastern elites such as Theodore Roosevelt, Henry Stimson, and Woodrow Wilson as well as some western Bryanites. Progressives had diverse and sometimes contradictory policy objectives, but they shared a common vision that informed, civic-minded elements of the citizenry (especially educated, middle-class professionals and small businessmen) and an enlightened, professionalized government could relieve the hardships caused by industrialization and other dislocating forces, and could otherwise work to create a better society. Their biases can be characterized as moralistic (in that they wanted to reform government and society) and elitist (in that they tended to distrust the lower classes and wanted to invest power in well-trained professional experts). Progressives believed that corrupt party bosses, allied with increasingly powerful and selfish corporate interests, had seized control of representative government (especially legislatures) and were using government to retard social progress. It was imperative, they believed, to liberate representative government from these corrupt forces so that it might become an effective instrument for social reform. The Progressive strategies for restructuring and reforming representative government were many. They included campaign finance reform, regulation of lobbyists, direct primaries, direct election of U.S. senators, civil-service reform, and the adoption of the initiative, referendum, and recall. Unlike Populists, Progressives did not intend for their reforms (including the initiative) to undermine representative government; instead, Progressives wanted to redeem and strengthen government (Cronin 1989, 54).

Progressivism cut across party lines—both Rooseveltian Republicans and Wilsonian Democrats claimed the label. In 1912, when Roosevelt was denied the Republican presidential nomination, he formed the short-lived Progressive Party and (with Hiram Johnson as his running mate) ran for president on its platform, which summarized many of the movement's core principles. The party was so closely identified with TR, however, that after he lost the election, it quickly folded. As a focused movement, Progressivism lasted through most of that decade (and the administration of Woodrow Wilson), winning important victories. In all, 1900–1920 was an era of wide-ranging reform. Progressives during that period achieved suffrage for women, direct election of senators, prohibition, significant regulation of the economy, graduated income tax, and in many states, the mechanisms of direct democracy. By the beginning of the 1920s, the Progressive movement was a largely spent force. But the Progressive impulse has endured in various reformist individuals and groups, and has maintained its moralistic and elitist characteristics. Modern Progressives distrust Populists and their attempts to undermine representative government. Instead they continue to believe in the importance of enlightened, well-managed government institutions. Present-day "good government" groups, such as the League of Women Voters and Common Cause, stand squarely in the Progressive tradition. Such groups support efforts to clean up government and reduce the influence of special interests; however, they oppose term limits and other Populist attempts to reduce the power of government officials.

In this discussion of the origins and impact of the initiative process, we use the terms "Populist" and "Progressive" to refer not only to the specific movements of the late nineteenth and early twentieth centuries, but also to the longer term impulses of American politics.

Competing Motives and Expectations for Direct Democracy

Political coalitions often succeed by accentuating areas of agreement over disagreement. Focusing on the goal of achieving a particular policy or reform diverts attention from differences in the expectations and goals that various coalition members might have. It is clear from historical accounts that both the Populists and the Progressives sought to adopt the mechanisms of direct democracy, but had different motives and expectations in doing so. Progressives wanted to use direct democracy to curb the power of corrupt corporate and partisan interests that controlled the state legislatures at the time. Populists shared this goal, but they had a more radical ultimate vision. Populists mistrusted legislatures generally and wanted to substitute direct popular control for representative government, which they regarded as a less pure form of democracy. Progressives, by comparison, wanted voters to check the legislature, but they did not want to replace representative government altogether. Progressives rejected the mediation of political parties and corporations, but that did not mean that they thought the public could govern without mediation. Quite the contrary, Progressives believed in the importance of expertise and administrative competence.

Consider the thrust of other Progressive reforms. The city manager form of local government sought to place local government in the hands of a neutral city manager, who in many ways was more removed from electoral pressures than a city mayor or city council member would be. Progressives sought to depoliticize the civil service because they recognized the need for neutral competence in policy matters. The evolution of public policy as a discipline derives from the Progressive idea that experts can give scientific, neutral advice free of partisan tint. Nonpartisan politics was an attempt to weaken political parties and to promote the influence of individuals in the political process, but on the assumption that people had to take the responsibility to inform themselves and that lazy voters could be easily corrupted by other influences. Progressives' wariness of unmediated public opinion helps to explain another controversial reform, the introduction of electoral registration procedures. Progressives were aware that voters could be led to commit voter fraud and sought to diminish the risk of fraud by introducing reforms that registered and accounted for voters more accurately. But as critics have pointed out, the thrust of these Progressive reforms was elitist—they effectively cut out many working-class and minority voters. By placing the onus on individuals to register themselves at some point well in advance of the election, Progressive reformers established a screening device that filtered out the less-interested and less-involved individuals. Progressives did not have a blind faith in the wisdom of the people to make policy. Instead, they thought that an informed, middle-class electorate could recognize when policymaking was corrupt, and act to adopt good proposals developed by competent people when they saw them.

In short, the Progressives sought to use the initiative to enhance the responsiveness, professionalism, competence, and expertise of government. By contrast, the Populists sought, then as now, to substitute the wisdom of the people, such as it is, for the deliberations of elected officials. This tension between Populist and Progressive notions of direct democracy is echoed in the current debate over initiative lawmaking.

The Populist position today supports the extended use of direct democracy and little or no reform of the initiative process. Pro-term limit groups are good examples of contemporary Populists. They support not only term limits but also unconstrained initiative lawmaking, in part because both mechanisms weaken legislatures, and they believe that legislatures tend to enact unwanted laws and create wasteful expenses. Moreover, they oppose any initiative reforms that would give the legislature the ability to amend or respond to initiatives in circulation and favor the direct over the indirect initiative. Many academic writers, by contrast, fall into the Progressive camp (e.g., Elisabeth Gerber 1999). While they view the initiative process as a useful supplement to representative government, they also believe in government professionalism.

THE POPULIST MODEL CRITIQUED

The typical analysis of the initiative process focuses on a conventional laundry list of problems posed by the increasing use of the initiative. Hence, there are scholarly debates over whether voters are sufficiently competent to handle the responsibility of voting on initiatives, whether money spent on measures needs to be limited and regulated, and the like. These are perfectly sensible questions to ask, but they miss the big picture, and without the right context it is hard to begin to determine the right answers. How can we discuss whether voters are sufficiently competent unless we stipulate the role they are meant to play? In the Progressive model, the voter's role is to check representative government when it fails to be sufficiently responsive or when it acts in a biased way. Cognitively, this demands less than the Populist conception, in which voters are the primary lawmakers and need to be informed about the minutiae of policies and programs. Even if, as Professor Arthur Lupia (1994) has argued, where voters do not have to know about policies but only about someone who does know and can be trusted, the Populist conception would require an infinitely richer world of information cues than the Progressive one. It is one thing occasionally to check the work of the government; it is another to replace it.

So we propose to step back from the microdebate over features of the initiative and consider the larger problem, namely, that the Populist vision of direct democracy has prevailed over the Progressive, and that this has important implications for the structure of state government and the balance between majority will and minority rights. As a consequence, increasing use of the popular initiative has placed an extra burden on the courts, leaving them as the check of first and last resort. This is particularly true in two areas where one might expect representative and initiative government to most diverge: governmental reform and individual rights. In this section, we will consider the divergence between the initiative and representative processes. Later, we will look at the court's role and the problems it faces handling this burden.

Undermining Checks and Balances: Initiative vs. Recall and Referendum

In retrospect, there was no way that the two conceptions of direct democracy could have coincided equally for very long. The implications of one inevitably precluded the full operation of the other. Since in politics power flows down the path of least resistance, those elements of direct democracy that furthered the Populist goal of unmediated, plebiscite decision making (i.e., the initiative) undermined those elements (i.e., the recall, the referendum, and the legislative constitutional amendment) that supported the Progressive ideal of supplementing the existing representative system in order to redeem it. Decision-making power at that point had two potential paths: the representative one with multiple veto points and requiring much negotiation, and the popular initiative, which placed matters before the people directly and with fewer institutional obstacles. Which way would power eventually flow? The answer is clear—in the direction of the popular initiative.

To elaborate, the Progressive model sought to supplement the existing balance among the legislative, judicial, and executive branches in state governments with the check of a direct popular vote. To understand the logic of this, one needs to appreciate the special features of many state constitutions, particularly in the western states, where the popular initiative has flourished. State constitutions, with one exception, mimic the tripartite structure of the federal system. But there are some critical differences. Significantly, most states have plural executives, reflecting the early suspicion of concentrated executive power. Hence, for example, California elects a governor, lieutenant governor, secretary of state, attorney general, controller, state insurance commissioner, treasurer, and superintendent of schools in statewide races. In addition, the resources available to executive officials were relatively meager until the Progressive Era. Consistent with their commitment to expertise, gubernatorial resources began to grow substantially at the turn of the century. But in the nineteenth century the fear of concentrated executive power and the fracturing of that power into separate, understaffed executive offices led to legislative dominance.

In that context, interest-group influence flowed to the source of power and legislatures became the focal point of special-interest activity. The Progressives faced a situation in which the balance of power tilted significantly toward the legislature, and even more so in the states than in the federal government. Hence, they sought to create new institutional arrangements to check legislatures. One such arrangement was the development of a more expert administrative structure; another was the institution of direct democracy.

It is important in our analysis to distinguish between the ways in which the recall, referendum, and initiative operate, since some modes in which these mechanisms operate are more compatible with Progressive intentions than others. The recall, for instance, allows citizens to remove elected officials from office for reasons of incompetence or malfeasance before their terms of office expire. In recent years, the recall has also been used at the local level to rebuke public officials who pass unpopular taxes or other measures. While this might seem problematic in the sense that special election turnout is much lower than general election turnout and can lead to biased outcomes, it is not problematic from the point of view of checking legislative power. Rather, it seeks to enhance the electoral control that voters have over elected officials, making representatives more responsive to public opinion.

The recall thus operates within the framework of representative government, because it is based on the assumption that elected officials will make decisions and that voters will retrospectively judge whether they approve of those decisions. If we define responsiveness as the rate at which changes in public opinion are reflected in changes in representation, then a heightened threat of removal from office, or even the inconvenience of having to defend one's position off-cycle, should increase responsiveness so defined. In theory, it could also lessen legislative bias. Here we define bias as movement away from the median voter outcome (a concept which is itself controversial). So conceived, the recall is in some sense a way to keep electoral pressure constant in order to offset pressures from nonelectoral sources. In practice, of course, there is nothing to stop interest groups from exerting their own pressure through the recall process, particularly if the turnout is low. So the frequent use of the recall, especially for policy reasons, is troublesome and potentially biased, but it does not challenge the basic framework of representative government and adds a check to the whole system.

Similarly, the referendum works within the representative government framework and supplements existing checks in the system. In a referendum, the legislature and governor sign a bill into law and then, if enough citizens sign a petition to qualify a referendum, the bill is sent to the voters for final approval. The referendum rarely makes legislatures more responsive, since it is a reactive mechanism: the government must act first to trigger reaction by the people. But the referendum does serve to check biases in the median voter sense that a bill which does not meet voter approval can be rejected at the ballot box.

As Butler and Ranney (1994) have noted, the referendum is widely used by other countries in a somewhat different way, more like a legislative constitutional amendment (LCA) in several American states. In the LCA process, typically both houses of the state legislature have to pass a measure by a supermajority vote (sometimes twice) and then the measure goes before the people. In Europe, major constitutional questions that divide the parties or policy issues of major importance are occasionally referred to the people for resolution. Examples of this are votes in Britain on the Common Market and in France on the Algerian war. Both the European referendum and the LCA in the United States are compatible with representative government, even in the cases where the legislature has used the referendum to avoid making a difficult decision. The point is that the legislature was given the opportunity to act first, and even if it ultimately decided to pass the matter over to the voters, it was not bypassed in the process.

The direct democracy mechanisms that pose the greatest challenge to representative government are the forms of the popular initiative. There are two: the statutory and the constitutional initiative. In both cases, citizens are able to propose measures directly that would either become statutes or would amend the constitution. The legislature and the governor are formally left out of the loop, although it is increasingly common for statewide candidates in particular to sponsor and sometimes finance initiative campaigns as a means of promoting their own candidacies. Initiative constitutional amendments (ICAs) most seriously undermine representative government because they can only be altered by another constitutional amendment. Some groups consider this a particularly objectionable feature of ICAs, because it means that they cannot be easily modified by elected officials and that they lock in policies formed by the uncertainties of shifting political coalitions.

As defenders of the initiative are quick to point out, popular initiatives are more likely to fail than to pass in most years. Voters seem to have the practical wisdom to vote "no" when measures are confusing or long. Even so, as discussed further below, voters frequently approve measures that violate basic rights or constitutional provisions, leaving the court to check or modify these flawed measures. A system with multiple checks and veto points is more likely to weed out unconstitutional or otherwise flawed measures than a system with few or none. Even if the people are no more flawed in their judgment than elected representatives as a whole, the probability in the representative system that a bad idea from one house will become law is lowered by the ability of another house or the governor to modify or veto it. Put another way, the probability that a representative system with checks and balances will adopt a constitutionally flawed proposal is the conditional probability that each of the actors within the system will make the same misjudgment. That scenario, in general, is less likely than one body making the mistake by itself.

It is true, of course, that the checks and balances system can produce unhealthy inertia. Indeed, it was the pathological inertia orchestrated by corporate interests and party bosses at the turn of the century that led both Populists and Progressives to urge adoption of direct democracy, and it can be argued that legislative gridlock in recent years has led to increased use of the initiative in many states. For example, Proposition 13 in California and Proposition 2 1/2 in Massachusetts (both of which reduced property taxes) appeared on the ballot and were approved by voters because the legislatures in those states were too slow in addressing public distress over high tax rates. In any event, there is no doubt that the relatively high level of inertia in the checks and balances system explains why the initiative has taken off in America but not in Europe outside of Switzerland. Since the parliamentary system is more responsive to begin with and the U.S. system is slower and more preservative of rights, it makes sense that the initiative would appear in the U.S. context. The problem with the initiative process, however, is that instead of simply making the legislature more responsive (as the Progressives had hoped and which it sometimes does), it has also evolved into a method for bypassing the checks in the legislative system altogether. As we shall see, this has implications for the substance of what is produced. Initiative government leads to a higher level of policy responsiveness to the median statewide voters, but it produces biases against individual and minority rights—precisely what the checks and balances system was meant to protect.

Undermining Representative Government

In the interest of greater responsiveness to the statewide median voter, the popular initiative not only weakens checks and balances in state governments, it clearly undermines core functions of representative government—especially legislatures. Specifically, it undermines the legislature's ability to set the policy agenda, frame policy options, balance competing interests, and make the final decisions on difficult policy choices. In these ways, the popular initiative creates a majoritarian, plebiscitary alternative to representative government. But again, we return to the question: Why does it matter if initiative lawmaking undermines representative government? Simply put, legislatures and other institutions of representative government promote certain democratic opportunities and reinforce certain democratic norms in ways that the initiative process does not, and these procedural differences have important implications.

Undermining Democratic Opportunities

A well-functioning democratic system provides opportunities for refinement, informed deliberation, consensus building, and compromise. Legislative procedures tend to maximize these opportunities, whereas the initiative process by its nature undermines them. More specifically, in the legislative process, after a bill is drafted by its author, it is referred to committee, hearings are held, the original language is scrutinized and marked up in open meetings, the bill is sent to the floor of one house (where it can be further amended), and if it is approved, it is referred to the other house, where the process is repeated. If the second house approves a modified version of the bill, differences are reconciled in joint committee, and, finally, the bill is sent to the governor's desk for signature or veto. Along the way, expert staff on committees and in specialized legal and policy offices, as well as outside lobbyists and experts, review and comment on the bill, often providing legislators with detailed analyses for use in their deliberations. In addition, committee members generally are well versed on the policy area the bill addresses (although in the term-limits era, member expertise is less certain). Throughout the process, interested parties can identify drafting flaws, unintended consequences, more optimal solutions, etc., and urge modifications. Opponents often can work with an author to seek amendments that resolve their concerns. If a minority of members intensely object to the bill, they can often find ways to force changes or delay. In addition, the system requires the bill to win concurrent approval of two houses of the legislature and the governor's office (which may be controlled by different political parties). Moreover, depending on the state, some of the legislature's voting rules are expressly supermajoritarian. As a result of these institutional arrangements, proponents are required to compromise their most extreme positions, harmonize differences, and build a large consensus in support of the bill if it is to be enacted. Most bills (especially complex or controversial ones) are amended multiple times prior to final adoption. Accordingly, a bill that emerges from the legislative process most often is well vetted and is accepted by a fairly broad majority.

By comparison, in the initiative process, private individuals or groups draft a measure's language, usually with the help of private attorneys specializing in election law. Opponents and other interested parties are routinely excluded from the drafting process. Once drafting is complete, sponsors file the initiative with the state officials, who prepare a title and summary but have no power to amend the proposal. The initiative's sponsors then have a specified number of days to gather enough signatures to qualify the measure for the ballot. Once the proposed initiative is submitted for signatures it *cannot* be amended. Sponsors in large states usually turn to a professional petition-gathering firm, which charges from one to two dollars per signature, depending upon the urgency of the deadline. The signed petitions are then submitted to the secretary of state, who reviews them for their validity and places the measure on the ballot. Voters, who have limited time and other resources, often are overwhelmed by the length and complexity of the ballot pamphlet and are forced to rely on a range of cues (endorsements, television advertisements, etc.) to inform their decisions. The process gives voters no opportunity to harmonize competing interests, request compromise language, or seek other more optimal alternatives. Instead, voters are forced to make a binary choice— either "yes" or "no"—in response to the fixed option presented by the initiative's proponents. In addition, with a few exceptions for local tax measures and the like, a simple majority vote of those participating in the election prevails. Typically, initiatives are enacted by considerably less than a majority of registered voters, particularly when the election is held in the off year. As a result, initiative proponents are not required to forge a broad consensus in order to enact major changes in law. A fleeting, simple majority will do, even if the initiative's opponents are intense and the supporters are relatively apathetic. Moreover, aside from seeking the measure's defeat, opponents have few opportunities to participate in the process. Again, unlike in the legislative process, opponents have no opportunity to seek amendments or compromise. Accordingly, if they cannot defeat the initiative outright at the polls, their only recourse is to litigate. As we discuss later, initiative opponents who lose at the polls more often than not challenge the initiative in the courts. We suggest that the initiative process's paucity of opportunities for refinement, informed deliberation, consensus building, and compromise fuels this litigiousness and makes it nearly inevitable.

Violating Democratic Norms

In addition, the actual operation of the initiative process violates a number of norms that have evolved in advanced democracies. These norms have been widely adopted by many modern state legislatures and are central to the Progressive conception of good government, but they are not required features of the initiative process. Conceivably, some of these norms could be grafted into the initiative process, but to date there has been little movement in that direction.

The first norm is *openness*. Openness means that the public and press are entitled to know about the information and motives that legislators have when they make policy decisions. This expectation is codified in open meeting laws, which require that legislatures or city and county boards give public notice before they hold hearings, that the meetings in which decisions are made should be accessible to the press and constituents, and that votes should be taken in public. Typically, open meeting laws make some important exemptions, such as for confidential personnel or contracting matters. For most matters, however, the norm requires that the front end of policymaking be an observable activity, if not by the public directly, then by the press, who report it to the public. The openness norm is based on the premise that voters need to be informed as to the true intent of legislation and the interests supporting and opposing it.

The initiative process violates the openness norm in several ways. First, meetings held to formulate proposed initiatives, even if they include public officials, are not covered by open meeting laws. There are no public notice requirements, nor hearings to solicit public input. The press is not privy to the machinations behind a particular measure, except in after-the-fact interviews (see, e.g., Chavez 1998). The process of devising an initiative can best be described as a black box. There are no constraints on and little public knowledge of what goes on at this stage. Measures simply appear at the circulation stage and the story behind how they got written and the motives behind them filter out selectively. What we do know suggests that many of the same kinds of political tactics and manipulations that occur behind closed legislative doors also occur in the meetings of the initiative proposers—provisions are added solely for the purpose of getting groups to endorse a measure, language is altered to maximize ambiguity and misunderstanding, popular provisions are combined with unpopular ones to maximize the chances of passing the unpopular ones, and the like (Schrag 1998).

The second democratic norm is *accountability*. We typically associate the accountability norm with representative government. Because voters (as principals) delegate lawmaking authority to elected officials (as agents), there is a possibility that the agents will fail to do what they have promised, or will otherwise fail to act in the principals' interest. Hence a major concern of representative government is how to give constituents more control over their representatives. This requires that voters know what their representatives have done in office and through their ballots appropriately reward or punish them. But can there also be accountability problems in direct democracy? In the formulation of the initiative measures, decisions are made by various actors who shape the choices that voters will have. An individual with enough money can essentially purchase the right to put an initiative before the people. What gets included in that measure or left out is decided by the proposer. If a measure proves to be poorly drafted, deceptive and illusory, or unconstitutional, the proposer is not personally accountable in any way.

Moreover, if, as Arthur Lupia would have it, voters rely on cues from experts such as Ralph Nader, then they delegate a great deal of power to a new class of mediators who are also unaccountable if something goes wrong. This is particularly a problem with measures that hide conflicts of interest at their core. Conflict-of-interest laws assume that powerful financial self-interest distorts political judgment in ways that are detrimental to the public interest. Legislators are prohibited from proposing pieces of legislation that would personally benefit themselves. However, there are no conflict-of-interest prohibitions in the initiative process. If a citizen wants to propose a massive increase in highway money and happens to stand to profit financially from the business that the state will generate if the measure passes, there is nothing in the law to stop the citizen from profiting in this way. Indeed, many initiatives are proposed by groups (teachers, insurance companies, trial lawyers, lottery entrepreneurs, etc.) who either want to line their own pockets or limit the ability of their adversaries to do so. In short, while legislators often try to undermine accountability and sometimes fail to observe prohibitions on conflict of interest and bribery, none of these regulations even apply to private citizens who propose initiatives. As a private citizen, for example, Ralph Nader could be given a million dollars for his endorsement of a seemingly pro-consumer measure or could participate in deceptive advertising or profit from business the initiative generates, and under current law he would be totally unaccountable, except perhaps in reputational costs. If we believe accountability norms matter in legislatures, why do we disregard them in the initiative process?

The third democratic norm is *competence*. The evolution of state government in the past century has been heavily influenced by the Progressive idea that expertise is important for good policymaking. As government programs and policymaking have become more complex and technical in the twentieth century, staffing for both the legislative and executive branches has increased exponentially, and thousands of policy experts are now trained in the nation's universities every year to staff the government. The Progressive philosophy acknowledges that voters must have experts they trust, either inside or outside the government, because they do not have the time and training to become expert on all policies and decisions. Populists, as we have discussed, disbelieve these premises. In their view, the average citizen cannot trust representatives or experts to make choices for them, because although experts have informational advantages, they may or may not share the public's values. The Progressive faith in legislative expertise is premised on value neutrality, but Populists believe that government decisions often favor elite interests, and they become suspicious when value choices are wrapped in the mystery of neutral scientific language.

But even Populists recognize that information and guidance are needed to negotiate the complexities of modern government. Aside from the press and the ballot pamphlet, expertise is provided by the private market in the form of lawyers and other professionals whose services can be purchased to draft and qualify measures. But without the guarantee of accountability, these consultants are not publicly responsible for the services they provide, except in the market signal sense. There are reputational costs to them if they err, deceive, or fail in a way that harms those who paid for their services, but not if they help their clients but harm the public. More typically, courts are left with the task of coping with measures that are illegal or badly crafted.

The fourth democratic norm is *fairness*. Fairness is typically built into the legislative process in a variety of ways. Fairness means such things as giving adequate time for the expression of dissenting opinions, consulting with the opposition and the public generally before promulgating a proposal, and having regular, preannounced voting rules for making decisions. But in the formulation of initiatives, there are no such requirements. The wealthiest person or group in the room might prevail over the objections of others because they are willing to finance the campaign. The objections of those who might be harmed by a measure need not be heard. There are no formal procedural rules or expectations. Moreover, it would be hard to develop fairness in this process. As game theory teaches us, fairness is hard to achieve in the absence of repeated play. If a group or individuals know that they have to deal with another group or individuals on future matters, then they are less likely to defect and more likely to cooperate. For instance, if a group thinks that its interaction with another is limited, it will be more tempted to break a promise, since it does not have to worry about retaliation at some later point in time. Since the formulators of initiatives may or may not come together in the future, there are fewer incentives to be fair and to cooperate than in a legislative setting. This creates more situations where the temporary majority will take unfair advantage of the temporary minority. This may also help to explain the large number of court actions needed to protect against rights infringements by initiatives.

In sum, the popular initiative, as it is practiced, undermines basic opportunities and critical norms associated with advanced democratic practices and central to the Progressive conception of good government. It is extremely ironic that initiatives have the reputation of being a more pure form of democracy when the process undermines democratic opportunities and violates procedural guarantees observed by almost every freely elected legislature in the world. In important ways, direct democracy can be less democratic than indirect, representative democracy. As we discuss in the conclusion, some of direct democracy's problems could be addressed through future reforms, but the implementation problems are complex.

POLICY IMPLICATIONS

The discussion so far has focused on process. In a democracy, process has independent value because how a decision is made and who participates in making it affect the decision's legitimacy. But process can also affect outputs, that is, policy. As initiative lawmaking has grown dramatically in recent decades, it has become increasingly important to ask in what ways the process has affected policy. Academics are divided as to whether initiatives introduce an overall policy bias. Gerber (1996) argues that one should not look for left- or right-leaning biases, but rather ask whether the policies produced by the initiative process are closer to the median voter. Since her critics do not adopt a similar approach, it is hard to say whether Gerber's findings can be widely replicated. But they seem plausible and for the moment we will take them as an assumption. If we assume that the initiative is median-voter enhancing, where would we expect the greatest policy differences between the products of legislatures and initiatives to appear? Two areas where voters and representatives will likely diverge are government reform and minority rights. We will discuss each in turn.

Government Reform

The representative system is bedeviled by the vested interest problem, which is to say that representatives can develop a self-interested, careerist perspective by virtue of the positions they occupy. Incumbents who want to make their lives more secure and comfortable will do all they can to keep political competition at bay, or will make the conditions and pay of their jobs as favorable as possible. Sometimes, the lawmakers' perspective regarding their working conditions is valid because they understand the requirements and stresses of public office holding better than the public; but sometimes it is completely self-serving. Reforms that threaten legislative self-interest will not pass a body of elected officials unless and until the public clamor for reform becomes so great that the legislature must act to prevent electoral backlash. Often reform that passes a legislature depends on a "fouling the nest" cycle; that is, if a major scandal causes the legislative "nest" to become so foul that it is widely acknowledged it must be cleaned up, legislators reluctantly will enact reforms. However, the normal inertia built into the checks and balances system is multiplied when it comes to measures that adversely affect the legislature, and it is extremely rare for legislatures to adopt such reforms. The biggest gap between median voter preferences and legislative response is in the area of government and political reform and it is no surprise that in recent years such reforms have dominated initiative ballots.

The most striking example of this dynamic is term limits. Over the past decade, polls have consistently shown that Americans overwhelmingly favor term limits for elected officials. Remarkably, with the exception of North Dakota, Illinois, and Mississippi, in every state where citizens have the opportunity to place initiatives on the ballot (i.e., in twenty-one of the twenty-four states with the initiative process), term limits have been adopted. By contrast, with the exception of Louisiana, none of the twenty-six states that lack provisions for initiative lawmaking have adopted term limits through the legislative process. Similarly, despite strong pressure for congressional term limits, members of Congress have voted down proposals to limit their own terms. It is clear that legislatures have been resolutely unresponsive to the public's demand for term limits, and direct democracy generally has been the only means by which these reforms can be imposed.

Term limits are only one example of a recent flood of Populist efforts to constrain representative government—efforts that generally can only attain their goals through the initiative process. Other examples include mandatory tax limitations, caps on state spending, reductions in legislative budgets, restrictions on legislative pensions, and imposition of legislative rules. One advantage of the popular initiative is that it allows government and political reforms to bubble up from below and circumvent the self-interested inertia of the legislators. However, if legislative self-interest can distort institutional reforms, citizens also can frame reforms in a self-serving and distorting way. Take the term-limits issue. While it is true that legislators have a self-interest in job security, groups in the electorate often have an interest in changing the rules so as to increase the odds of achieving partisan advantages or obtaining the policies they like. For example, in 1990 Republicans in California supported Proposition 140 (which imposed term limits and cut back on the legislature's resources) at least in part because that initiative shifted power to the governor (who up to that time typically had been a Republican) at the expense of the Democratic-controlled legislature. Similarly, groups that seek to use the initiative process to control legislative redistricting often harbor partisan objectives. In other words, many groups, including legislators, will have a self-interested perspective on reform. If we believe that governmental rules should be above normal politics to the greatest degree possible, then the rules should not be dictated by a temporary majority in the electorate at a particular election, but should represent some larger consensus in the polity. As we discuss further in our conclusion, some potential reforms to the initiative process, such as requiring a supermajority vote for major changes in government structure and rules, may help achieve this goal.

Minority Rights

One also can expect the initiative process to produce different outcomes than the legislative process will in the areas of protecting minority rights and promoting minority interests. This is so for several reasons. First, the checks and balances system of representative government contains numerous features expressly designed to strengthen the position of minorities and constrain majority rule. For example, bicameralism, the executive veto, and supermajority voting rules require the building of broad coalitions (larger than a simple majority); the committee system provides minority groups with additional points of access and often places brakes on the legislative process; the party system and logrolling provide opportunities for minorities to aggregate and leverage their strength; publicly recorded votes and electoral competition build accountability into the system; and the mere presence of minorities in a legislature may deter the worst forms of legislative prejudice (Bell 1978; Eule 1990; Linde 1993). By contrast, the initiative process, at least in theory, allows even a fleeting majority of citizens, in the secrecy and anonymity of the voting booth, to enact a law that adversely affects an unpopular minority. Moreover, some scholarly evidence suggests that voters do not very well understand or appreciate basic constitutional rights and thus may be prone to violate them through the initiative process.

In addition, the initiative process may be more likely than legislatures to produce laws that adversely affect minorities due to the two constituencies problem, in which, under certain demographic conditions, it is possible to have a statewide median that is very different from the median in the legislature. If this difference has racial overtones, then the initiative may be used to voice the interests of the statewide racial majority against the interests of the racial minorities. This can currently be seen most clearly in California. There, at present, the statewide electorate is disproportionately white and middle class relative to the population. Specifically, while the state population is nearly 50 percent nonwhite, the state electorate is over two-thirds white. Currently, initiatives in California are in effect at-large elections controlled by a white electorate. By contrast, legislative districts are based not on the number of people who vote, but on total population. The operation of the one-person-one-vote principle, combined with vigorous application of section 2 of the Voting Rights Act of 1965, has resulted in the creation of a large number of minority-controlled legislative districts. As a consequence, in 2000, the California legislature (with 120 total members) had 24 Latinos, 5 African Americans, and 2 Asian Americans, many of whom served in key leadership positions— three of the last four speakers of the Assembly have been members of racial or ethnic minorities. Given this discrepancy between the composition of the legislature and the initiative electorate, it is not surprising that the recent language, immigration, and affirmative action changes were adopted as initiative measures rather than as ordinary legislation. Again, without expressing an opinion as to whether these were good or bad policies, we can safely state that they would not have been passed by the legislature at the time they appeared on the ballot.

Empirical studies regarding the fate of minority rights in the initiative process compared to the legislative process are difficult to come by. Most comparative analyses are merely anecdotal and their conclusions range across the map. Some scholars emphasize that representative government has an imperfect record of protecting the rights of minorities and that direct democracy has not fulfilled the most dire predictions regarding its potential to tyrannize minorities. Thomas Cronin, for example, has argued that "direct democracy devices can only rarely be faulted for impairing the rights of the powerless" (Cronin 1989, 92). Moreover, initiative defenders argue, at least with respect to women, that the initiative process has been used to promote the rights of persons historically marginalized in the political process. (Several states, for example, adopted women's suffrage through the initiative.) Other political scientists, however, point to specific instances in which initiatives restricted minority rights and conclude that the initiative process endangers minorities. David Magleby, for example, argues that direct democracy is a danger to the rights of minorities, "unless the courts are able and willing to protect these groups from attacks from direct legislation" (Magleby 1994, 241). Two recent empirical studies have measured voters' propensity to approve initiatives that restrict the rights of minorities—and have reached different conclusions. Gamble (1997) found that while voters more often than not reject proposed initiatives at the polls, they approve three-fourths of initiatives and referenda that seek to repeal existing civil rights laws (e.g., with respect to fair housing and accommodations, school desegregation, gay rights, English-language laws, and AIDS policies) or prevent elected officials from enacting such laws (248). Donovan and Bowler (1998) challenge Gamble's findings, at least with respect to statewide measures affecting the civil rights of homosexuals. They found that voters approved initiatives restricting the rights of homosexuals at a lower rate than they approved other initiatives (267).

Kenneth Miller's recent study of three high-use initiative states (Oregon, Colorado, and California) over the past four decades found that voters in these states approved eleven initiatives that overturned or preempted efforts by representative government to promote the rights or interests of racial or other minorities (Miller 1999, 21). These initiatives should not be too easily caricatured as majority efforts to tyrannize minorities, although many of them at least presented that danger. Some of the measures (e.g., shifting from a policy of bilingual education to English immersion) arguably represented bona fide (if controversial) efforts to promote the interests of minorities and enjoyed some support in affected minority communities. The problem, however, is that initiatives that directly and differentially affect minorities can easily tap into a strain of antiminority sentiment in the electorate. The initiatives from the three states in this category sought to ban state efforts to prevent "private" racial discrimination in housing, restrict busing to desegregate public schools, restrict state efforts to protect the rights of homosexuals, establish English as the state's official language, restrict illegal immigration, ban state affirmative action for women and minorities, and restrict bilingual education. (As discussed further below, several of these initiatives were overturned by the courts.) By contrast, no voter-approved initiatives in those states during that period expressly expanded the rights of minorities. In addition, voters in these states adopted fifteen initiatives during this period that imposed burdens and restrictions on criminal defendants (surely an unpopular minority group.) Among other things, these initiatives authorized the death penalty, increased minimum sentences, restricted parole, and modified evidentiary rules and other criminal justice procedures. (Courts also invalidated, at least in part, several of these initiatives.) Again, by contrast, no initiatives in these states during this period expanded defendants' rights. The limited evidence does suggest that the initiative process, with its Populist orientation and its lack of institutional filters, is sometimes prone to produce laws that disadvantage relatively powerless minorities—and probably it is more likely than legislatures to do so.

To summarize our argument to this point, we have said that Populist-oriented initiative lawmaking weakens checks and balances and the government's representative function. This has procedural and policy implications. Procedurally, initiative lawmaking fails to maximize opportunities for deliberation, refinement, consensus building, and compromise and violates important democratic norms such as openness, accountability, competence, and fairness. In terms of policy, it produces big differences in the areas of governmental reforms and minority rights. What prevents initiatives from unfairly undermining individual rights and altering the constitutional structure of government? The courts. But putting pressure on the courts, as we shall see, raises some serious concerns.

INITIATIVE POLITICS AND THE COURTS

As we have seen, through the initiative process, Populists have discovered an increasingly effective way to bypass legislatures and enact law directly. They have not found a way, however, to bypass the courts.[3] Courts are a filter through which all laws potentially must pass, and thus they constitute the one institutional constraint on the initiative process's freedom of action. In this section, we discuss how courts have approached this uniquely important filtering role.

Judicial Review and the Counter-Majoritarian Difficulty

Judicial review (i.e., the courts' power to invalidate laws) is a unique and controversial mediating feature of the American constitutional system. From its inception, the purpose of judicial review has been counter-majoritarian. In exercising judicial review, the courts' responsibility is to check majority actions that run counter to constitutional principles (including individual rights, especially those of unpopular minorities). In any democratic system, judicial review is controversial because it can threaten popular sovereignty, thus posing what has been called the "counter-majoritarian difficulty" (Bickel 1962). Accordingly, when exercising their power of judicial review, courts must balance popular sovereignty with other constitutional principles, including protection of minority rights. And more specifically, since the New Deal era, courts have given priority to the constitutional protection of certain rights over others. Namely, in *U.S. v. Carolene Products*,[4] the U.S. Supreme Court set forth a differential standard of review whereby government actions affecting property rights are subject to lesser scrutiny than government actions that infringe on civil rights and liberties, political rights, or the rights of protected "discrete and insular" minorities.

Most analysis of judicial review focuses on its operation within the context of representative government, usually at the federal level. Thus, the "counter-majoritarian difficulty" is understood as the nullification by unelected judges of laws enacted by elected representatives. Judicial review of direct democracy, however, is a more acute counter-majoritarian act. When a court strikes down a voter-approved initiative, it is not checking a coordinate branch of representative government; it is checking the people themselves. As former California Supreme Court justice Joseph Grodin noted, "It is one thing for a court to tell a legislature that a statute it has adopted is unconstitutional; to tell that to the people of a state who have indicated their direct support for the measure through the ballot is another" (Grodin 1988). Overturning a direct vote of the people thus has its own dynamic, different from judicial review of "ordinary" legislation. But what is the legal significance of this difference?

Judicial Review of Direct Democracy: Competing Views

The U.S. Supreme Court has held that it is irrelevant for purposes of judicial review whether a challenged law has been enacted by a legislature or by the people directly.[5] But in the lower federal courts and state courts, where most legal battles over initiatives are waged, judges increasingly seem to recognize that the process for adopting initiatives is radically different from standard legislative proceedings and—one way or the other—that those differences matter when reviewing challenges to initiatives. This has stirred increasing analysis and debate about how courts should treat initiatives.

Populists argue that, in exercising their power of judicial review, courts should give extraordinary deference to initiatives, because initiatives represent the "pure" will of the people, and the will of the people is entitled to great respect. Many modern Progressives, however, have developed increasing concerns regarding the Populist orientation of the initiative process and advocate vigilant judicial review of initiatives as a legitimate means for protecting individual rights and representative government. Both views have adherents in the courts.

Juris-Populists

Judges who adopt the Populist view can be characterized as "juris-populists." One example is former U.S. Supreme Court justice Hugo Black. Black asserted that the initiative process was "as near to a democracy as you can get" and that a challenge to a law has less force if the law is enacted by the people directly than if it were enacted by the legislature.[6] Black voted to uphold initiatives against attack in several high-profile cases, including *Reitman v. Mulkey*,[7] *James v. Valtierra*,[8] and *Hunter v. Erickson*.[9] Justice Antonin Scalia offers a more recent example. In a dissenting opinion in *Romer v. Evans*[10] (which overturned Colorado Amendment 2, a voter-approved statewide initiative that would have prevented homosexuals from claiming rights as a protected class), Scalia wrote: "[The initiative] put directly to all the citizens of the state, the question: Should homosexuality be given special protection? They answered no. The court today asserts that this most democratic of procedures is unconstitutional. . . . Striking [the initiative] down is an act, not of judicial judgment, but of political will."[11] Similarly, Ninth Circuit Court judge Diarmuid O'Scannlain, in an opinion reversing a federal district judge's decision striking down California Proposition 209 (which dismantled the state's affirmative-action programs), wrote: "A system which permits one judge to block with the stroke of a pen what 4,736,180 state residents voted to enact as law tests the integrity of our constitutional democracy."[12] And in a series of opinions, justices of the California Supreme Court have argued that initiatives are entitled to "very special and very favored treatment";[13] that "it is our solemn duty jealously to guard the initiative process, it being one of the most precious rights of our democratic process";[14] and that the [state] constitution's initiative and referendum provisions should be liberally construed to promote the democratic process."[15]

The Populist view that judges should be extra deferential to initiatives has much intuitive appeal. However, as Julian Eule noted, if one accepts the underlying rationale for judicial review, this is in fact 180 degrees off the mark (Eule 1990, 1508). If the role of the courts in exercising judicial review is to act as a filter to protect constitutional principles and minority rights against majoritarian attack, then the courts need to be more vigilant, not less, when reviewing initiatives. This is so because of the following:

(1) As noted above, in a representative system, the courts are but one of many institutional checks on majority rule, whereas in the initiative process, the courts are the only institutional filter, the check of first and last resort. As we have argued, it is easier for violations of minority rights or other constitutional norms to emerge from an otherwise unfiltered majoritarian process than one in which there are multiple checks and balances.

(2) Conventional canons of judicial review maintain that courts should defer to a legislature's policy judgments in part due to considerations of competency. The idea is that a legislature has comparative institutional advantages over the courts in developing policy. But this assumption that gives rise to judicial deference in the legislative context is often inapposite in the context of initiatives. Specifically,

as we have noted, the initiative process lacks many of the comparative advantages of the legislative process (i.e., openness, accountability, competence, fairness, and opportunities for refinement, informed deliberation, consensus building, and compromise), and
thus it lacks much of the standard rationale for judicial deference.

Progressive-Oriented "Initiative Watchdogs"

Progressive-oriented judges who are concerned about procedural deficiencies in the initiative process and who argue for judicial vigilance in
reviewing initiatives may be characterized as "initiative watchdogs." Examples include the dissenting justices in *Brosnahan v. Brown*,[16] a 1982 California Supreme Court case that upheld California Proposition 8 (a 1982
statewide criminal justice initiative called the Victim's Bill of Rights). In
arguing that courts should not give special deference to initiatives, then-
chief justice Rose Bird (who was famously disliked by Populists because
of her liberal judicial activism), cited some of the defects of the initiative
process:

> Initiatives are drafted only by their proponents, so there is usually no inde-
> pendent review by anyone else. There are no public hearings. The draftsmen
> so monopolize the process that they completely control who is given the op-
> portunity to comment on or criticize the proposal before it appears on the
> ballot. This private process can and does have some detrimental conse-
> quences. The voters have no opportunity to propose amendment or revisions
> . . . [and the] only expression left to all other parties who are not proponents
> is the "yes" or "no" they cast. Since the only people who have input into
> the drafting of the measure are its proponents, there is no opportunity for
> compromise or negotiation. The result of this inflexibility is that more often
> than not a proposed initiative represents the most extreme form of law that
> is considered politically expedient.[17]

In the same case, Justice Mosk, joined by Justice Broussard, stressed the
potential consequences of the initiative process's unfiltered majoritarianism:

> Initiative promoters may obtain signatures for any proposal, however radical
> in concept and effect, and if they can persuade 51 percent of those who vote
> at an ensuing election to vote "aye," the measure becomes law regardless of
> how patently it may offend constitutional limitations. The new rule is that
> the fleeting whims of public opinion and prejudice are controlling over spe-
> cific constitutional provisions.[18]

Another initiative watchdog, federal district judge Thelton Henderson,
made it clear that he gave no special deference to initiatives when he is-

sued a preliminary injunction against Proposition 209, the 1996 California initiative banning state-sponsored affirmative action programs:

> The issue is not whether one judge can thwart the will of the people; rather, the issue is whether the challenged enactment complies with our constitution and Bill of Rights. Without a doubt, federal courts have no duty more important than to protect the rights and liberties of all Americans by considering and ruling on such issues, no matter how contentious or controversial they may be. This duty is certainly undiminished where the law under consideration comes directly from the ballot box and without benefit of the legislative process.[19]

In short, Progressive-oriented judges in the watchdog camp believe that initiatives have become dangerous lawmaking instruments that deserve no special deference. When initiatives have been challenged in the courts, these watchdog judges have been quite willing to overturn them.

The Problem of Backlash: Populist Pressure on the Courts

Since Populists place the highest value on popular sovereignty, they generally dislike judicial review, even in the context of representative government. For them, judicial review raises the specter of elitist, insular, activist judges overturning popular laws. Indeed, during the past century, judicial review of legislative enactments has often run counter to Populist interests and led to backlash against the courts. For instance, during the Warren Court era (the 1950s and 1960s) and the years that followed, activist courts invalidated policies that restricted civil rights and individual liberties (e.g., laws that segregated public facilities on the basis of race, restricted the rights of criminal defendants, and prohibited abortion). This liberal activism expanded rights for many persons but at the cost of Populist backlash against the courts. In recent years, a new judicial activism has emerged that seems to enjoy Populist support. In a number of so-called reverse discrimination cases, courts have exerted a socially conservative judicial activism to dismantle policies enacted by legislatures to assist minorities, such as affirmative action programs and redistricting plans designed to maximize minority representation. Populists would argue that the challenged policies lack legitimacy (i.e., they do not enjoy majority support) and thus in these cases the interests of the median voter are more closely represented by the courts than by legislatures. And, indeed, these cases present an apparent role reversal: it is legislatures that are attempting to protect the rights and promote the interests of historically marginalized minority groups, while it is the courts that are protecting and promoting majority interests.

But in most cases, the courts' responsibility for overturning unconstitutional laws places them in the unpopular position of opposing majority preferences. When a court makes a counter-majoritarian ruling, it places itself at risk of public opposition and even defiance (Rosenberg 1991).

The risk is most acute for state court judges, who in many states are subject to voter recall as well as periodic retention elections. Respect for judicial independence is a long-held tradition in this country, and this reservoir of respect generally provides judges sufficient authority to make unpopular decisions without risking their jobs. But there have been exceptions. One notable exception occurred in California in 1986, when voters removed three justices of the state supreme court (Rose Bird, Joseph Grodin, and Cruz Reynoso). Critics accused these judges, among other things, of being soft on crime for reversing on appeal a series of death penalty convictions. In 1996, voters in Tennessee removed Justice Penny White from the state's supreme court shortly after she voted to overturn a death penalty judgment. In Florida, pro-life forces mounted vigorous campaigns in 1992 and 1994 against two justices, Leander Shaw Jr. and Rosemary Burkett, who had voted to overturn a state statute requiring minors seeking abortions to obtain parental consent. Voters retained these justices, but only after expensive and heated campaigns. In Nebraska, voters targeted state supreme court justice David Lanphier after he authored an opinion overturning the state's voter-approved term-limits law. The term-limits initiative had received 70 percent of the votes at the polls; in his retention election Lanphier received only 32 percent of the votes and was removed from the bench (Uelmen 1997).

In some cases, coercion of judges is overt. Uelmen (1997, 1134) notes that after voters in California approved Proposition 8 (a victim's rights initiative) in 1982, and the measure was challenged in court, several elected officials publicly suggested that the state supreme court justices' chances in a retention election depended on whether they upheld the initiative. Critics of Chief Justice Bird threatened to wage a recall election against her if the court invalidated the measure. (The initiative was upheld on a 4–3 vote, with Bird dissenting.) One former California Supreme Court justice, Otto Kaus, described the pressures he faced in ruling on this initiative challenge. Acknowledging that his vote to uphold the initiative may subconsciously have been influenced by thoughts of his upcoming retention election, Kaus noted that trying to ignore the political implications of his decision in the case was like "finding a crocodile in your bathtub when you go to shave in the morning. You know it's there and you try not to think about it, but it's hard to think about much else when you're shaving" (Redlinger 1987, 58). Former justice Grodin similarly noted that his votes in high-profile cases may have been subconsciously affected by his upcoming retention election, and argued that "the potential that the pendency or threat of a judicial election is likely to have for distorting the proper exercise of the judicial function is substantial, and palpable" (Grodin 1988).

As discussed above, pressure on the courts is most acute when judges overturn the "will of the people" as directly expressed through the initiative process. And as the recent Nebraska term-limits case indicates, the same Populist impulse (and campaign machinery) that drives initiative campaigns can quickly be retargeted at state court judges who play that counter-majoritarian function. Populist anger is sometimes directed at federal judges who overturn popular initiatives. For instance, shortly after federal judge Thelton Henderson overturned Proposition 209, the California initiative banning state affirmative action programs, there were calls for his impeachment. Fortunately for Judge Henderson, the federal system of judicial life tenure provided him full insulation against direct threats of removal. Conversely, in state courts, where most initiative challenges are filed, judges lack the same measure of protection. It may be argued that any judge worth his or her robes should be willing, if necessary, to stand up to public pressure and overturn a popular initiative because such willingness is the foundation for the court's counter-majoritarian role. But as Kaus and Grodin have noted, judges are human and at least at a subconscious level they may be less likely to make an unpopular decision if their career rests in the balance.

As initiative lawmaking becomes more prevalent (and there is no sign that the dramatic increase in initiatives is abating), the stakes for courts will increase. If courts continue to invalidate voter-approved initiatives at a high rate, there is a danger that public resentment against the judiciary will grow. State court judges may face increasing pressures in retention elections, and the courts' legitimacy, independence, and capacity to protect minority rights may erode.[20] At that point, the Populist ideal of the unmediated power of the people will have moved a step closer to realization, but at a cost. Populism will have undermined not only legislatures, but courts as well.

CONCLUSION

Progressives hoped that the initiative process would act as an occasional "safety valve" to make representative government more responsive and effective; instead, the device has increasingly provided an opening for the forces of Populism. The gradual triumph of the Populist conception of the initiative process has undermined representative government, required unpopular minorities to defend themselves against hostile majorities, and placed courts in the perilous position of frequently overturning the will of the people. Understanding the initiative process's increasingly Populist orientation helps clarify the reform debate. Progressives should not harbor illusions that the initiative process works exclusively, or even primarily, to perfect representative government and produce enlightened policies. In some instances, the process may achieve Progressive ends, but more often its tendency runs in the other direction, toward battering representative government and producing poorly drafted, discriminatory, or unconstitutional laws.

Neo-Progressives thus should recognize the necessity of checks on and reforms of initiative lawmaking. As noted earlier, the primary check on the initiative process currently resides in the courts. Given the initiative process's lack of checks and balances and its many polarizing characteristics, it should come as no surprise that initiatives are challenged in court as a matter of course, or that courts frequently invalidate initiatives in whole or in part. Neo-Progressives should be heartened by the work of "initiative watchdogs" and should encourage more aggressive judicial review of initiatives than of "ordinary" legislation. And, since electoral pressures potentially limit state judges' ability to invalidate popular initiatives, neo-Progressives should encourage federal courts to exercise the judicial check with vigilance, especially when initiatives threaten individual rights.

Realistically, however, if courts are required to invalidate initiatives at a high rate, tension between courts and the public will grow. Modern-day Progressive reformers should be acutely concerned about the potential for Populist backlash against the courts. To help alleviate this pressure on the courts, neo-Progressives should consider backing reforms that build new institutional checks into the initiative process. At a minimum, the initiative process should be governed by the same requirements of openness and fairness that are currently placed upon legislative bodies and rulemaking administrative agencies. Such reforms should include mandatory public hearings prior to and during the circulation period for initiative petitions and opportunities for amendment as part of the initiative process, potentially including participation by the legislature. In addition, conflicts of interests need to be more clearly disclosed by those who write and back initiative proposals when the passage of a measure brings material benefits to them.

However, it is our contention that beyond these minimal procedural reforms, there is a great, and perhaps insurmountable, divide in reformist thinking. Reformers who consciously or unconsciously adhere to Populist principles want to focus reform efforts on saving the initiative process from special-interest capture. For instance, they would like to require that all signature gatherers be volunteers, or to propose prohibitions or limits on corporate giving for initiative causes. The purpose of these reforms would be to make sure that the initiative process serves the interests of the people and not wealthy and powerful groups. The major obstacles they face come from the courts, which have ruled in both instances that such regulations violate basic constitutional rights. Assuming for the moment that these reforms could be realized, they would not address the issues of democratic representative government that we have raised in this chapter. Their object would be to purify direct popular control over policy, not to embed it in a more representative government system.

By comparison, reforms in the Progressive spirit would strengthen the role that initiatives play in checking, as opposed to replacing, representative government. These fall into two types: (1) measures that increase the pressure that initiatives can place on representative government prior to the vote and (2) measures that allow the legislature to amend initiatives after they pass. An example of the first type of reform would be the following: Once a proposed initiative measure has received a requisite number of signatures, the legislature would be given the opportunity to respond with a measure of its own. The initiative sponsors then would have the choice to accept the legislative bill or to go forward with both measures on the ballot. The original initiative thus serves the function of goading the legislature into a decision, or facing the prospect of having matters taken out of their hands. Such a proposal is consistent with Progressive assumptions because it checks representative government (in this case by stimulating action) without supplanting it.

The second type of reform allows the legislature to amend measures that are passed by initiative. There are several ways that measures inoculate themselves from legislative amendment. Putting legislation in the form of an initiative constitutional amendment requires that changes in, amendments to, or the repeal of that measure also be done through constitutional amendment. In essence, an initiative constitutional amendment takes the matter out of the hands of the legislature. Similarly, statutory initiatives often specify the timing and extent of legislative amendment. If it were more difficult to place ordinary legislation in the constitution (e.g., by limiting the subject matter of initiative constitutional amendments or by raising the vote threshold to two-thirds or more) and if it were more difficult to place restrictions on amendments to statutory initiatives, more initiatives would have the status of ordinary statutes and it would be easier for the legislature to amend initiatives that prove at a later date to be flawed or unpopular. For those who value representative government, this type of initiative reform is more consistent with its basic premises.

For these sorts of modifications to the initiative process to have a chance, however, requires persuading the public to abandon its Populist conception of initiative lawmaking and to replace it with a more Progressive vision. This will require a sustained effort by leaders in the government and the private sector to expose the weaknesses, limitations, and dangers of initiative lawmaking, and promote the relative advantages of the representative system. Perhaps more important, it will require representatives to restore trust with the voters. During the 1950s and 1960s, representative government enjoyed a high level of public trust—and initiative lawmaking was almost totally dormant. The subsequent rise in distrust of government has fueled the public's desire to bypass legislatures and enact laws directly. Through improved responsiveness and efficacy, representative government can defuse the forces of Populism and the type of initiative lawmaking they drive.

Time to Walk the Talk

Mike Gravel

Over the last quarter century, awesome improvements in communications technology have enhanced the ability of the citizenry to participate in lawmaking. In states that permit citizen initiatives, the people have enacted meaningful reforms, such as campaign finance reform and term limits. This assertion of legislative power by the people has led to reforms by representatives operating under the guise of correcting abuses of the initiative process.

This contest over who will rule—government officials or the people—has attracted the attention of the political science community and media pundits. Their articles, papers, and books address all aspects of citizen lawmaking, but often in a vacuum. Most of the references to the practices of legislatures and initiatives are familiar to me due to my sixteen years in elective office: four in the Alaska legislature (two as speaker), and twelve in the U.S. Senate. My experiences have taught me the dangers of legislative monopoly by representative government.

THE INFLUENCE OF MONEY

Money is the mother's milk of politics. This statement is immutably true and vital. However, empirical evidence has shown it is less true with respect to the initiative process than the representative legislative process. The failure of money to buy the enactment of initiatives discredits the disingenuous arguments of initiative opponents. Yet, the substantial sums spent in initiative campaigns do affect some initiatives negatively. The amounts of money spent on initiatives will continue to grow, as they have in candidate elections. The main culprit is not money itself but soft money coming from unidentified sources. The likelihood of Congress reforming meaningfully either candidate- or initiative-funding practices is remote.

THE COMPETENCE ISSUE

Questioning the competence of the people in the initiative process touches the foundation of human governance. It is an argument commonly used to discredit direct democracy and, frequently, an unconscious assumption. The obvious retort to this unflattering judgment of others is: What are the options? Since the Age of Enlightenment positioned the individual to be as sovereign as any king, who is there to rule other than the people? If the people are not competent to govern themselves, then we must suffer whatever kind of government the people's competence chooses. This principle operates in Borneo or in New York City, where former mayor Jimmy Walker is reported to have said, "I may have been a jerk in office, but it took a lot of jerks to put me there."

Considerably less competence is required to set policy or enact laws, since both usually involve straightforward decisions, than to select agents with complex personalities, with bundles of positions and indiscernible motivations. Or, as James Madison put it in *Federalist 10:* "Men of factious tempers, of local prejudices, or of sinister designs, may, by intrigue, by corruption, or by other means, first obtain the suffrages, and then betray the interests, of the people."

THE INFORMATION ISSUE

The lynchpin of competency is the information people acquire or can cue on to make their decisions. While cues may come from many sources, information about the types of groups that support an initiative and the partisan affiliation of politicians who endorse a ballot measure are two examples of important voting cues. While reading about the information cues people rely on to make decisions, I often say to myself, "That's exactly the way we did it in the Senate."

Let me share a recent conversation I had with my good friend, Senator Alan Cranston, as an illustration of the extent to which legislatures rely on cues. I asked his reaction to my estimate that 75 percent of the members of Congress did not read 75 percent of the legislation they voted on. Alan's view is informed by greater experience, since he served longer in the Senate than I did (including as majority whip, in which he performed the task of monitoring votes). He thought my estimate was off, that more than 90 percent of the members of Congress did not read 90 percent of the laws on which they voted.

THE COURTS

The courts dare not interfere with the legislative branch prior to the enactment of legislation, absent overt fraud. The executive is less restricted in its legislative participation, at least informally. Nevertheless, the separation of these two branches from the legislative branch is a mainstay of our checks and balances system. But the executive and judicial branches wantonly interfere with the people's legislative venue, the initiative. Their reasons for this interference—usually self-serving—are that initiatives lack the deliberative procedures of legislatures.

FIRST PRINCIPLES

The chapter by Cain and Miller traces the origins of the initiative to Populists and Progressives. This is correct with regard to the explicit aspects and procedures of initiative, referendum and recall laws introduced in the first quarter of the twentieth century. However, tracing the lineage of the initiative back no further than this skews the dialogue and falsely suggests that the people's involvement in lawmaking lacks an adequate foundation in history.

The dialogue is better served by tracing the initiative's lineage, at least with respect to our nation, further back, to its proper beginnings: to the era of the Mayflower Compact, Jamestown, and the New England town meeting. The initiative originated with the "First Principles" of governance—wherein people initiate and enact rules themselves. First Principles are embodied in the initiative process. James Madison pointed to the primacy of First Principles on August 31, 1787, at the Constitutional Convention in response to a Maryland delegate who feared that the proposed adoption of the federal constitution would violate procedures in Maryland's constitution.

The difficulty in Maryland was no greater than in other states, where no mode of change was outlined by state constitutions, which officers were under oath to support. The people were, in fact, the fountain of all power, and all difficulties could be surmounted by deferring to them. The principle that the people could alter the Constitution as they pleased was embedded in the Bill of Rights.

Opponents of initiatives cite Madison's *Federalist 10* as the prime justification for representative government's supremacy over the people's legislative power. Two points need to be made with regard to this. First, Madison made those arguments in the heat of the ratification campaign. Earlier, at the Constitutional Convention, James Wilson described the deeper context of republican governance: "The Legislature ought to be the most exact transcript of the whole society. Representation is made necessary only because it is impossible for the people to act collectively." The framers had no choice but to build and defend a representational structure. However, what was impossible in 1787 has become possible with the incredible level of technology we enjoy today.

Second, Madison, in the last seven paragraphs of *Federalist 10*, argues that state governments, with more people and larger areas, are well suited to resolve the problems of local, smaller governments. He then extends that argument to sell the federalism of the Constitution, arguing that a national government is well suited to resolve difficulties that plague the smaller state governments. Extending Madison's logic, the people, our highest venue of authority, can address and have the responsibility to address today's problems of an unresponsive national government. As James Wilson stated, "All power is originally in the people and should be exercised by them in person, if that could be done with convenience, or even with little difficulty."[1]

CONCLUSION

Direct democracy, which may seem radical to some, is the essence of our Constitution, as expressed in the initial words of the Preamble, "We, the People . . . do ordain and establish this Constitution." Alexander Meiklejohn, the great constitutional scholar, defined the real meaning of self-government: "The citizens of this nation shall make and shall obey their own laws, shall be at once their own subjects and their own masters."[2]

Dumber than Chimps?
An Assessment of Direct
Democracy Voters

Arthur Lupia

In "The Populist Legacy: Initiatives and the Undermining of Representative Government," Bruce E. Cain and Kenneth P. Miller compare the current practice of direct democracy to the ideal of its Progressive Era advocates. Their comparison is thorough and multifaceted. They claim that "the actual operation of the initiative process violates a number of norms that have evolved in advanced democracies." My essay focuses on the claim that initiatives violate one specific norm—the norm of accountability.

Cain and Miller claim that direct democracy violates the norm of accountability. They say that accountability occurs when "voters know what their representatives have done in office and through their ballots appropriately reward or punish them." In other words, Cain and Miller claim that direct democracy voters do not know enough to appropriately reward or punish those who put measures on the ballot.

In an ideal world, direct democracy voters research the issues before them. But, as Cain and Miller point out, ours is not an ideal world. Instead, citizens learn much of what they know about ballot measures from bumper stickers, sound bites, interest-group endorsements, and slick thirty-second advertisements. At the same time, public opinion polls show that citizens are bad at answering questions about politics. Like many observers, Cain and Miller take facts such as these as evidence of voter incompetence.

Are Cain and Miller correct to doubt the competence of direct democracy voters? To answer this question, it is important to define competence precisely. Following definitions of intelligent performance from the cognitive sciences, I define voter competence as follows: A voter's choice is competent if it is the same choice that she would make given the most accurate available information about its consequence. Would she cast the same vote if fully informed about its consequences? If yes, then her choice is competent. An electorate containing a large number of competent voters satisfies Cain and Miller's accountability norm.

This definition of competence stipulates only that the voter chooses as if she were well informed. It leaves open the possibility that encyclopedic information about issues is not required. This definition stands at odds with prevailing definitions of competence in political science—definitions that demand encyclopedic levels of knowledge and focus on attentiveness to political detail. For something like knowledge of details to be a necessary condition for competence, however, people should be able to make reliable predictions about the consequences of their actions only if they know a particular, detailed set of facts about these actions. But this assumption is false. Citizens can and do use limited amounts of information to make the same choices they would have made if they had more information.

Suppose, for example, that knowledge of a particular set of facts is sufficient for a competent choice (e.g., suppose that knowing Bill Clinton's position on one hundred political issues is sufficient for a competent vote in the 1996 U.S. presidential election). Then, if a person does not know these facts, and cannot access any other facts that allow her to make the same choice, she cannot choose competently. If, however, there exists another, perhaps simpler, set of facts that leads her to make the same choice (i.e., the Sierra Club and the AFL-CIO endorse Clinton), then knowing the initial set of facts is not a prerequisite for competence. When a few, simple pieces of information can lead citizens to make the same choices that many, complex pieces of information do, citizens can be competent without having detailed information. In sum, competence and information are different. Competence is the ability to make accurate predictions; information is data.

Of course, direct democracy confronts voters with choices that are very complex. So, it is reasonable to ask, "How does complexity affect voter competence?" The answer to this question is that voter competence is helped by a common attribute of initiatives and referendums—nearly all ask voters to make a binary choice. The typical ballot measure asks voters to choose one of two alternatives—the piece of legislation described on the ballot or the status quo policy. A direct democracy voter is competent when she chooses the same alternative that she would choose given the best available information about the consequences of doing so. Even if both alternatives are very technical, a competent voter need only figure out which of the two alternatives is better than the other—having more detailed information will not change her vote.

Cain and Miller's accountability concern, which is really a concern about voter competence, can be restated as: Can voters (or electorates) choose the better of two alternatives? To begin to answer this question, I propose a simple thought experiment. Suppose, for a moment, we allow the outcome of a direct democracy election to be determined by chimpanzees. Suppose further that instead of reading newspapers, watching television, and talking to others, the chimps base their voting decisions on the flip of a coin. What can we say about the competence of this electorate? To clarify the example, suppose further that one of the two alternatives is indeed better for the voters in question—a luxury not universally afforded to political choices. Let "heads" represent the policy outcome that is best for all voters. So, if the coin-flipping voters choose tails, then we can all agree that they are incompetent.

In this scenario, one chimp with a fair coin can make a competent choice (heads) 50 percent of the time, on average. In many decision-making venues, a 50 percent success rate is regarded as a good thing. In politics, however, many people desire a higher rate of competence, something approximating 100 percent. If this is true, then one chimp with a fair coin is insufficient.

Now let's change the example a bit by giving each chimp a coin that is slightly unfair. In particular, imagine that each chimp has a coin that gives the correct choice (heads) 51 percent of the time. This is not much greater than 50 percent and is far short of the 100 percent correctness that we desire. But there is no reason to make any single chimp a policy dictator. So let's determine society's choice by a referendum of coin-flipping chimps, using majority rule to determine whether heads or tails wins the election.

When we do this, things change dramatically. To see why this is true, we rely on a bit of eighteenth-century mathematics, the Generalized Condorcet Jury Theorem (Grofman and Feld 1988). The theorem shows that collective decision-making processes can overcome the errors of individual decision making. The theorem states that if each voter is more likely than not to make a correct choice, then as the number of voters goes to infinity, the probability that a majority will make the correct choice goes to one.

What does the theorem tell us about the competence of our chimp electorate? Grofman and Feld (1988, 571) give a preliminary indication, where p is the probability that a single coin generates the right answer and "a competence of .98" implies that an electoral majority makes a competent choice ninety-eight times out of one hundred.

Even for average group competence p near .5, the expected judgmental accuracy of large assemblies is considerable. For example, even if p is only .51, a 399-member assembly has a competence of .66, while if $p = .55$, a 399-member assembly has a competence of

.98. For a reasonable level of p (e.g., $p = .6$), even relatively small assemblies (of size greater than 41) have a group competence level PN above .9. For $p = .7$, an assembly of only size 11 will have a group competence level of above .9.

The electorates that students of direct democracy are used to dealing with number somewhat more than 399, but somewhat less than infinity. So I close this thought experiment by citing the result for two different-sized electorates—one of one million chimps (the approximate size of electorates in many U.S. states) and one of ten million chimps (the approximate size of electorates in the largest U.S. states). In both cases, the Jury Theorem tells us that a majority chooses the correct answer approximately 100 percent of the time. So, for electorates of the size of most U.S. states, even an electorate filled with 51 percent coin-flipping chimps chooses correctly about 100 percent of the time.

If an electorate of chimps with slightly unfair coins can choose the best alternative approximately 100 percent of the time, what does this imply about competence of human voters in direct democracy elections? Are we dumber than chimps?

While this question may seem fanciful at first, the human voters' superiority cannot be taken for granted. The chimps have at least one advantage that human voters do not. The coins do not try to mislead the chimps. Indeed, the Jury Theorem works only if every voter on average is more likely than not to make an accurate prediction. If large segments of the electorate are easily or systematically led to vote against their interests, then the competence of the electorate is in peril.

As recent research (Sniderman, Brody, and Tetlock 1991; Lupia 1994; Bowler and Donovan 1998; Lupia and McCubbins 1998) shows, our ability to choose competently depends on how we use the limited information to which we attend. This is true not only of voting, but of nearly every conscious decision we make. We collapse complex phenomena into simple categories that we can later use and process quickly. We do not take these actions randomly, but when we observe aspects of the environment that have systematic and similar properties, we convert them into informational shortcuts, some of which are better known as brand names, interest-group endorsements, personal reputations, or political ideologies.

Cain and Miller assert that if voters rely on shortcuts, "then they delegate power to a new class of mediators who are also unaccountable if something goes wrong." Their concern is valid, though it presumes that using shortcuts is a recourse used only by lazy voters rather than a general attribute of human cognition (Marcus, Neu-

man, and MacKuen 2000). The key to competence in direct democracy is the voters who use shortcuts (which is to say nearly all direct
democracy voters) for making correct decisions about whom to
trust. The research cited above reveals that transparency and feedback regarding the interests of those who attempt to persuade voters are essential elements of voter competence. The research further
implies that ensuring publicly visible competition among initiative
proponents and supporters induces transparency and feedback—
for if someone has the opportunity to expose the opposing side's
weaknesses, the competitive nature of politics gives them a strong
incentive to go public.

The theory and evidence produced by scientists over the last two
decades reveal that common stereotypes about voter incompetence
rely on shaky theoretical and empirical foundations. They show that
if there are people who are willing to provide simple cues to voters
and there is sufficient competition for voters to learn the motives of
people they listen to, then voters can approximate the binary choices
they would have made if better informed. And if the electorate is
large enough, then the Jury Theorem shows that not everyone in the
electorate must choose competently for an electoral majority to do
so.

Direct democracy voters are far more competent than commonly
perceived.

3

Campaign Financing of Ballot Initiatives in the American States

Daniel Smith

A century ago, Populist and then Progressive reformers advanced the devices of direct democracy in the United States. While the two groups of reformers were not always in agreement on policy outcomes, one of their shared goals was to limit, if not eliminate altogether, the corrosive effect of corporate money on the legislative process. The champions of direct democracy argued that by empowering ordinary citizens to participate in the making of public policy via the initiative, "the people" would be able to circumvent state legislatures that were controlled by political bosses and entrenched special interests. Acting as election-day legislators, citizens would approve ballot measures and reclaim the right of "government by the people." By devolving policymaking decisions directly to the people, the leading proponents of the process thought they could break the political stranglehold on state legislatures by party bosses and vested special interests.

Far from eliminating special-interest money from politics, as the advocates of the initiative process had hoped, the process has permitted campaign financing to play a central role in ballot measures. Today, as a century ago, ballot measures are susceptible to the same kind of financial pressures present in the legislative process. As political scientist John Shockley (1985, 427–428) laments, "As long as wealth is as unequally distributed as it is in American society, and political interest groups are organized around private rather than public rewards, ballot proposition campaigns, like American politics generally, will reflect the power of the best-organized and wealthiest groups in society." Reflecting on the past century, it becomes fairly clear that the process of direct democracy, and most notably the initiative, has not been any more immune from the in-

71

fluence of money than has our representative system of government. This is not to say that money can outright buy ballot measure elections. The initiative process potentially does offer average citizens a different institutional venue to vent their frustrations and stake their public policy claims. Nevertheless, wealthy financial interests are more able to assert themselves through the initiative process than are citizen groups for which the process was originally intended to bolster (Schumacher 1932, 257–259; Shockley 1985, 427–428; Magleby 1984, 186–199; Garrett 1997, 22–24; Daniel Smith 1998, 157–167). In this chapter, I examine the topic of campaign financing of ballot initiatives.

CAMPAIGN FINANCING OF BALLOT MEASURES: A HISTORICAL GLANCE

Defenders of direct democracy often portray the initiative as a "pure" and unmediated process (Wilcox 1912, 3–10). In particular, proponents have claimed over the years that the so-called citizen initiative is essential to the preservation of democratic practices. It serves as a safety-valve mechanism when representative government is not responsive or accountable to the electorate. As a case in point, the 1911 California Ballot Pamphlet— which was made available to citizens who voted in the October special election to add the mechanisms of direct democracy to the state constitution—advanced the proponents' argument that the direct initiative would serve as a "safeguard [by] which the people should retain for themselves" the ability to pass laws that "reflect the will and wish of the people," and not moneyed special interests (California Commission 1992, 263; Allswang 1991, 10–11). David Schmidt (1989, 25–29), a contemporary advocate of the process, goes so far as to call the initiative "a safeguard against the concentration of political power in the hands of a few" which "is effective not only in venting popular discontent, but in channeling it constructively to make the necessary changes." Without question, the initiative over the years has played a major role in the shaping of public policy in half of the states. At times, it has even realized the goal of Populist and Progressive reformers of providing a democratic vehicle for injecting into public policy "the will of the people."

Early proponents of the process, however, freely admitted that the use of the initiative by special interests would inevitably occur. Professor Delos Wilcox (1912, 103), for example, fully "expected" that "the people . . . will have to rebuke not only public service corporations [utilities] seeking to get favors from them, but also many other kinds of special interests having a pecuniary stake in legislation proposed by themselves." Wilcox noted that special interests of all stripes and colors—from "the schoolteachers" to the "letter-carriers, or the policemen" to the "brewers" to the "labor unions"—would likely use the initiative to offer "some legislation for their own benefit or for the advancement of their pet ideas." But advocates such as Wilcox nevertheless reasoned that an "aroused majority will still have the power of repeal" and that public-regarding citizens "have less reason to fear the tyranny of the minority under the initiative than we now have under the unchecked caprices of representative bodies" (103).

Over time, it has become quite clear that "the people" have never taken exclusive control over the initiative process. Special-interest groups—as much as citizen groups—have used the initiative to advance their private interests. What proponents like Wilcox have failed to recognize is the immense financial resources that special interests, as opposed to most citizen groups, have at their disposal. Since the turn of the twentieth century, special-interest money has flowed uninterrupted into the coffers of issue committees promoting and opposing ballot measures. With the possible exception of the first decade of its use, there is little evidence suggesting that the initiative has ever been dominated by grassroots operations run by amateurs and citizen groups.

Perhaps somewhat surprising, extraordinary levels of campaign spending by special interests on ballot measures are nothing new. As such, the "populist paradox" (Elisabeth Gerber 1999, 5)—the notion that special interests rather than the "plain people" have come to dominate the initiative—is not an illusion. Rather, the populist paradox is accurate because special interests, since at least the 1920s, have played an important, if not a decisive role, in the initiative process. Despite the good intentions of the original reformers, the systematic lack of restrictions on campaign contributions and expenditures on ballot measures has concentrated an immense amount of power in the hands of a few well-financed interests. As law professor Elizabeth Garrett (1997, 23) writes, "Ordinary citizens do not determine the agenda of direct democracy any more than they determine the agenda of the legislatures," as "direct lawmaking requires resources, and organized groups are better able to raise and deploy those resources than are the putative citizen-lawmakers."

SPENDING ON BALLOT MEASURES

Unfortunately, there is little research documenting the level of spending on ballot measures during the early part of the twentieth century. Public records of campaign expenditures made by ballot committees are either sketchy or do not exist at all. In Colorado, as in many other states, no formal records were kept by the state on campaign contributions and expenditures until the second half of this century, and many of those records have not been kept on file. Campaign contribution records in California date to the turn of the century, when the state legislature passed the Purity of Elections Act in 1907. Although the law required the full disclosure of campaign receipts and expenditures for every candidate and campaign committee, the "financial statement [was] only partly enforced" by the secretary of state (Crouch and McHenry 1949, 63–64). As Winston Crouch and Dean McHenry reported in the late 1940s, the California campaign disclosure law was "hopelessly inadequate," existing in name only:

> The persistent citizen who seeks full information on campaign contributions may work through the files in the Secretary of State's office in Sacramento, only to discover, in addition to the conditions discussed above ["wholly incomplete or unintelligible returns"], that large sums are listed as gifts of campaign managers and camouflage committees, obviously acting as fronts for persons who did not wish their names known as contributors. (64)

In 1923, the state tightened its disclosure law by requiring any group raising or spending more than $1,000 on a ballot measure to file with the secretary of state, but frequently no reports would be made, even though ads on billboards and newspapers were ubiquitous (Crouch and McHenry 1950, 31).

The research on initiative campaign contributions and expenditures contemporaneously conducted by scholars during the first decades of the twentieth century is scant, but it does reveal that campaign financing of some ballot measures was quite substantial. In South Dakota in 1910, for example, eleven out of twelve ballot propositions were rejected by the voters. Historian Charles Beard (1912, 49) submits that the defeat of the measures—which included a popular referendum invoked by the railroads to overturn a law requiring electric headlights for locomotives and a referendum regulating embalmers—was directly attributable to the "activity of certain parties, especially interested in the defeat of one or two propositions, who filled the newspapers with advertisements and plastered the fences with billboards advising the electors to 'Vote No.' " Undoubtedly, substantial expenditures were also made by rival fishing interests in Oregon during the months leading up to the June 1908 election. Upstream and downstream fishermen each placed an initiative on the ballot that would have effectively eradicated the other's right to fish for salmon on the Columbia River (Cushman 1916; Beard 1912; Eaton 1912; Bowler and Donovan 1998, 118–128).

In Colorado, as in other states, official records of early ballot campaigns are in short supply. The City Club of Denver, which assessed the initiative and referendum process in Colorado after its first fifteen years in existence, reported that the costs to groups submitting initiatives were "im-

possible to ascertain" (City Club of Denver 1927, 20). During the formative years of the initiative, proponents and opponents evidently incurred
few costs: petitions were drawn without compensation and signatures
were obtained without assistance of paid solicitors. However, during the
second decade of the initiative's existence, the City Club found a noteworthy change in the process. During the 1920s, legal talent was employed to
draft petitions, solicitors were paid to circulate petitions, and substantial
campaign funds were collected and disbursed for and against measures.
In 1926, for example, proponents were paying circulators upwards of
three cents per name, and a "flat sum of $1,000" was paid to a circulator
by one group of proponents to secure their petition on the ballot. During
the 1920s, the City Club reported that $10,000 was routinely spent pro-
moting initiatives. In one case, $15,000 was spent by "friends" of a mea-
sure and $9,000 by those who opposed it. In sum, the City Club report
found that "a very substantial sum of money in the aggregate has been
disbursed"(City Club of Denver 1927, 20).

   In California, the initiative process started to become centralized and
capital intensive as early as the 1930s (Key 1936; Cottrell 1939; Kelley 1956;
Crouch and McHenry 1950; McCuan et al. 1998). At the forefront of the
industrialization of the initiative process was the husband and wife team,
Clem Whitaker and Leone Baxter. The savvy public relations couple
joined forces in 1933 to promote candidates as well as ballot initiatives.
They pioneered numerous campaign techniques in California, including
direct-mail solicitation, television ads, "building public attitudes," and
the use of "gimmicks," all of which drove up the costs of ballot campaigns (Kelley 1956: 39–66). It was even common for Whitaker & Baxter's
Campaigns, Inc., to run five or six ballot campaigns every election (Mc-
Cuan et al. 1998, 59).

   Tied to the industrialization of the initiative industry in California was
the explosion in spending on ballot campaigns beginning in the 1930s.
In 1936, more than $1.2 million was spent by proponents and opponents
fighting over a referendum taxing chain stores, and nearly $1 million was
spent by groups battling for and against an initiative on a retirement life
payment proposal (Crouch and McHenry 1950, 32). During the 1940s and
1950s, campaign financing of initiative and referendum campaigns would
often "run into the millions" (Heard 1960, 95), with the payment of circulators to qualify an initiative costing upwards of $65,000 (Crouch and
McHenry 1950, 14). In 1956, Whitaker and Baxter represented four of the
wealthiest corporations in California—Pacific Telegraph and Telephone,
Standard Oil, Pacific Gas and Electric, and Southern Pacific Railroad—
which joined together to fight an oil conservation initiative, Proposition 4.
Despite a war chest of $3.45 million, which was more than double the
$1.42 million the proponents spent, Whitaker and Baxter suffered a rare
defeat (Pritchell 1959, 287; Heard 1960, 95). Typically, though, during the

first half of the century in California, scholars such as Crouch and Mc-Henry (1950, 32) found that "the old adage of politics that 'the side that spends the most wins' has been proven true."

Even before the initiative process became centralized and industrialized, ballot measures were attracting big money in California. A circumspect examination of the campaign financing of ballot measures—especially in comparison with candidate elections—reveals that the large-scale spending on propositions is not really a new phenomenon. A California Senate committee in the 1920s unearthed the "startlingly large expenditures in [ballot initiative] campaigns" (McCuan et al. 1998, 57). Investigating the rise in campaign spending on ballot measures, the committee reported that in excess of $1 million was spent on seven measures on the 1922 ballot. In one ballot campaign alone—the Pacific Gas and Electric Company's effort to defeat the Water and Power Act—proponents and opponents spent more than $660,000.

Several other studies support the notion that big campaign spending on ballot measures is nothing new in California. Adjusting for inflation, a historical survey by John Owens and Larry Wade (1986, 679–680) found that in California initiative expenditures had not increased appreciably since the 1930s. In fact, Owens and Wade found that spending on ballot measures, in constant dollars, actually dropped over the years. "Between 1924 and 1962 per capita costs in 1972 dollars averaged $.10 per election," they show, "while for the period 1964–1984 they averaged $.08" (680). Research by political scientist David Magleby (1984, 149) shows that during the 1950s, 1960s, and early 1970s—a period noted for its lack of ballot measures (Schmidt 1989, 21–23)—total spending on ballot propositions in California occasionally outpaced that of all statewide and state legislative races. In 1958, a gubernatorial election year in California, proponents and opponents spent over $6 million on ballot propositions, half a million more than the combined candidate races for constitutional offices and the state legislature. The same held true for the presidential election years of 1964 and 1972. When controlling for inflation, total spending on ballot propositions in 1958, 1964, 1972, and 1976 remains roughly equivalent (Magleby 1984, 150). It was not until 1982, when issue committees spent more than $36 million promoting and opposing propositions, that ballot measure spending began to increase exponentially in California. Before that time, special interests were waging relatively inexpensive campaigns in California and other states for most of the century.

While sizable campaign spending on initiatives dates back to the turn of the century, spending reached new heights in the 1990s. Without money, groups backing or opposing ballot measures are now almost by definition excluded from the game. In 1998, issue committees across the country spent nearly $400 million promoting and opposing measures on the ballots in forty-four states (Initiative and Referendum Institute 1998).

In comparison, the national Republican and Democratic parties raised only $193 million in soft money during the 1997–1998 election cycle; congressional committees raised another $92 million in soft-money contributions. While both figures set new records, the combined amount of unregulated soft money flowing to the national parties was less than the total amount raised and spent on ballot measures across the country (Common Cause 1999).[1]

California, with the largest population of any state in the union, not surprisingly leads the way in ballot measure spending. In 1998, issue committees spent roughly $250 million on twelve general election and nine primary ballot measures, approximately the same amount spent by all the political candidates running for the California General Assembly and statewide offices (Morain 1999c). The amount spent on ballot measures was double the $117.9 million that gubernatorial candidates doled out during the primary and general elections, which was by far the most ever spent on the race for governor in California (Morain 1999a). Furthermore, campaign spending on ballot measures was more than twice that of all the legislative races combined, which topped the $100 million level for the first time ever (Morain 1999c).

Spending on the 1998 California ballot measures broke several state campaign expenditure records. The quarter billion dollars spent on ballot measures broke the previous state record of $141 million, set just two years earlier. More than $88.6 million was spent on a single November 1998 ballot initiative, Proposition 5. The successful measure allowed Native American tribes to operate casinos on their reservations. The amount spent for and against the measure—which included $63.2 million by Indian tribes supporting the measure and $25.4 million by casino operators and organized labor opposing it—easily broke the previous spending record of $55.9 million set in 1988 on an auto insurance measure (Morain 1999b). The San Manuel Tribe alone spent $25.5 million promoting the measure. For comparative purposes, the total given by all the American Indian tribes to the national Republican and Democratic parities in unregulated soft-money contributions during the 1997–1998 election cycle amounted to less than $1 million ("American Indians Raise the Stakes" 1999). In addition, electric companies spent $38.1 million to defeat Proposition 9, a measure that would have deregulated the electric utility industry, and tobacco companies drained $29.7 million (including more than $20 million from Philip Morris) from their corporate coffers in a failed bid to defeat Proposition 10, which raised taxes on cigarettes by 50 cents a pack to pay for early childhood education and health programs (Morain 1999a).

During the past decade, spending on ballot campaigns in California has grown beyond even the wildest expectations. In 1996, for example, groups supporting and opposing measures in California spent an average of $8 million per ballot measure, up from $3 million in 1976 (Elisabeth Gerber 1998, 2). In addition, by 1988, spending on ballot measures in the Golden State exceeded for the first time the amount of money spent by special interests lobbying state legislators. In 1976, $20 million was spent in California by interest groups lobbying state legislators, double the amount spent on ballot measures. Just twelve years later, issue committees expended nearly $130 million on ballot measures, a third more than the total amount spent on lobbying in the state (California Commission 1992, 264). Indeed, as the California Commission on Campaign Financing stated in its 1992 report, *Democracy by Initiative,* "today . . . money often dominates the initiative process even more than it does the legislative process" (263).

Less populous states also have witnessed a dramatic rise in spending on initiatives during the late 1980s and 1990s. In Colorado, a state with one-eighth the population of California, more than $10 million was spent on eight ballot campaigns in 1998. This was nearly double the total spending on all statewide races, including the race for governor (Hubbard 1998). The amount easily surpassed the previous spending record on ballot measures of $8.8 million set in 1994. While in the past spending on ballot measures would occasionally exceed the total spent on races for political office (Shockley 1980, 8–9), in the 1990s the amount spent on ballot initiatives in Colorado regularly surpassed that of all candidate races.

The rise in ballot initiative spending in Colorado is hardly unique among smaller initiative states. In Montana in 1996, opponents of Initiative 122, a measure which would have required tougher water treatment standards in mine operations, spent nearly $9 per vote to defeat the measure (Billings 1998). The proponents of Question 2, the "clean money" and public-financing measure in Massachusetts in 1998, spent upwards of $1 million promoting it (Goldberg 1998). In Washington, more than $5.6 million was spent in 1998 by the proponents and opponents of five ballot initiatives (Washington State Public Disclosure Commission 1999b). And in Nebraska, AT&T spent $5.3 million in its successful campaign to defeat a single 1998 initiative that would have lowered long-distance access charges (Cordes 1999).

THE LINK BETWEEN INITIATIVE CAMPAIGN SPENDING AND INITIATIVE USAGE

The increase in aggregate levels of spending on initiatives during the 1990s was closely linked to the rise in the number of citizen initiatives on the ballots in the states that permit the process. Citizens in the two dozen mostly western states currently permitting the initiative are increasingly serving as election-day lawmakers. In the states that allow the process, voters have come to expect a handful of (if not more) ballot initiatives—statutory or constitutional measures petitioned on the ballot by citizens—to appear on their ballots on election day. Voters in 1998 considered 235 referendum and initiative measures, including 60 statewide "citizen" initiatives. In the general election, Arizona led the way with 14 initiatives and referendums. Several other states—Oregon, Florida, California, Colorado, and Nevada—had at least 10 statewide measures on their ballots. With respect to just initiatives, the total number of statewide measures has increased dramatically, with more than 300 initiatives making it on the ballot during the 1990s, an average of 60 per general election nationwide. The number of statewide initiatives on the ballot across the nation during the 1990s surpassed that of all other decades, even the previous high, which was set during the 1910s (Price 1975; Schmidt 1989; Cronin 1989; Magleby 1994). During the 1990s alone, California voters considered over 60 initiatives placed on the ballot via citizen petition. As the number of measures on the ballot has grown, there has been an attendant increase in spending on individual propositions. "It's a growth industry," says Katy Atkinson, a prominent Colorado campaign consultant (Hubbard 1998).

Why are more measures—which coincidentally have become more expensive—reaching the ballot today? One school of thought views the increased use as being derivative of either legislative action or inaction. If a state legislature fails to respond, or if it acts contrary to public opinion, citizen-based or special-interest groups will turn to the initiative process to address their grievances. According to these scholars, citizen groups and special interests—just as the founders of direct democracy encouraged them to do a century ago—will turn to the initiative process to promote their legislative agenda, through either direct or indirect means. As a result, more and more contentious policy decisions are being decided at the polling booths, rather than in state houses (Rosenthal 1998, 31–34). Many of these ballot measures deal with highly controversial matters that for one reason or another the legislature does not want to touch. Theoretically, at least, ballot initiatives can serve as "the gun behind the door," keeping the legislature close to the "will of the people" (Matsusaka 1995; Elisabeth Gerber 1996; Tolbert 1998; but see Lascher et al. 1996). In addition, because powerful interest groups either launch or are impacted by statewide ballot initiatives, many special interests view the initiative process as an extension of their business operating expenses. In sum, direct legislation matters to special-interest groups, and they are willing to pay to advance their agenda.

A second school of thought suggests that the "initiative industrial complex" is driving up the number of initiatives on the ballot, as well as the attendant costs (Schrag 1998, 210–214). The growth of the initiative industry, which dates back to at least the 1930s, assisted both narrow special interests and so-called amateur or citizen groups in placing their measures on the ballot, soliciting funds, framing the issues, and packaging their messages for the voters (McCuan et al. 1998, 71–73). The aggregate increase in spending on ballot measures, this perspective suggests, has been fueled in part by the dramatic rise in the role of political consultants (Magleby and Patterson 1998). The classic example is that of William Butcher and Arnold Forde, the consulting team that ran Howard Jarvis's monumental Proposition 13 in 1978. Butcher and Forde signed a nineteen-year contract with Jarvis's group in 1979 that provided them with virtually all responsibility for running subsequent initiative campaigns (Daniel Smith 1999). By the mid-1980s, "Butcher and Forde were paying themselves $3 million to $5 million a year, while their firm was pulling in up to $12 million a year" (Weber 1996). Campaign consultants have even gone so far as to sponsor initiatives in the hopes of generating business for their firms. In 1984, Kimball Petition Management, a California signature-gathering firm owned by Kelley Kimball, advanced Proposition 37, a state lottery measure. Kimball hoped he could lure a lottery company to bankroll the measure and hire his firm for the signature-collection phase of the campaign. Scientific Games of Atlanta, a manufacturer of lottery tickets, bellied up to the table and anted $2.3 million (of the $2.5 million raised) to advance the successful measure (Magleby and Patterson 1998, 167; Schrag 1998, 211–213; California Commission 1992, 278).

In addition to the rise of the initiative industry, home-grown "populist entrepreneurs" (Daniel Smith 1998, 48–49)—citizens who are able to tap into the public mood and advance an ameliorative ballot measure—are often drawn to the initiative because there is easy money to be made. Sherry Bockwinkle, an erstwhile liberal grassroots instigator of the term-limits movement in Washington during the early 1990s, has turned her political organizing savvy into a profitable business as a campaign manager/consultant for a variety of ballot measures, including Initiative 200 in Washington, the anti-affirmative action measure that copied the California measure of 1996. David Biddulph of Florida has advanced a variety of conservative ballot initiatives over the years, and has tapped the sugar industry for several million dollars to bankroll his measures. Furthermore, numerous nonprofit "educational" groups, most notably the Washington, D.C., based Americans for Tax Reform and Term Limits, Inc. (Rausch 1996, 121; Daniel Smith 1998, 16–17), understand that sponsoring initiatives helps to excite a disaffected portion of the electorate and can stimulate contributions from their national donor lists. Over the years, both organizations have profited substantially by promoting what amounts to permanent ballot campaigns across the country coupled with year-round fundraising.

THE EFFECT OF MONEY ON BALLOT INITIATIVE OUTCOMES: A REVIEW OF THE EVIDENCE

Some scholars contend that, in comparison to races for political office, money may play a larger role in ballot initiative elections. This is due to the fact that voters generally have less information on which to base their decisions on ballot measures than on candidate races. With ballot measures, voters often do not have convenient party cues, elite endorsements, or other informational shortcuts to assist them in making their choices (Magleby 1984, 146; Bowler and Donovan 1998, 31; Lupia 1994). Magleby (1984, 146) points out that "most voters begin the campaign knowing little about most propositions, a situation quite different from that in candidate contests." Campaign expenditures, especially on paid advertisements, enable proponents and opponents of measures to impress upon the voters the various strengths and weaknesses of the propositions. This spending, some scholars contend, allows all kinds of voters—well educated and poorly educated, well informed and poorly informed—to evaluate ballot questions better. As Bowler and Donovan (1998, 159) suggest, "Spending brings more attention and more awareness to an issue . . . which somehow allows voters with different cognitive abilities to see an initiative in partisan or ideological terms."

In answering the question, "Does money influence ballot initiative outcomes?" scholars have examined the effect of campaign finance on ballot measures from two different perspectives. First, a number of scholars have tried to document the effect of campaign expenditures on ballot outcomes. Second, and more recently, a few scholars have tried to document the effect of campaign contributions on ballot outcomes. This section reviews the evidence.

Expenditures

Of the handful of studies that examine the initiative process in some detail, many have found that campaign spending has an impact on whether or not a ballot measure is successful on election day. In one of the earliest studies on the effect spending has on ballot outcomes, Shockley (1978, 239–240) examined twelve ballot initiatives in eleven states dealing with mandatory bottle deposits and the regulation of nuclear energy. In his cross-state examination, he documents how the initial public support for all twelve measures was largely favorable prior to the election.

Industry opponents of the initiatives, however, were able to outspend the proponents of the measures by an average of three to one. The heavy level of negative spending during the campaign, Shockley argues, had a direct effect on the outcomes of the ballot measures: nine of the twelve measures, despite being favored in public opinion polls early in the campaign, were defeated on election day. The power of negative advertising by the opponents of the measures showed up most prominently in the mandatory deposit initiative in Colorado. A postelection poll conducted by the opponents of the measure found that 40 percent of those who voted against it thought it was "the wrong solution"—which just happened to be the primary slogan the opponents used during the campaign (Shockley 1978, 240). In two subsequent analyses, Shockley (1980; 1985) extended his investigation to more ballot elections, concluding in his latter study that "the impact of money seems to have been crucial to the outcome of the vote."

Research by law professor Daniel Lowenstein (1982) on the effect of campaign spending on ballot outcomes in California is largely consistent with Shockley's findings. Lowenstein's carefully selected sample of ballot measures comprises twenty-five high-spending initiatives in California between 1968 and 1980. In each campaign, the spending levels by the proponents and opponents exceeded $250,000, with one side spending at least twice as much as the other side. His analysis reveals that the higher spending side won sixteen out of the twenty-five campaigns, or 64 percent. More telling, the higher spending sides that opposed ballot measures had an extremely good rate of success defeating the measures. Opposition committees with a two-to-one spending advantage defeated nine out of the ten measures they opposed. "During the study period in California," Lowenstein contends, "one-sided spending in support of ballot propositions did not constitute a major social problem," but analysis of "propositions opposed by one-sided spending shows that in some cases the spending was almost certainly decisive" (543–544). Furthermore, Lowenstein suggests that the one-sided campaigns were plagued by "gross exaggeration, distortion, and outright deception" (570).

Other research confirms the role of money in ballot campaigns. In his path-breaking study of direct legislation in the American states, Magleby (1984, 146–148) found that proponents with at least a two-to-one spending advantage over their opponents won less than half of the time, whereas opposition groups with a two-to-one spending advantage were successful 87 percent of the time. Similarly, in her detailed analysis of campaign expenditures in fifty ballot campaigns between 1976 and 1980, political scientist Betty Zisk (1987, 92–98) found that the high-spending side prevailed on election day in 80 percent of the cases, regardless of the total spending, the source of the money, or the type of issue. More recently, in a comprehensive examination of 329 statewide ballot measures (initiatives and referenda) in California between 1976 and 1998, sociologist Chang-Ho Ji (1999) found that opposition campaign spending is one of the few variables that influences ballot outcomes. Importantly, Ji controlled for a variety of factors, including the economic growth rate of the state, divided government, campaign spending by proponents, initiative or referendum, number of propositions on the ballot, placement on the ballot, substantive type of measure, type of election, and turnout (14).

Not all scholars agree that money calls the shots in ballot campaigns, however. Owens and Wade (1986) present the most compelling argument that higher campaign expenditures do not lead to ballot success. Analyzing the success rate of eighty-five ballot measures (sixty-eight initiatives, seventeen legislative referendums) between 1924 and 1984 in which spending was one-sided, they report that opponents were able to defeat ballots 89 percent of the time, even when they had less than a two-to-one spending advantage. "Money," concluded the authors, "has simply been overemphasized as a determinant of voting on direct legislation" (686). Other scholars have also argued that money by no means assures victory or defeat on election day (see, for example, Price 1988; Schmidt 1989; Ernst 1999).

Whether or not they conclude that "money matters" or that negative spending has a significant effect on a measure going down to defeat, most studies examining campaign expenditures contain what some would argue is a fatal flaw: they focus on aggregate spending levels by groups proposing and opposing initiatives. While convenient to analyze the total amount of money spent by initiative groups, such an approach has problems. First, the few cross-state studies that examine total spending by initiative committees do not account for the great disparity between states in the amount of expenditures needed to wage an effective campaign. Simply put, it takes considerably less money to wage a winning ballot campaign in Montana than it does in California. Second, aggregate campaign expenditures provide a poor reflection of the type of spending made by groups supporting and opposing ballot measures. Indeed, studies using aggregate campaign expenditures typically do not account for the substantial proportion of proponents' total finances that are depleted during the petitioning stage—and which are thus unavailable during the later stages of the campaign. Third, the use of aggregate expenditures overlooks the importance of the timing of campaign expenditures. *When* money is spent on paid advertising is perhaps even more crucial than *how much* money is spent. Finally, reliance on aggregate spending data disregards nonmonetary sources that may influence ballot outcomes. Cronin (1989, 113–116) notes that when the low-spending side wins (which happens about 20 percent of the time), it is usually because the victorious side has put together a well-organized, grassroots coalition with skillful campaign leadership who know how to obtain free publicity.

Contributions

By examining solely the spending side of the ballot campaign equation, the previously mentioned studies have not taken into account where the money comes from to finance ballot measures. Recently, rather than examining the effects of campaign expenditures on initiative campaigns, a couple of scholars have begun to look at how campaign contributions may effect the outcomes of ballot measures. They argue that the source of initiative money, rather than the total amount of money that is expended by proponents or proponents, is perhaps a better measure of the impact money has on the initiative process.

The scholarly focus on how campaign contributions influence ballot outcomes makes some analytic sense. Since information costs for voters are often high for ballot measures (Lupia 1994; Bowler and Donovan 1998; Magleby 1994), knowing what interests support a measure can serve as an important cue to those voters who are looking for informational shortcuts. In particular, less-educated voters often rely on cues provided by the groups that either support or oppose a measure (Bowler and Donovan 1998, 151–153; Lupia 1994; Magleby 1984, 128–140). Thus, the groups financially supporting ballot measures through their contributions to issue committees may be an important source of information to voters.

In one of the few studies that examine the campaign contribution side of ballot measures and the impact on ballot outcomes, Elisabeth Gerber (1999) presents the most compelling research. Gerber's analysis demonstrates that ballot measures receiving a majority of their financial support from individuals, labor organizations, and citizen groups are more than twice as likely to pass than those receiving the bulk of their funding from corporate sources. These findings run counter to the "populist paradox" hypothesis—that special interests are able to buy influence through the initiative process. Similarly, examining fifty-five ballot issue committees in California and Colorado between 1992 and 1996, Richard Braunstein (1999, 10) found that two-thirds of the ballot measures supported by committees receiving a majority of their funding from individuals passed, while only one-third of the measures supported largely by organizational donors passed. Braunstein argues that voters "are sensitive to the funding source of ballot measures, when they are aware of these differences, and respond more positively to those funded by fellow citizens" (12).[2]

Money and Ballot Initiative Outcomes: Inconclusive Evidence?

As should be clear by now, studies examining the effect of money—either expenditures or contributions—on ballot initiative outcomes have produced varied and sometimes conflicting findings. The principal reasons for the lack of scholarly consensus on this question seem fairly obvious. There is tremendous variation among the twenty-four states that permit the initiative. Should we expect that raw spending on ballot measures has the same impact in California as in Colorado? As in Washington? As in Montana? As in Maine? Political, cultural, economic, and procedural differences exist among the states and each factor may impact the outcome of ballot measures. Interest-group strength, political party dominance, voter registration, and turnout vary among the states. Voter ideology, public opinion, and the coverage of ballot campaigns by the media also differ widely. There is tremendous variation among the states in terms of their physical geography, ethnic and racial demographics, urban density, and economic prosperity. There are significant differences with respect to the typical number of initiated and referred measures on the ballot, how the ballot title and ballot language is set, and the professionalization and amount of money spent on campaigns. Laws regulating the initiative process also differ. States have different signature-gathering and petitioning requirements, and some only allow statutory or indirect initiatives. A few states allow ballot measures to be offered during special, primary, or odd-year elections. Each of these factors, of course, may only partially explain why some ballot initiatives happen to garner a majority of electoral support on election day. Because there are so many differences among the states that permit the initiative, it is exceedingly difficult to measure and control for these independent variables in order to specify precisely the impact that money alone has on the process.

Furthermore, the subject matter and salience of ballot issues within and across states vary widely. Should we expect money to affect the initiative process equally across all substantive policy areas? In the 1990s alone, citizens voted on state initiatives concerning school vouchers, gay rights, the official language, affirmative action, euthanasia, legalization of marijuana, term limits, crime victims' rights, abortion and parental notification, environmental regulation, gambling, child pornography, tax limitations, spending limitations, campaign finance reform, health care reform, insurance reform, smoking and cigarette taxes, welfare reform, and tort reform. Some of these measures were highly controversial and hotly contested; others went barely noticed by the media and the voting public. It seems unrealistic to expect that campaign contributions and expenditures would have the same impact on such dissimilar ballot measures across such disparate states. Most quantitative research examining the outcomes of ballot measures, however, either ignores or fails to control for the array of variables that affect ballot campaigns. As Thomas Cronin (1989, 110) wisely cautions, "Explaining outcomes over a broad range of issues and in diverse states is a challenge that defies tidy causal analysis."

Still, the plethora of conclusions outlined above should not be allowed to obscure an empirical finding that appears with remarkable regularity in these studies: that the amount of money spent by opponents is typically among the best predictors of ballot initiative outcomes. And while this finding might be construed as illustrating the limits of money in the initiative process, it can also be interpreted as evidence of money's influence. Indeed, group interests are often protected by preserving the status quo as much as they are by changing it. Clearly, therefore, it seems safe to conclude that money has at least some influence on ballot initiative outcomes, and even such a tempered conclusion would seem to stand in stark contrast to the vision of direct democracy held by its earliest proponents.

BALLOT MEASURES AND CAMPAIGN FINANCE LAWS

While money's influence—potential or real—in the ballot initiative process would seem to warrant strict campaign finance regulations, few regulations actually exist in this area. Indeed, of the twenty-four states that permit the initiative, no state currently limits the campaign contributions or expenditures of ballot initiative campaigns, even though at one time or another roughly half of them had some regulations on ballot campaign finances (Shockley 1980, 8). The explanation is fairly straightforward. The federal courts have not looked favorably toward state campaign finance regulations of ballot measure campaign contributions or expenditures. As this section will illustrate, however, the Supreme Court has hardly been consistent in its reasoning when it comes to ballot initiative campaign finance law.

The first case to deal directly with ballot initiative campaign finance was *First National Bank of Boston v. Bellotti*.[3] In *Bellotti*, the Supreme Court invalidated a Massachusetts statute that banned corporate expenditures in ballot initiative campaigns. In its decision, the Court relied on its ruling in *Buckley v. Valeo* (1976), in which it held that campaign contributions and expenditures are a type of speech and can be regulated only if such regulations advance the government's interest in halting corruption related to quid pro quos.[4] With the possibility for quid pro quo corruption nonexistent in ballot campaigns, Massachusetts had no legitimate justification for banning corporate expenditures in these campaigns, the Court reasoned. The Court rejected Massachusetts's argument that the ban on corporate expenditures in ballot campaigns was necessary to preserve the integrity of the electoral system, prevent the dangers associated with corporate dominance of the political arena, and protect corporate shareholders from contributing to political causes with which they disagree.[5]

Although the Court in *Bellotti* struck down expenditure limits in ballot initiative campaigns, it did not consider whether contribution limitations in such campaigns would withstand constitutional scrutiny. Three years later, however, in *Citizens against Rent Control (CARC) v. City of Berkeley*, the Court addressed precisely this question and invalidated a local statute limiting contributions to ballot campaigns to $250.[6] Relying on *Bellotti*, the Court reiterated that the government's legitimate interest in preventing quid pro quo corruption in ballot campaigns was irrelevant because no danger existed in the initiative and referendum setting.[7] By 1981, then, the Court had fashioned a body of law in which the prevention of quid pro quo corruption was the only state interest compelling enough to justify government limits on campaign contributions and expenditures (Garrison 1989, 190).

Beginning in the mid-1980s, the Supreme Court began to develop a new line of campaign finance decisions that retreated from much of the Court's reasoning in *Buckley, Bellotti*, and *CARC*.[8] In *FEC v. Massachusetts Citizens for Life (MCFL)*,[9] the Court ruled that as applied to noneconomic groups such as MCFL, a federal requirement that independent expenditures be made from a segregated campaign fund (independent of the corporation's treasury) was a violation of a group's First Amendment rights.[10] Whether such requirements violated the First Amendment rights of business corporations was left open by the Court. Importantly, however, the Court in *MCFL* recognized a corruption justification distinct from the quid pro quo corruption rationale used in Buckley: "the corrosive influence of concentrated corporate wealth . . . [on] the marketplace of political ideas."[11] As the Court asserted, "direct corporate spending on political activity raises the prospect that resources amassed in the economic marketplace may be used to provide an unfair advantage in the political marketplace."[12] Clearly, the Court had expanded its notion of corruption from that of *Buckley* and *Bellotti*.

Four years after *MCFL*, in *Austin v. Michigan Chamber of Commerce*,[13] the Court continued down this path, upholding a Michigan statute that prohibited corporations from making contributions and independent expenditures in state candidate elections (but allowing corporations to make political expenditures from a segregated fund).[14] Again broadening its definition of corruption, the Court ruled in *Austin* that Michigan had a legitimate interest in preventing "the corrosive and distorting effects of immense aggregations of wealth that are accumulated with the help of the corporate form and that have little or no correlation to the public's support for the corporation's political ideas."

While the Court's decisions in *Austin* and *MCFL* expanded the definition of corruption in the context of candidate campaigns, the federal courts have continued to employ *Bellotti*'s narrower definition of corruption in reviewing government regulations on corporate financial activity in ballot campaigns. Many scholars, however, question the continuing validity of the Court's reasoning in *Bellotti* as applied to ballot campaigns (Garrison 1989, 200–202; Lowenstein 1992, 403-405; Winkler 1998, 133–134). As long as the state interest in preventing corruption was limited to the prevention of quid pro quo corruption, that is, improper political favors done in exchange for campaign contributions, the *Bellotti* Court's reasoning was sound (Lowenstein 1992, 402–403).[15] *MCFL* and *Austin*, however, supplement *Bellotti*'s quid pro quo corruption reasoning with a state interest in preventing corporations from using state-created advantages to gain an "unfair advantage in the political marketplace."[16] In the view of several scholars, this additional state interest undermines the *Bellotti* Court's reasoning and assails the judicially imposed distinction between candidate campaigns and ballot measure campaigns imposed by *Bellotti*—a distinction that scholars argue is "utterly nonexistent" in light of the Court's recognition of a state interest in preventing unfair corporate advantage (Tolbert et al. 1998, 48; Lowenstein 1992, 402; Garrison 1989, 202).

The latest court battle over ballot initiative campaign finance—a case concerning a 1996 Montana initiative that banned corporate contributions to ballot measure campaigns—provides an excellent opportunity for the Court to resolve the different lines of reasoning developed in *Bellotti* and *Austin*. Sponsored by the Montana Public Interest Research Group, the measure stipulated that corporations "may not make a contribution or an expenditure in connection with a ballot issue" (though the measure did include a provision allowing corporations to fund political speech through a segregated fund consisting only of voluntary contributions.)[17] Seeking to challenge the logic of *Bellotti*, the authors of the Montana initiative intentionally used the language of the Court's decisions in *MCFL* and *Austin* (Winkler 1998, 211–213). Nevertheless, advocates of more stringent campaign finance regulations in ballot campaigns should not be overly confident of victory.

CONCLUSION: THE FUTURE OF BALLOT MEASURE CAMPAIGN FINANCE

Former speaker of the California Assembly Jesse "Big Daddy" Unruh once characterized money as "the mother's milk of politics." The well-worn adage usually is applied to the legislative process and candidate races, but it is equally applicable to the initiative process. According to John Hein of the California Teachers Association, which spent more than $20 million on ballot measures in 1998 alone, "the initiative process is not going to go away. It's going to grow. . . . That is just a hard, cold fact" (Morain 1999c). Another hard, cold fact is that the amount of money spent on ballot measures is only likely to continue to grow. Despite some incongruous decisions, there is little chance that the Supreme Court will uphold even the mildest of limitations on the campaign contributions or campaign expenditures in initiative politics. And because there are no limits on what groups sponsoring and opposing ballot measures can raise or spend, there is a good probability that special interests, public interest groups, and wealthy individuals will continue to use the initiative process to promote their causes or defend their turf. Big money in direct democracy is here to stay.

Ironically, the citizen initiative, as some scholars and journalists are still wont to call it, has always had at its foundation moneyed interests. Although numerous scholars have suggested that the use of the initiative somehow deviated from its Populist and Progressive roots during the latter part of the twentieth century, there is considerable evidence from many states that special interests have played a leading part in ballot campaigns since at least the 1920s. This should not come as a surprise. The system of direct democracy is no less susceptible to the corrosive influence of money than is representative government. It is merely a different process of public policymaking. Except in the mythic abstractions advanced by some Pollyannaish supporters of the process, the initiative has never functioned purely as a citizen endeavor.

Scholarship on the effect of money in the initiative process—including some recent innovative research—tends to reinforce the finding that substantial campaign spending by opponents can be effective in defeating ballot measures. Shockley's keen observation continues to be supported by the empirical evidence: "big-money interests—whether corporate or union—are more successful in defeating proposals they do not like than in insuring the success of measures they strongly support. It seems easier to sow seeds of confusion about initiatives (which will lead people to vote against them) than to get voters to support measures positively" (Shockley 1980, 43). Yet, even if money cannot buy ballot measure elections, the presence of unconstrained campaign contributions and expenditures on initiatives should raise some concerns about the practice of democratic governance, as the process has become an arena for unfettered special interests to advance or protect their policy agendas.

While certainly not a decisive factor in all ballot measure elections, the ability to raise and spend a substantial level of money is a necessary condition in most of them. The *Los Angeles Times* (1998) recently editorialized that in California "well-heeled special interests" are able to "write their own wishes into state law or the Constitution." This apprehension is nothing new, nor is it confined to the residents of the Golden State. Nearly ninety years ago (1911), the editorial board of the *New York Times* raised similar concerns about the initiative, commenting how, "This new method of handling the basic law of the state is advocated in the name of democracy. In reality it is utterly and hopelessly undemocratic. While pretending to give greater rights to the voters, it deprives them of the opportunity effectively and intelligently to use their powers." Concurring, Alan Rosenthal (1998, 331), a strong proponent of representative democracy, notes how "organized interests, and not common folks, are most frequently the initiators" of ballot initiatives. Even citizen groups promoting ballot measures usually need to amass substantial financial resources along with their labor power if they are to be successful on election day.

Direct democracy was forged out of the public concern over money dominating the political process. It is inconceivable that the Populist and Progressive reformers at the turn of the century would approve of the enormous spending by special interests on ballot measures today. It is equally unlikely that they would condone "citizen" interests waging faux Populist or astroturf campaigns bankrolled by sugar daddies or vested special interests (Daniel Smith 1998). It is quite possible that the citizen initiative in the twenty-first century will become even more dominated by the same interest groups the public generally bemoans for capturing representative government. If direct democracy is no purer or no more egalitarian than representative government, and if the campaign financing of ballot measures is boundless, is there any reason to assume that the outcomes of the initiative process will be more democratic than representative government?

Regulations on the Ballot Initiative Process: Interfering with Political Liberty

Paul Grant

Appellees seek by petition to achieve [peaceable] political change . . . [and] their right freely to [participate in activities] concerning the need for that change is guarded by the First Amendment.

—*Meyer v. Grant*, 486 U.S. 414, 421 (1988)

Professor Smith examines the impact of money on ballot issue campaigns and determines that initiative and referendum processes have never been pure and egalitarian, that is, uninfluenced by financial special interests. He seeks to discredit special-interest-dominated initiative processes, while he also recognizes (not with approval) the increasing importance that initiative politics is playing in America today. What he overlooks is the vital and essential role that initiatives do serve.

Rather than debate whether money spent on ballot issues is effective, I will discuss whether regulations restricting ballot issue processes are lawful or necessary or proper in this free society. Below, I discuss First Amendment protections for initiative and referendum processes from a broader perspective than the free-speech analysis typically employed by the courts. I do this in part to head off Professor Smith from where I think he is going: arguing for greater regulation and restriction of what he sees as special-interest-dominated, nonegalitarian, low-quality initiative processes so as to diminish the quantity of citizen lawmaking occurring in this country.

When courts come to understand that ballot issues involve more than free speech, that they also involve the First Amendment right of the sovereign people to petition the government, or to self-govern, then courts may more readily conclude that regulations limiting ballot issue expenditures and contributions, as well as regulations giving government control over initiative content and initiative processes, are simply unconstitutional. I don't, however, share Professor Smith's view that the courts will never uphold ballot issue contribution and expenditure regulations. The Supreme Court has shown a willingness to jettison First Amendment protections to allow regulation on contributions and expenditures in candidate campaigns, most recently in *Nixon v. Shrink Missouri Government*, 120 U.S. 897 (2000), and there is no reason to be confident that the Court won't do the same concerning ballot issue regulations.

The signers of the Declaration of Independence pledged their lives, their fortunes, and their sacred honor in support of American liberty. Campaign finance regulations dishonor those pledges and our history. The First Amendment does not tolerate government regulation of political speech, political association, or the right to petition, because the framers of the First Amendment understood that political power tends to corrupt, and that persons in power would use that power to suppress political dissent and change and to preserve and enhance their own power. The framers looked on any government, even our own, as a dangerous force which must be constantly restrained. They also recognized that any legitimate power originates with the people. Our system of separation of powers, and checks and balances, has been enhanced by adding initiative and referendum processes to the original design.

The right to petition—which is any peaceable nongovernmental effort to achieve political change—and the right of free speech were not gifts from the government. In seventeenth-century England, these rights were established after civil war and revolution. The founders fought a successful revolution to establish these rights on American soil. Presenting a petition for redress is an exercise of popular sovereignty and is precisely what the petition clause of the First Amendment protects. Although the petition clause does not require that states establish initiative processes, it does protect initiative and referendum processes once they are established.

The right to petition involves a fundamental exercise of self-government by the sovereign people, a right which is inconsistent with the political interference posed by campaign finance and other regulations. Those who argue that laws are better made through traditional representative bodies should understand they are arguing that hired agents are superior to their principals and that sovereigns should speak only through their representatives. That argument for aristocracy contradicts basic notions of republican government. A republican government belongs to the people. *Res publica* means property of the people.

As citizens have become more effective at achieving political change through initiative and referendum, advocates of more traditional government processes have struck back, finding ways to limit what the citizens can accomplish through direct legislation. Some states tried restricting petition collection efforts to amateurs, banning commercial circulation. The effect was to preclude many grassroots efforts from ever getting started. On the other hand, corporations with large numbers of employees or unions could place their measures on the ballot through the volunteers' efforts of their employees or members. The difficulty of petition signature requirements blocked many worthwhile measures from ever getting the ballot qualified. In 1988, the Supreme Court declared unconstitutional Colorado's criminal ban on paid petition circulators, in *Meyer v. Grant*, 486 U.S. 414. In most initiative states today, very few initiatives could or do qualify for the ballot without using paid circulators.

The proposal espoused by many that contributions and expenditures in issue campaigns be restricted, to minimize the influence of special interests, suffers from many flaws, not the least of which is that such restrictions clearly violate the First Amendment. Laws that would inhibit the right to petition for political change through limitations on contributions or expenditures must be seen as unconstitutional interference with popular sovereignty. The American Revolution could not have succeeded with such campaign contribution restrictions.

A second major flaw of such restrictions is that they would have unintended consequences and discriminatory impacts as they would reduce only one type of special-interest money—that given openly to support a campaign. As with candidate campaigns, there would remain many ways for soft money to influence outcomes. It is naive to believe that major money interests will not remain active participants in initiative and referendum processes (or other political processes), even if contributions, or expenditures, could be limited. Further, many special interests already control legislative agendas, so those interests would be favored over interests to which legislatures are not as responsive. More important, initiative and referendum provide a real alternative—and a safety valve—for those who feel shut out of traditional legislative processes. It would be a mistake with explosive potential to curtail initiative and referendum processes. The founders understood that the most dangerous special interest that exists is the special interest of entrenched power. Initiatives provide a means to challenge entrenched power.

Those who criticize money being spent to influence election outcomes focus on idealized processes or on results they perceive as problems, without first dealing with the source of those problems. The reason that special-interest money is spent on influencing political outcomes is simply that political outcomes are important. If one's economic welfare depends on government policies, then one will to attempt to influence those policies in one way or another. Financial resources will always be brought to bear to influence political outcomes. Politicians know they have the power to affect fortunes, and it is only human nature for those affected to do what they can to protect or advance their economic interests. If initiative processes are curtailed, then special interests will simply focus their financial energy where political decisions are still being made: on elected and appointed officials. We must allow those threatened by politics to spend their money and pursue alternative politics so they don't have to resort to violence. The problem lies with the importance of politics, not with the influence of money.

Government has considerable power to determine economic winners and losers. Persons and corporations whose lives and fortunes are affected have a right to speak up to protect their interests. Rather than view the initiative and referendum process (I&R) as having failed, we should recognize I&R for its real significance: that sovereign citizens who reject nonresponsive government-by-legislature have taken back some of their own original power to legislate directly. I&R provides an alternative and a safety valve for those persons who can't protect or advocate their interests through elected or appointed officials. Fewer than eight hundred initiatives have been passed into law in this country during the past century, while many state legislatures pass that many bills *per year*. Thus, whatever problems there may be with initiative measures, we should be much more concerned with laws passed by legislatures. Initiative and referendum processes do not bring perfection in government, but they can help limit the damage inflicted by legislatures.

CONCLUSION

Current efforts to control and limit the I&R process through further regulations, whether campaign finance regulations or single-subject regulations—or through other means—are misguided and offend against the sovereign right of the people to self-government. This is an unwise effort in light of American revolutionary history.

The Initiative Process: Where People Count

Paul Jacob

In contemporary America, much is said about the power of money. Money is proclaimed "the mother's milk of politics," known to "make the world go 'round," and feared as "the root of all evil." But money is merely an inanimate object. Its goodness or evil depends completely on the people who use it.

Daniel Smith investigates the effect of money on the citizen initiative process. But Smith's analysis is, in Shakespeare's words, "full of sound and fury, signifying nothing."

"Big money in direct democracy is here to stay," asserts Smith. Yet he never explains at what threshold money becomes "big"—or what harm comes from spending more money, rather than less, in an initiative campaign. Apparently, at some indefinable quantity of spending, Smith presumes a campaign to be corrupted, which at just a dollar less was a wholesome endeavor.

When initiatives to give women the vote were on state ballots earlier this century, how much money could the proponents have spent before the effort would have been deemed corrupt? Spending money for a good cause is positive. It doesn't become negative on the basis of the amount. Smith's examination falls short because it never gets beyond the amount of money in order to reflect on the more important question of what the money actually buys.

BUYING WHAT?

In 1998, the *Los Angeles Times* editorialized against the initiative, arguing that "well-heeled special interests" can "write their own wishes into state law or the Constitution." Can they? It's true that anyone can write his or her own language for an initiative. But getting the initiative on the ballot and passed by a majority of the people—which is the requirement for making it a law—is quite another matter.

A peek at the twelve measures on the ballot nationally in 1999 and in the California 2000 primary suggests a far different emphasis than one would expect from "well-heeled special interests." The measures consisted of two term-limits proposals, a ban on partial-birth abortion, a tax-reduction measure, medical marijuana, repeal of a cigarette tax, establishing marriage as only between a male and female, a prohibition on commercial fishing, increasing criminal penalties, campaign finance reform, lowering the threshold of voter support to approve school bonds, and allowing voters the electoral option of "none of the above." One can agree or disagree with the ideas expressed by these propositions, but all are issues citizens care about on the basis of general public policy concerns and not for any targeted financial benefits.

Certainly, there have been and will again be initiatives where the primary goal is the selfish economic advancement of certain interests. But, while Congress and state legislatures have established a plethora of subsidies and special regulations that advance the economic interests of various industries or occupations at the expense of the general public, these special interests—or "economic interests"—have experienced little success through the initiative (see Ernst in this book).

Elisabeth Gerber (1999) compared ballot measures that receive most of their funding from "citizen interests" to measures financed by "economic interests." Her conclusion: "Spending by citizen interests to support initiatives leads to higher passage rates, whereas spending by economic interests to support initiatives leads to lower success rates." Gerber discovered that voters enacted 60 percent of those issues funded primarily by citizen interests, while only 22 percent of propositions bankrolled by economic interests were passed. Ernst's (1999) study found similar results. So much for well-heeled special interests nonchalantly writing their wishes into law.

THE FACTS PROVE OTHERWISE

The initiative process presents an environment that consistently allows financial advantages to be offset by other political assets. Separate studies by Lowenstein (1982) and Magleby (1984) show that even when proponents of initiatives outspend opponents by a two-to-one margin or more, most of these "big spending" measures lose at the ballot box. The California Commission on Campaign Finance (1992) found "no significant relationship between money spent in support of an initiative" and victory for the proposition. Owens and Wade (1986) concluded, "money has simply been overemphasized as a determinant of voting on direct legislation."

Spending against initiatives is statistically much more likely to be successful. Voters have a conservative mentality. If uncertain about the benefits of a measure, they will stick with the status quo. That means voting "no." Opposition campaigns know that initiative voters are volatile and can be moved to vote "no" simply on doubts about a proposition. Therefore, opposition campaigns have at times produced much more heat than light.

Still, many political reforms and other measures have withstood massive advertising assaults and won. Proposition 140 won in California in 1990 despite being outspent better than three to one. Term limits had the public support to overcome then-speaker Willie Brown's statewide television ad blitz, without running a single TV ad in favor of the initiative.

Even political scientist John Shockley, who sees spending as a strong determinant of initiative outcomes, admits, "I'm afraid money can buy an election. But it's not money alone. It's money well spent." Yes, money can purchase communication with large numbers of people. And if the message is compelling, people can make a decision, even change their minds, because of the new information. Is this really a problem? Or more evidence that free speech is exceedingly valuable?

COMPARING INITIATIVE ELECTIONS
WITH CANDIDATE ELECTIONS

Money is much more a determinant of outcome in candidate elections than in initiative contests. In 1998, not a single challenger who spent less than $800,000 won a seat in Congress. The Center for Responsive Politics reports that only nineteen victorious candidates spent less than their opponent. That amounts to a tiny 4 percent of U.S. House and Senate races—96 percent were won by the bigger spending candidate. Eight of the nineteen lesser spenders were incumbents with valuable built-in advantages such as the franking privilege, staff, websites, and more. Include their taxpayer-financed advantages and the spending gap would be reversed.

In comparing the initiative with legislatures, Smith fails to come to grips with the depth of the crisis in our representative institutions—a crisis that calls the term "representative" into question.

Political scientists can expound at length on what most voters know in their gut: elections between incumbents and challengers are no longer fair contests. The powers of incumbency have rendered elections a mere formality, certainly not an effective check on power. In 1998, the incumbent reelection rate was 98.3 percent in the House. Not a single member of Congress with four or more years of incumbency was defeated. One of five incumbents had no major party opposition at all.

A political monopoly of incumbency has swallowed up our electoral process and, with it, the connection between representatives and the people. Monopolies are dangerous because their customers don't control them; they control their customers. The initiative process has become the only effective check the people have on the monopoly power of politicians.

IN SEARCH OF CORRUPTION

Unlike candidates, for whom a contribution may change policy in ways unseen by the average citizen, initiatives are written down in black and white. Not only can every voter read them, but they can vote them up or down as well. Most comforting to the public, initiatives cannot renounce their legal wording after passage the way politicians discard campaign promises once in office. The potential for corruption is nil.

No wonder the courts, as Daniel Smith freely admits, have found a conflict between First Amendment rights and restrictions on the contributions and expenditures of ballot measures. We have reason to fear the corruption of our elected representatives. A long history exists of legislators taking bribes and doing the bidding of special interests. But special interests cannot pay off the voters of an entire state. As the U.S. Supreme Court wrote in *First National Bank of Boston v. Bellotti*, 435 U.S. 765 (1978), "The risk of corruption perceived in cases involving candidate elections . . . simply is not present in a popular vote on a public issue."

CAMPAIGN FINANCE REGULATION

Campaign finance reform is popular precisely because Americans feel that their legislators are easy prey for special interests that offer campaign contributions. Support erodes considerably when citizens conjure the details of allowing government to regulate the speech of political candidates, initiative advocates, and other political actors. Especially frightening is the dominant role played by the very incumbent legislators with such a large personal stake in the outcome of campaign rules.

Campaign finance regulations have not merely failed when applied to initiatives; they have been seriously counterproductive. Just to understand the complex law and correctly fill out the forms for contributions and expenditures often require professional legal and accounting help, which better-financed efforts are better able to afford.

For those who complain that initiatives have become too costly, the solution lies in reducing the restrictions and barriers that discourage less wealthy people from participating in the process. For instance, research cited by Smith shows that between 1978 and 1986 fully 72 percent of expenditures by California proponents were made just to qualify a proposition for the ballot—legal assistance and petitioning—not to campaign for it on the merits. We need to ease rules for qualifying initiative measures, not increase state regulations.

CONCLUSION

Arrogance and corruption run rampant in our legislatures—especially in Congress and the twenty-six states that suffer without any citizen initiative check on their power. The initiative is the one process where government operates with the consent of the governed. It's where the people count.

4

Political Consultants and the Initiative Industrial Complex

Todd Donovan, Shaun Bowler, and David McCuan

It cannot be denied that ballot access, advocacy campaigns, and opposition campaigns in a state as large as California often require what seem to be extraordinary sums of money. This money, furthermore, represents the demands for and employment of a sophisticated array of campaign professionals. However, it remains to be seen exactly what the roles of these professionals are. Are they corrosive to the process of democratic politics? Are they a disease in and of themselves or simply a symptom of the difficulty of conducting issue-based politics in a large, diverse polity?

Some of the more vocal consultants themselves fuel perceptions of mercenary campaigning by claiming that they search for measures that are a "big score" in terms of the money they make them (Kimball 1997). Offering scholars an evaluation of the industry, the owner of a large California petition firm, Kelly Kimball, reported, "I've never met a consultant who is in this because he believed in the causes." Commenting on consultants' motives, he added, "you can find me a consultant who tells you that money is not the issue, and I'll find you a liar" (Magleby and Patterson 2000, 9, 12).

Today, this "initiative industrial complex" is quite sophisticated, specialized by task and extending beyond California, although its centers remain in the Golden State and in Washington, D.C. Magleby (1984) noted the existence of at least twelve California-based campaign management firms working on initiatives in the 1980s. One publication listed nineteen "major" California consulting firms as of 1986 having expertise in initiative politics (Peterson 1986). Depending on the size of their firm, professional consultants might claim expertise in communications, media production, media purchasing, opinion research, focus group studies, public relations, and direct-mail advertising.

Firms with a national presence in congressional and gubernatorial campaigns also have initiative proponents and opponents as major clients. These firms include but are by no means limited to Fenn & King Communications, Joe Slade White, Strubble Opel Donovan, and Trippi McMahon Squier. For others, such as Goddard Clausen/1st Tuesday, initiative work and "issue campaign" work are a dominant portion of their client base. Furthermore, large public relations firms which handle political work that is not primarily campaign oriented, such as Storris, Zeeger and Mesker, have offices and/or associated firms that work heavily on campaigns, including initiatives. For example, the campaign arm affiliated with the Storris firm is Candidate Strategies.

In addition to the consultants who are primarily engaged in what they refer to as "communications," there are at least fifty attorneys who are members of the California Political Attorneys Associations, and a small number of law firms, who specialize in political law, some having expertise in initiative politics (McCuan et al. 1998). These professionals work with clients on drafting the language of initiatives, as well as assisting with regulatory compliance issues.

It is problematic to characterize the initiative campaign industry by describing firms working specifically on initiative politics, since many large and small firms work candidate and initiative contests alike. The 1990 *California Green Book* listed 161 general campaign consultants, 14 polling firms, 22 fund-raising firms, and 15 law firms offering general advice to campaigns (Bowler et al. 1996). By the time the periodical *Campaigns & Elections* had released its 1999–2000 "Political Pages," the extent of specialization in initiative campaign politics in the three West Coast states (overwhelmingly dominated by Californian firms) had expanded to include the variety of actors listed in table 4.1. In addition to 104 general consultants who work both candidate and initiative contests, and 47 who claimed specialties in initiative and referendum, the list includes specialties as narrow as "internet consultants," campaign software, and video production.

There is certainly some double counting buried in these figures. Furthermore, some of the smaller firms involved (as we found out when conducting a mail survey) seem to be in business no longer. On the other hand, several known firms are not counted in the list provided by *Campaigns & Elections* (three based in the city of Oakland alone are left out). Nevertheless, despite their problems, these numbers make it clear that the infrastructure of professional campaign services has both grown and grown more specialized—even over the course of the past ten years—in the West Coast states.

Throughout this chapter, we make reference to interviews conducted with California-based consultants and to results from a broader mail sur-

Table 4.1   Number of Campaign Professionals by Specialization, 1999

7	Attorneys
9	Campaign management
14	Database/File Management
25	Direct mail (processing)
38	Direct mail (strategy and creative)
4	Education and training
12	Field operations
36	Fund-raising
47	Initiative and referendum consultants (in all of United States)
6	Fund-raising software
104	General consultants
2	Internet consultants
10	Mailing and phone lists
17	Media buying consultants
38	Media consultants
6	Media and speech training
2	On-line information
10	Petitions and signature gathering (in all of United States)
23	Polling and Survey Research
8	Polling—focus groups
4	Polling—interviewing
21	Printing and promotional
6	Print ads
18	Political publications and newsletters
17	Press relations
11	Research opposition
3	Research issues—voters and legislative
29	Software
4	Speech and copy
1	Speakers, analysts, and press sources
9	Targeting
15	Telephone contact services
5	Videotape duplication
14	Video production

Source: "Political Pages (1999–2000)." *Campaigns & Elections* magazine. California, Oregon, and Washington, unless noted otherwise.

vey. We obtained from *Campaigns & Elections* magazine the addresses of the 151 general and initiative consultants listed in table 4.1 in order to survey industry insiders knowledgeable about initiative campaigns. In the spring of 1999, these professionals were sent a brief mail survey asking about their firms and the services they provide. Thirteen of the addresses proved to be invalid. A filter question eliminated those respondents who had not worked on initiatives. We received 50 replies (36 percent of 138 working addresses) and, after filtering, had 45 valid responses from professionals experienced with initiative campaigns. Thirty percent of these respondents had worked on more than thirty initiative campaigns, and 53 percent had worked on at least thirteen initiative campaigns. Our respondents thus have a solid working understanding of initiative politics. The number of people employed in their firms averages around ten, with more being employed during election periods. One-third of our sample reported that their staff levels grew by more than 50 percent during elections.

Table 4.2 lists the frequency of various services that consultants reported providing for their clients. Taken together, tables 4.1 and 4.2 illustrate the extent of specialization in this field. Most of the respondents for table 4.2 report that they give clients advice on political strategy (89 percent), provide general campaign management (73 percent), and design and produce advertisements (70 percent). Few provide services such as fund-raising (22 percent), polling (20 percent), and signature gathering (9 percent), a reflection of a level of specialization in the industry that makes it possible for these activities to be subcontracted.

Receiving at least as much media and scholarly attention as initiative consultants are the firms that specialize in petition management—the collection of signatures, for a fee, to secure access to the ballot. Table 4.1 suggests that ten of these firms were in operation in all of the United States in 1999.

In the 1950s, Robinson and Co. engaged in this work in California (Bowler et al. 1996). Other more contemporary operations include Advanced Voter Communications (AVC) of Newport Beach, California (which has ceased operations), and Kimball Petition Management, Inc., of Los Angeles. In the early 1990s, the firm AVC advertised its ability to fully qualify a constitutional amendment in California in forty-five days on a

Table 4.2   Services Offered by Professional Initiative Consultants, 1999

Opinion polling	20
Media buying	56
Designing/producing campaign ads	70
Advice on political strategy	89
Signature gathering	9
Fund-raising	22
Legal advice	9
Direct mail	69
General campaign management	73
Research	31
Other	27

Source: Authors' survey of forty-five campaign professionals, spring 1999.
Note: Numbers reflect the percentage of firms providing the service.

"money-back basis" using direct-mail technologies (*California Journal* 1990a, 77). Kimball, founded in the 1960s by Fred Kimball, is the oldest firm in existence, and one of the largest. Fred Kimball's sons now operate the firm. A number of former Kimball employees have established smaller firms discussed below. A few of the larger, multioffice consultant firms (such as Goddard Claussen/1st Tuesday) that offer a wide array of "in-house" media and consulting services also advertise petition-management services.

Our discussion of the professionals employed in a campaign begins from the perspective of a proponent—typically an issue-advocacy group such as those discussed above—since proponents move first in initiative contests and often make full use of the professional resources dedicated to initiative campaigns. Our perspective on the structure of the industry is informed by the existing academic and journalistic literature, by dozens of interviews with people employed in various stages of the process, and by our mailed survey of campaign professionals who work on state and local ballot initiatives. One thing we have learned from our observations is that there is no single model that describes how every group contesting an initiative utilizes the services of campaign professionals (see, e.g., Mc-Cuan et al. 1998). But by focusing on the sequence of campaign actions we can begin to show how the campaign specialists come into play at different points in the campaign.

Actually getting onto the ballot by running through the sequence that we examine below contains many pitfalls for the would-be proponent. Between 1912 and 1998, 1,043 propositions in California received a formal title; only 272 of these qualified for the ballot, and of these only 87 were approved by voters. Not only do roughly 70 percent of propositions fail at the ballot, over 70 percent of proposals never actually reach the ballot (Jones 1998b). The road from being an idea to being an actual proposition is clearly a difficult one. In what follows, then, we concentrate first on the road to appearing on the ballot. This process of actually getting on the ballot—the jockeying and politicking before the actual vote occurs—is not especially relevant to discussions of candidate races. Yet, as we illustrate, this stage is in fact a quite crucial part of the campaigns for ballot propositions.

THE SEQUENCE OF INITIATIVE CAMPAIGNS AND THE INVOLVEMENT OF PROFESSIONALS

Step 1: Drafting the Initiative

Prior to petition circulation, an initiative proponent must translate its idea into a formal law and, along the way, address the political feasibility of how the initiative campaign will, or can be, conducted. At this stage, some pure "amateur" groups go it alone, choosing to draft their proposals without concern for the opinions of the electorate, their adversaries, or other groups who may be potential allies. Several prominent initiatives, including California's famous antitax, Proposition 13 of 1978, and California's term-limit initiative (Proposition 140 of 1990), were drafted without professionals but were subsequently "picked-up" by interested groups who hired professional campaigners (Zimmerman, p. 1). For many others, proponents hire consultants prior to the crafting of the final initiative proposal. Table 4.3 displays results of a question asking consultants when they are typically brought on board an initiative campaign. Fully half of our respondents indicated that they are hired relatively early, "at or before titling and summary."

Nevertheless, consultants and managers who work on initiatives indicate that they may often be brought on board after initiatives are drafted, even when they are working for established interests. They recognize, however, that established business and issue-advocacy groups are more likely to hire them earlier in the process, compared to amateur groups who have used the process rarely (McCuan et al. 1998). Regardless of the point at which they are employed, consultants emphasize that they have a limited role in shaping the formal, legal content of a measure.

Even if they are brought in to advise a campaign prior to the initiative being filed, many consultants leave the language of the proposal, its title, and the summary that appears in the state's official pamphlet to other professionals—the attorneys who specialize in political law. In response to a question about his influence over the summary and content of initiatives he assisted as a consultant, one professional noted, "usually they have lawyers for that" (Dash 1997, 1). Another responded to the same question, "I'm not an expert. You need attorneys for that" (Zimmerman 1997, 1). The consultant's role at this early stage is to advise clients of potential political liabilities that might end up in a measure, and to be on guard for provisions in the measure that opponents could use to undermine support. One professional indicated that he would read proposals

Table 4.3   When Consultants Typically Join Initiative Campaigns (percent)

At or before titling and summary	50
At the petition or signature-gathering stage	14
After qualification	33
Just a few weeks before the election	2

Source: Author's survey of 45 campaign professionals, spring 1999.

Note: Responses to the question, "At what stage in the campaign process are you usually brought in?"

after they are written "to make sure there is nothing politically incorrect in there, or something that will really bite you" (Zimmerman 1997, 1). Others indicate the importance of finding a measure's "Achilles heel" (Schultz 1996, 16).

Amateurs who draft initiatives on their own face substantial risks. One UCLA law professor was so dismayed with the ambiguities of Howard Jarvis's Proposition 13 that he charged its author with "drunken drafting" (Hamilton 1982; California Commission 1992, 10). Confusion over Proposition 13 "spawned dozens of court cases and stimulated sixteen clarifying ballot measures" (California Commission 1992, 10). As the California Commission on Campaign Finance (1992, 10) report concluded, "Many problems with initiatives stem from poor initial drafting" that can lead to "litigation, legislative inaction, judicial invalidation, and voter confusion."

Poorly drafted proposals can also cause ambiguities that might be successfully attacked by opponents during the campaign. If a poorly drafted initiative is approved, opponents will be in a good position to use the courts to block its implementation. Holman and Stern (1998, 1224) note that interests opposed to various California initiatives can select between different benches that are more or less sympathetic to overturning voter-approved initiatives. From 1964 to 1990, less than half of the twenty-one California initiatives challenged in court were upheld. After 1990, California initiatives have been contested and overturned at a similar rate. However, initiatives were more likely to land in federal courts after 1990, as opponents filed their challenges in courts known to be less sympathetic to initiatives than state courts (Holman and Stern 1998, 1250–1256). Professional attorneys used in the drafting stage give proponents some ability to anticipate litigation that might weaken the impact of an initiative proposal.

Step 2: Opinion Research during the Drafting Stage: Focus Groups and Polling

Tools used to find what in an initiative might "bite" a proponent include the consultant's intuition and, if funding is available, focus groups and opinion polling. Focus groups, a standard technique used in commercial marketing, involve a discussion with a small number (twelve to twenty) of citizens, with consultants (overtly or covertly) monitoring responses to open-ended questions about an initiative's topic. Participants are typically paid a nominal fee for participation in the hope that they express sincere, plain-language views that can be translated into effective themes for advertising campaigns. Follow-up polling can be used to further test the effectiveness of themes discovered in focus group sessions

(Schultz 1996, 15). A solid, twenty-five-minute, one-hundred-question poll on an initiative in California will cost at least $20,000 to $25,000, according to Schultz. "Campaigns that can afford it will typically run at least two polls. The first one is to guide the drafting process—testing language, emphasis, and key policy provisions" (Schultz 1996, 16).

As Schultz reports in his *Initiative Cookbook*, a "how-to" guide for progressive-liberal groups considering the use of direct democracy, "polling takes the language, opinions and arguments raised by the focus groups and tests them with a representative sampling of state voters" (1996, 16). Polling can also be used to determine how far proponents might reach with their measure, or to tell opponents what provisions of a measure are most vulnerable. In addition to testing pro and con arguments, polls can be used to "test messengers" by asking respondents their evaluations of a list of groups and individuals who might take a position on the initiative. One fund-raising consultant, Matt Kuzins, reports that polls can also be used to demonstrate the viability of a campaign to potential contributors (Schultz 1996, 15). As for polls being used to craft campaign messages, Schultz offers an example of the successful campaign opposing Governor Pete Wilson's initiative to cut welfare (Proposition 165 of 1992). Opponents used focus groups and polls to discover messages that they believed would move opinions. Trudy Schafer, of the League of Women Voters, claimed that research on the welfare issue "revealed that welfare wasn't as popular an issue as [was] concern over the power of the governor" (Schultz 1996, 18). Opponents played down welfare policy, while attacking the issue as a "power-grab" by the governor.

Consultants indicate that groups most familiar with the initiative process will be more likely to use polling early, in the formative stages of drafting the initiative. Amateur groups, or individuals working without input from elements of a broader coalition, are probably less likely to utilize opinion research at the drafting stage. According to Bill Zimmerman, with the controversial illegal immigration initiative of 1996 (Proposition 187), "the people behind it put it together without any discussion with campaign people, without any focus groups, without any polling, they just did their thing." On the other hand, proponents working with established interests and advocacy groups behind them, as with the automobile insurance measures of 1988, "went to pollsters and political people and said this is what we want to do" (Zimmerman 1997, 1).

Step 3: Building Coalitions at the Drafting Stage

The small number of law firms that specialize in the process provide technical and legal advice for drafting initiatives, as well as for managing the regulatory apparatus associated with modern campaigns. Firms such as Wilke, Fleury et al., and Bagatelos and Faten specialize in political law and campaign reporting. In addition to ensuring compliance with standard campaign finance regulations, Federal Communications Commission reporting requirements, and internal auditing requirements that apply to modern campaigns, lawyers assist in drafting the formal text as it evolves from negotiations among the groups proposing an initiative. Initiatives can go through multiple drafts as the concerns and interests of numerous elements of the proponents' coalition are incorporated.

At this initial stage of the process, the role of the private lawyers is not unlike that of the legal staff consulting a legislative committee marking up a bill, and the process of drafting an initiative can appear very much like the slow process of the majority party drafting a bill in a legislature. It is rarely appreciated that numerous groups are involved in the coalitions that develop initiative proposals. This applies to initiatives funded by individual patrons, by broad-based issue groups, and by narrowly based economic interests.

Coalition building can take many forms. In attempting to build support for their parkland purchase initiative at the drafting stage, the California Planning and Conservation League (PCL) adopted logrolling strategies reminiscent of a congressional committee drafting a bill authorizing highway projects. The PCL negotiated with local conservation and environmental groups throughout the state, agreeing to include a group's local park project in exchange for its support (Williams 1994, 47; Bowler and Donovan 1998, 110–113). The legislature was not flattered by imitation, and responded by passing legislation that banned overt spending logrolls in future initiatives. The PCL has also forged a coalition between environmentalists and corporate interests to promote a mass transit initiative. In this instance, the PCL allied with Southern Pacific (Schultz 1996, 37), the original target of California's Progressive reformers.

Coalition building at the drafting stage extends to proposals sponsored by narrow economic interests as well. Silicon Valley executives seeking to limit shareholders' lawsuits built a coalition with supporters of no-fault auto insurance to draft three propositions for the 1996 ballot. Ironically, one of the executives who sponsored the initiatives responded to an opponents' offensive commercial by filing a lawsuit (*California Journal* 1996a, 10). Some of California's more costly initiative battles emerge when drafting negotiations among various interest groups break down, and pieces of the failed coalitions draft and qualify their own rival initiatives. A pair of initiatives designed to regulate HMOs resulted from divisions among various labor associations that had been in negotiations to craft a single initiative (*California Journal* 1996b, 11–13). Some of 1988's rival auto insurance initiatives were also spawned from intra-industry differences of opinion about how to respond to the threat of regulation.

A number of consultants and attorneys relayed that negotiations over drafting an initiative can take months, if not years, as various groups bring their concerns to the table. One consultant stated that "If there is a coalition of organizations that is looking to support [a measure] it typically goes through quite a number of drafts . . . [and] the various groups kind of try to hammer out whatever their competing interests may be and get something that everyone is happy with" (Shepard interview, p. 4). An attorney specializing in political law noted that "some of these things go through many, many drafts to get it right." Participating in negotiations for a 1990 redistricting proposal developed by several bipartisan groups, he observed that "we must have gone through thirty drafts—that took a long time" (Bagatelos 1996, 2).

Schultz observes that "initiative coalitions are like a giant potluck dinner" where each potential member of the coalition brings something valuable to the table (Schultz 1996, 37). Some are brought on board by proponents because they can provide money for petition circulation and campaigning. Some can provide volunteers who can collect signatures and a mass base from which to draw votes. Having volunteers collect a large portion of required signatures might lower the costs of qualification. Some might provide staff resources, or expertise with initiative campaigns. Others might give the initiative an aura of credibility (Schultz 1996). Groups may expect something in return for their support, including favorable provisions in an initiative (or, at least, the absence of clauses that threaten them). As in a legislature, the proponent of an initiative law needs to form coalitions that can win. Building one with adequate resources to contest an initiative campaign can occasionally bring groups who might often oppose each other into temporary alliances. This was the case with a recent California political reform measure that brought Common Cause into alliance with Ross Perot's United We Stand America party, the League of Women Voters, the American Association of Retired Persons (AARP), and the California Taxpayers Association (Schultz 1996, 36).

Step 4: Negotiating Official Summaries

Once proponents agree upon the language of the proposal, the political attorneys enter into negotiations with state officials about how title and summary will portray the measure. Negotiations might also occur over how the state's Legislative Analysts' office will calculate projections of the measure's fiscal costs. Since title, summary, and the analysts' projections are printed in the pamphlets that the state mails to all voters, consultants and attorneys indicate that great importance is placed on these negotiations. Lawyers will represent their clients in negotiations with state officials over each of these items, and these negotiations may proceed through several stages as a measure is redrafted.

The state's title and summary will also appear on the official petitions that proponents circulate prior to qualification. For some voters, if not all potential petition signatories, the summary and title of the initiative are all they may ever know about a measure. "If you can't get a title and summary that is satisfactory, often times they will go back, the supporters will go back, and redraft the entire initiative just to try to get a more favorable title and summary from the attorney general" (Shepard interview). If political attorneys are employed, they redraft proposals as negotiations progress.

After drafting and negotiations over summaries and titles, during the election phase, the role of the political attorneys is fairly limited. They do not provide campaign communications consulting services, nor solicit endorsements for clients. However, they will continue to assist their clients throughout the campaign and after the election, managing regulatory compliance and "clean-up." During a campaign, they may serve as legal counsel, as well as provide language for disclaimers used in broadcast and mail advertisements. Clearly, the political law firms play much less of a role for opposition campaigns that do not need to draft a proposal.

Step 5: Securing Endorsements

As indicated by the discussion of coalition building above, proponents of initiatives recognize that endorsements are a valuable resource. By lining up support from well-known groups, proponents may secure a base of potential volunteers for petition circulation. And endorsements can add to the proponents' ability to raise money for campaigns by establishing credibility. During campaigns, endorsements also provide many voters with what might be their single most useful source of information when attempting to figure out how to vote on an initiative (Lupia 1992; 1994; Bowler and Donovan 1998). It is important to secure endorsements well before the campaign in order for them to appear in the official pamphlet that is sent to all state voters. In states such as California and Washington, proponents and opponents may list themselves, or supporting groups, in the pro and con arguments (and rebuttals) published by the state. In Oregon, any group or individual willing to pay a fee (or have the fee paid for them) may enter an argument for or against an initiative in the state's official pamphlet.

The value of these endorsements relative to all other sources of campaign information is illustrated in table 4.4. In an attempt to determine how voters decide on initiatives, random-dial telephone surveys of regis-

Table 4.4 Reported Sources of Information Used for Deciding on Initiatives (percent reporting use of source)

	California Voters	Washington State Voters
Voter's pamphlet	54	73
Newspapers	n/a	66
TV news	n/a	55
Word of mouth	n/a	53
Radio news	n/a	51
Newspaper editorials	47	n/a
TV editorials	33	n/a
Campaign mailings	20	35
Friends/neighbors	22	n/a
TV ads	21	20
Other (unspecified)	n/a	23
Radio ads	6	19
Newspaper ads	18	n/a
Radio editorials	10	n/a

Sources: California: Field California Poll 1990. Washington: authors' poll of Washington voters conducted by Applied Research Northwest, spring 1999.

tered voters conducted in California and Washington asked "whether or not you rely on each [information source] when deciding on ballot initiatives." Respondents were offered a list of several sources of information about propositions. In each state, the pamphlet ranks at the top of the list of potential information sources, with nearly three-quarters of Washington voters claiming they used it as a source of information. A study of those who read the pamphlets, moreover, demonstrated that more than 80 percent use them to determine who is endorsing the pro and con positions—far more than who report reading the title and summary (Dubois et al. 1991). As Schultz puts it, endorsements define the "sides of an issue in a way that can have a powerful effect on voter attitudes" (1996, 38).

Early in the process of developing an initiative, consultants will begin building their base of endorsees. Not all consultants indicated they were involved with securing endorsements. Some relayed that this task was left to the proponent or opponent group. But, as one put it, "the biggest hunk of activity that our Sacramento office has in most state initiatives is just going out and securing endorsements and arranging for editorial board meetings with newspapers" (Shepard 1997, 2). As an example of the power of endorsements, another consultant cited the crucial role that Ralph Nader's endorsement played in pulling the consumer group's insurance initiative to victory over four competing proposals from economic interests (see also Lupia 1994; Bowler and Donovan 1998, 60), noting that "endorsements are very important to all kinds of campaigns because people tend to look and see who is supporting what" (Dash 1997, 2).

Consultants recognize that people use endorsements to figure out what to vote against, as well as what to vote for. Some voters "always look to see whether the governor comes down on an issue," then vote for or against it. "A lot of issues come down and [people] see where Willie Brown is and vote the other way" (Dash 1997, 2). On some occasions, then, proponents walk a fine line over who to list as an official supporter, for fear of losing more support than is gained. Highly visible partisan officials (e.g., Republican governor Pete Wilson), or known groups (e.g., the National Rifle Association [NRA]) who might actually be movers behind an initiative, can mobilize strong partisans of one camp in opposition while bringing strong supporters of the other party on board as supporters (Bowler and Donovan 1998, 64–65). Well-known groups that offer a reputation for nonpartisanship or an aura of neutrality are highly sought after, since they may draw potential supporters on board without alienating many voters. Examples include the AARP, Common Cause, the League of Women Voters, and the PTA. The Jarvis and Gann associations' names are also powerful drawing cards. Other groups that act as powerful cues include mass-membership labor groups such as the California Teachers Association (CTA) and the California State Employees Association (Schultz 1996, 39).

Less commonly, celebrities are also used as endorsees and are featured as supporters or critics in broadcast ads. The impact of these endorsements probably depends on how viewers regard the celebrity and on how they translate the endorsee into partisan and policy considerations. It is likely that some voters can recognize the partisan stance of celebrities such as Ed Asner, based on their previous political activism and from the candidates and groups they have supported in the past. Celebrities can be cast in a partisan light because political parties and candidates frequently make use of the state's celebrity community.

Narrowly based groups lacking the ability to secure endorsements from well-known groups or individuals might be forced to publish their arguments and air ads using the banal names generated by their campaign organization. Examples include the Coalition against Unregulated Gambling (Nevada casino opponents of 1998's Proposition 5), Californians for Paycheck Protection (Yes on Proposition 226 of 1998), the Alliance to Revitalize California (Silicon Valley executives seeking tort reforms via Propositions 201 and 202 in 1996), and Californians for Affordable and Reliable Electrical Service (industry opponents of utility regulation initiative Proposition 9 of 1998). Since these single-campaign groups lack the enduring presence that would give them a reputation and credibility in the minds of voters, it is unlikely their monikers have much impact on voter decisions.

Indeed, vague group names might actually cause voters to evaluate a measure based on the unknown group's incentives for supporting or opposing a proposal (in a related vein, see Lupia and McCubbins 1998). Knowledge of the value of having a known versus an unknown (or questionable) endorsee attached to a proposal led opponents of a utility regulation initiative (Proposition 9, 1998) to hire David Horowitz, the consumer activist made famous by his show "Fight Back," for $100,000 to sign their ballot argument against the initiative (*Los Angeles Times* 1998; *California Journal* 1998, 32). The purchased endorsement, however, became the subject of media attention during the campaign. Upon hearing of Horowitz's fee for the endorsement, one observer noted that the show should be renamed "Kick Back" (*Los Angeles Times* 1998). We have not identified any other examples of such practices.

While the heavy spending on broadcast ads during the campaign phase is known as an "air war," competition for endorsements might be seen as the modern initiative campaigns' ground war. Even corporate interests proposing or opposing an initiative under the label of a single-election coalition will attempt to build an endorsement list of known organizations. The internal campaign organizing manual for the 1998 No On Proposition 5 Coalition against Unregulated Gambling (CAUG), for example, states that the campaign's primary objective was "to broaden our base of organizations and opinion leaders statewide and at the local level" and "use endorsements to demonstrate to the news media, other opinion leaders and voters" the groups opposed to Proposition 5 (CAUG 1998, 1). This involved local organizers trained to form steering committees and to solicit endorsements from groups sympathetic to the state coalition (e.g., local labor organizations, local law enforcement, local religious leaders, the PTA, school board members, and local elected officials). CAUG organizers were provided with training on how to publicize endorsements they secured—including the use of templates of press releases and samples of letters to editors. The No on 5 campaign—rare in its level of organization and funding—would then communicate to members of endorsing groups through their newsletters, with weekly faxes, and via campaign mailings directed to member lists obtained from endorsing groups (CAUG 1998, 9).

Step 6: Picking an Electorate: Timing the Election

Without prompting, several consultants we spoke with mentioned that one of the most important things they could provide advice on was the scheduling of an election. As one put it, "You're making a decision real early as to which electorate you want to be in" (Remer interview, p. 2). The timing of initiative elections depends on when proponents qualify their petitions. Typically, a proponent has a fixed period in which to qualify. If successful, the measure is automatically placed on the ballot in the next election where initiatives are regularly scheduled. Even if states schedule initiatives in general elections only, this might offer proponents the ability to choose between high turnout "on-year" elections and lower turnout "off-year" contests. In California, the state schedules elections biannually, including primaries and general elections, offering proponents a wide range in the type of electorate that might be voting on their proposal. Similar conditions apply with local initiatives. State laws start the clock for scheduling an initiative based on when petitions are put in circulation, so proponents can, in theory, schedule their vote by strategically selecting when to file their initiative with the state. Picking an electorate, if it can be done, requires factoring in "the kind of initiative it is, the kind of turnout you want, . . . Are you fighting? Are you proposing? Is it going to be a presidential election year? What will that do to your issue?" This consultant suggested that small turnout elections favor the opposition, "because opponents come out more than proponents" (Dash 1997, 1–2). Consultants seek an electorate shaped by "big forces" of turnout (candidate elections, contested party primaries) that favor the type of issue their client is proposing (Remer interview, p. 2).

Decisions about scheduling, however, can be affected by opponents (see below) and by partisan consideration. Discussing the California voucher initiative (Proposition 174 of 1993), one consultant said, "The governor did not want that affecting the Republican primary in June of 1994, so he created a special election just to get it out of the way" (Zimmerman 1997, 2).

Step 7: The Petition Circulation Stage

Working in the professional campaign hierarchy below the political consultants, who act in part as the general contractors of initiative campaigns, are the petition-management subcontractors, who provide services to clients that are more narrowly technical.

In addition to AVC—Butcher and Forde's former operation—and the Kimball firm, several operations founded by former Kimball employees compete in the petition-management side of the industry. These include Mike Arno's American Petition Consultants of Gold River, California, and Rick Arnold's National Voter Outreach of Carson City, Nevada (Broder 1998). Other major California-based firms include Masterton and Wright in northern California and Angelo Paparella's Progressive Campaigns of Santa Monica (Broder 1998).

While these firms pick up significant work outside of California, there are additional petition operations based in other states. At least one Portland-based firm, Klein Communications, works qualifying initiatives for the Oregon ballot. Klein Communications has worked on some of Bill Sizemore's petitions, although Sizemore subsequently opened his own Oregon-based petition firm. In the state of Washington, Shirley Bockwinkel established an enduring petition-management firm after gaining experience as a proponent of the state's first term-limit initiative (David Olson 1992). Most of these firms are dedicated to the single task of qualifying initiatives and are typically employed on a contract basis by initiative proponents or their consultants.

Even purveyors of technical services such as petition management can have reputations that are decidedly partisan, and their clients are often ideologically compatible. Examples of major California petition firms with partisan or ideological reputations include Butcher and Forde's ACV direct-mail firm, which in the early 1980s was clearly linked to Howard Jarvis's antitax efforts (Magleby and Patterson 2000, 20; Daniel Smith 1998). However, AVC later expanded from that base, while engaging in questionable fund-raising methods that produced a lawsuit from a former member of the Jarvis organization (Schrag 1998, 212). David Broder (1998) reports that the contemporary Kimball firm earned its reputation working with traditional Democratic constituents such as trial lawyers and teachers' unions—Kimball's founder was an archconservative, however (Price 1992, 545). Masterton and Wright's signature firm works with many environmental clients, and while Angelo Paparella of Progressive Campaigns "says his workforce and agenda reflect his liberal origins" as one of "Nader's Raiders," Progressive campaigns also circulated petitions for the initiative repealing bilingual education (Broder 1998). The Masterton firm is somewhat unique in that it has a history of working on petition efforts that utilize many volunteers (Price 1992, 548).

Like television stations that air ads, companies that print mailings, attorneys who represent candidates and campaigns, and corporations that own telephone infrastructure, petition-management firms profit from politics. Critical attention directed at the petition side of initiative politics focuses on this for-profit aspect of the industry (see, e.g., California Commission 1992; Lowenstein and Stern 1989). This stems, in part, from the idea that the petition phase should be a forum for deliberation and education about the proposed issue and from the hope that signatures should reflect an initial measure of public support (American Bar Association 1992). Volunteers, it is assumed, have greater incentives to discuss issues than paid signature collectors and thus educate voters while building support for a proposal. States such as Washington and Colorado attempted to preserve volunteerism via laws banning paid signature collection, but the Supreme Court's *Meyer v. Grant*, 486 U.S. 414 (1988) decision nullified these laws in 1988. Petition management firms have set up shop in these states since the Court's decision.

With signature collection driven by profits and time constraints, some observers suggest that deliberation and education cannot occur and that successful qualification is no measure of initial support. Others argue that discussion does occur. Unfortunately, evidence supporting these claims (e.g., Tolbert et al. 1998, 33–34; Cronin 1989, 63–64; Lowenstein and Stern 1989; Dusha 1975; Brestoff 1975, 944–945) relies heavily upon anecdotes (see, however, Neiman and Gottdiener 1985). Whatever the evidence, it seems likely that many people who sign initiative petitions come away with little or no familiarity with the issue.

Given the sheer volume of signatures needed for ballot access (discussed above) it is reasonable to assume that very few petitions can ever be qualified by relying exclusively on volunteer petition circulators. In Washington State, as recently as 1999, sponsors of a tax rollback initiative used a volunteer effort to gather 450,000 signatures, the second most collected in that state's history (Ammons 1999). As table 4.5 illustrates with data from 1990 (a year for which campaign spending data were published by expenditure categories), petition costs are frequently the single largest expense for a "yes" campaign. For twelve of the seventeen initiatives on California's state ballots that year, signatures (and prequalification surveys) accounted for the first or second greatest category of expenditure. Other categories included fees to consultants, literature, general expenses, fund-raising, broadcast ads, newspaper ads, outdoor ads, and travel. It is important to note that qualification costs have risen since 1990.

Despite the fact that few initiatives qualify via full volunteer efforts, many issue-advocacy groups utilize volunteers from their supporter base and effectively reduce the costs of ballot access. According to Schultz, "most campaigns combine volunteer and paid signature gathering" (1996, 35). The wide variety of expenditures on signatures in California— from $23,000 to more than $914,000 in 1990—reflects differences in each campaign's ability to use volunteers and may also result from discrepancies in reporting expenditures.[1] Only narrow interests, particularly those faced with a short time period for qualification, will rely exclusively on paid signatures.

But even an all-volunteer effort does not mean that there are no costs. Rick Arnold of National Voter Outreach indicated that volunteers can actually cost more than an efficient staff of trained for-hire circulators and that paid staff can sometimes bring in signatures at a lower cost per unit than volunteers. Proponents using volunteers will still require funding for coordinators, transportation costs, materials, lodging costs, training costs, administration, and overhead. Lacking experience and training, he

Table 4.5   Proportion of Proponent Expenditures on Paid Circulators: California 1990

Initiative	Topic	$ on Sigs and Survey	% of Budget	Sigs as % Budget on Broadcast Ads
Primary Election				
Prop. 115	Criminal justice	$609,924	29.1%	36.8%
Prop. 116	Rail transportation	418,000	32.8	12.7
Prop. 117	Wildlife protection	275,400	26.7	2.2
Prop. 118	Reapportionment/ethics	566,471	46.9	0.0
Prop. 119	Reapportionment	655,150	22.3	30.2
General Election				
Prop. 128	Environmental/Big Green	$141,358	2.5%	53.8%
Prop. 129	Criminal justice reforms	638,224	58.0	0.0
Prop. 130	Forests	914,230	12.9	66.2
Prop. 131	Term limits/campaign reform	568,199	48.8	0.7
Prop. 132	Gill net fishing	23,310	3.3	3.2
Prop. 133	Drug enforcement/prevention	461,917	57.6	17.3
Prop. 134	Alcohol tax	912,772	48.1	2.0
Prop. 135	Pesticide regulations	132,536	2.3	52.6*
Prop. 136/7	Taxes/initiative process	171,353	1.6	16.2
Prop. 138	Forest clear-cutting	461,411	8.2	45.6*
Prop. 139	Prison labor	527,635	39.8	0.9
Prop. 140	Term limits	596,723	30.5	38.7

Source: California Commission 1992, appendix F.
*Denotes industry counterinitiative. Published records include circulation expenses together with preelection opinion polls.

notes, volunteers can have lower rates of collecting valid signatures, further increasing proponents' costs (Arnold 1999). A 1990 California initiative to regulate mountain lion hunting confirms the cost of all-volunteer efforts. The measure was one of the few in the 1990s to qualify using only volunteer circulators, but proponents still spent $250,000—a relatively small sum now for California (Schultz 1996, 35). Ken Masterton, who operates a petition firm that specializes in volunteer efforts, also estimated in 1992 that it would cost $250,000 to run a volunteer qualification effort in California (Price 1992, 548). The 1999 all-volunteer effort that collected 450,000 signatures in Washington was funded with a "shoestring budget" of $78,000 (Ammons 1999).

How much does it usually cost to get on the ballot? It depends on the market. The highest amounts paid per signature we could identify rarely reach the $2 range, although Schultz (1996) reports $2.00 as the "record" paid per signature and Guetzloe of Advantage Consulting reports that his firm reached $5.00 a signature by the end of the signature campaign he ran in Florida on behalf of gaming giant Bally Inc. Price (1988, 484) reports the case of a single "no fault" initiative rapidly qualified by the insurance industry that had more than $14 million in qualification expenses, which equaled nearly $39 per signature. In California, at least eight petition efforts, including direct-mail solicitations for corporate interests, exceeded the $3.00 per signature range during the 1980s (Price 1988, 484), but such cases continue to be relatively rare. It is not always clear from these reports if the price paid is to the street-level signature collector, or if it is the total per-unit cost to the proponent.

The distinction is important. As table 4.6 illustrates, there are several layers of workers involved in petition-management operations, and each layer claims a share of the fees. At the top of the operation are the firms, who contract with the clients and manage the qualification efforts. They tend to have few full-time employees relative to the scale of their accomplishments. In 1998 alone Rick Arnold's operation had worked on seventeen initiatives by April (Broder 1998), but the firm typically employs fewer than six people full time (Arnold 1999). For street-level workers, firms work with independent contractors who act as regional coordinators and local crew chiefs in the field. Regional coordinators oversee local crew chiefs, who are responsible for managing and paying the people actually collecting signatures. There may be as many as fifty of these subcontractors in California alone (Broder 1998). Many specialize in conducting petition work in specific locations, and they may take contracts for work from several different petition-management firms simultaneously (Spero 1997). Circulators in the field will typically carry petitions for at least five initiatives at a single time (Spero 1997) and some make the best-paying petition their first and most emphatic pitch (Mapes 1994, 4).

When a petition firm signs up a subcontractor, it usually demands that a fixed proportion of signatures collected are valid—typically 70 percent (Spero 1997). This means that, in addition to recruiting individual petition circulators, part of the subcontractor's duties involve checking the validity of signatures prior to shipping signed petitions to the regional coordi-

Table 4.6 Costs of Paid Petition Efforts Per Signature

Consulting firm ("override" fee)	.15–.25
Regional/area coordinators	.10–.15
Local subcontractor/crew boss	.10–.15
Validators	.02
Circulator on the street	.50–.75
Average total cost to proponent = $0.87–$1.32 per signature	

nators. Some subcontractors pay fees to individuals who specialize in validating signatures, and validators may also have subcontractors working under them (Spero 1997).

Based on published reports cited above, and interviews conducted with the owner of a firm and with subcontractors, we estimate that when the average fees collected by all these elements of the petition-management operations are combined, in 1999 the cost for a median proponent in California ranged from $0.87 per signature to $1.32. If a proponent was using no volunteers and needed about 600,000 signatures to qualify a statute (this assumes a modestly high validity rate), costs would be between $522,000 and $792,000 for signatures alone. For a constitutional amendment, typical costs would be between $870,000 and $1.32 million. Since our estimates are based on average costs, many petition efforts will cost more than this, and some will cost less. It is important to stress that these are only the petition costs of qualification. As such, they do not include money that proponents spend on polling, consultants, and attorneys during drafting and qualification.

Costs vary as a result of many factors, including the size of the state, the amount of time left in the qualification process, the issue, the methods used to get signatures, and the number of petitions in circulation. If there are more petitions in circulation or one initiative is paying a premium fee, circulators will focus attention on that measure, potentially forcing other proponents to pay more out of fear that their petitions will be ignored.

With more initiatives qualified in the 1990s by professionals than in previous decades, the average qualification costs in California, Washington, Oregon, Colorado, and other states have increased enormously. The CCCF reports that, in the mid- and late 1970s, average qualification costs for a California initiative were only about $45,000 (California Commission 1992, 12). Costs are likely to continue to increase as voter registration rises in western states, or if turnout in state elections increases (thus raising the bar needed to qualify for the next election cycle).

Step 8: Countering Petitions and Counterpetitions

The maturity of the petition management industry brings with it two important phenomena associated with modern initiative campaigns: ballot access is costly, and, for groups with adequate funds, it can be nearly automatic. But costs are not fixed. Qualification battles have become a critical element of campaigns for both proponents and opponents, and effective opposition tactics can drive up qualification costs, delay qualification, and constrain a proponent's ability to schedule a vote before a favorable electorate. California's two largest petition firms, APC and Kimball, have both worked on antiqualification campaigns (Price 1992, 548). Opposition groups thus have at their disposal techniques, while rarely used, that allow them to intercept petition circulators in order to discourage citizens from signing.

It is difficult to determine how common countercampaigns are for initiative opponents, but it seems counterpetition efforts are a tool at the disposal of well-financed and grassroots opposition campaigns. Speaking of the former, one consultant indicated, "you hire a consultant early on to monitor and sometimes even run a countercampaign so people won't sign an initiative. Sometimes you will hire a consultant after the initiative qualifies, but in California and big-time elections, especially where big interest groups are attacked . . . opponents start in early before an initiative qualifies" (Dash 1997, 1).

A classic example of this is the heated battle to qualify California's first school choice initiative (Proposition 174 of 1993). The initiative was supported by conservative religious groups, the state GOP, and the Paul Gann organization. Proponents hired the APC (Arno) firm to qualify their measure. Opponents included the CTA, which is the state's main teachers' union, and other education organizations (Locke 1993). Proponents hoped to qualify for a November 1992 ballot, thinking this would improve their chances of winning by diluting the influence of the CTA in a low-turnout primary election.

The CTA's political organizers, having previously qualified their own initiatives, were familiar with petition-circulating strategies and used their experience to delay Proposition 174's qualification. They hired Kimball to work against qualification. Kimball claimed that "our strategy in the antiqualification campaign was to arm the potential signer with the information needed to say 'no' " (Price 1992, 548). Methods included dispatching CTA activists to locations where petitions were being circulated, then providing counterarguments to anyone considering signing petitions. Such tactics made it impossible for choice advocates to qualify for the election cycle they favored, and eventually forced them to spend more on collecting signatures. In the end, the choice measure qualified for the ballot much later, proponents spent more on qualification and had little cash left to wage a campaign, and opponents were given more time to raise funds. The initiative was defeated.

Campaigns designed to counter the qualification efforts of an initiative proposal have also succeeded in preventing proponents, even those using some paid circulators, from qualifying for the ballot. A coalition of gay rights activists in Washington (Hands Off Washington), for example, designed and funded a successful $1 million antiqualification campaign in 1994 that was credited with keeping two antigay initiatives off the state's

ballot (Gilmore 1995). The initial effort that blocked two initiative proposals, one which was modeled after an initiative from Oregon, included dispatching so-called Bigot Buster protesters wherever signatures were
being gathered (Simon 1994). In the end, proponents of one measure
hired a professional petition firm, but both proposals failed to collect sufficient signatures. Another successful Hands Off Washington campaign
against a third initiative involved creating opposition to an antigay proposal by asking citizens to sign a pledge that they would not sign the antigay initiative petition (Gilmore 1995). This benefited the opposition in a
number of ways. Circulating the pledge kept volunteer gay rights activists
mobilized politically and provided Hands Off with a database of potential supporters.

In an unusual twist on opposition groups collecting signatures to block
an initiative, Schultz (1996, 34) reports that in 1988, the tobacco industry
hired professional circulators to collect signatures on a noninitiative petition that expressed opposition to a tobacco tax initiative that was in circulation at the time (Proposition 99 of 1988). The industry's petition had no
possible way of affecting policy, but served as a device "to hire petitioners
away from the tobacco tax effort," thereby starting a signature pay war
and driving up the proponent's qualification costs (Schultz 1996, 34). The
tobacco tax initiative qualified nonetheless, and it was passed by voters
despite massive campaign spending by the opposition (*California Journal*
1988).

The existence of professional qualification services also means that opponents of an initiative have other tools available to fight a proponent's
initiative during the qualification phase: counterinitiatives. Counterinitiatives are actual initiative proposals that are developed as a defense
against a proposed or qualified measure that threatens some group's interests. Banducci (1998) demonstrates that the use of counterinitiatives increased dramatically in the 1990s as corporate and industry groups responded to initiatives by drafting and rapidly qualifying their own, rival
measures. In Oregon, for example, health care advocates and insurers
drafted and qualified a measure that would tax tobacco to fund antismok-
ing education. The tobacco industry responded by qualifying a measure
for the same ballot (Measure 39, 1996) that would have forced Oregon's
health care providers to recognize and fund "alternative healers" such
as acupuncturists and naturopaths (Donovan et al. 1998, 86). Other well-
known examples come from California's 1990 election. That year, industry groups countered a sweeping environmental initiative with a much
more modest proposal, and the alcohol industry countered a drink tax
with an industry-friendly proposal. Since counterpropositions are often
done within short time frames, they can cost much more than petition
efforts that begin early (see, e.g., Price 1988).

There are multiple incentives for opponents to qualify counterinitiatives as part of an opposition campaign. First, if a well-financed opponent is circulating its counterinitiative simultaneously with the proponent's measure while paying top-dollar for signatures, it can bid up the price of signatures and increase the proponent's costs. Second, qualification of a measure that threatens the original proponent's interests (such as in the Oregon tobacco tax case) might force it to divert scare campaign funds to fight the counterinitiative. Third, for some economic groups, the relative costs of qualifying a counterinitiative, which can exceed $2 million in California, are far less than what they may spend on a large-scale campaign against an initiative. Alcohol industry groups, for example, spent $25 million to defeat a "nickel-a-drink" tax initiative in 1990 (Proposition 134), while spending only a fraction of this to qualify their defensive "penny-a-drink" proposal (California Commission 1992, 16; Schultz 1996, 20; *California Journal* 1990a). Fourth, counterinitiatives can contain "killer-clauses" directed specifically at the original initiative—and if both measures pass the counterinitiative trumps. Finally, empirical studies and conventional wisdom suggest that, other things being equal, more voters will vote against a measure if it is on a longer ballot (Bowler et al. 1992; Bowler and Donovan 1998).

EVALUATIONS OF INITIATIVE PROFESSIONALS AND THEIR CAMPAIGNS

Professional Consultants: Will They Work for Anyone?

One of the things that bothers critics of consultant involvement in general, and in initiative campaigns in particular, is consultants' supposed mercenary qualities. A received view is that consultants often do not care about the underlying issue or ideology at stake and that this is a bad thing. Whether or not it is a bad thing when consultants do not care about proposals may be a matter for debate. What is less debatable is that consultants do—again by the self-report of our survey and interviews—seem to care about the issues at stake. All of the several dozen consultants we surveyed and interviewed were asked if they would work for almost any client, or if they specialized in working for specific clients, on specific issues, or on "yes" or "no" campaigns. Their responses challenge the conventional wisdom that consultants offer their services as ideological mercenaries to anyone willing to pay, and they reveal how specialized the industry of campaign professionals has become.

The vast majority of initiative campaign consultants consider the ideological perspective of a client when deciding for whom to work. In our mail survey, we asked consultants, "Does the political or ideological leaning of the client affect whether you accept the job or not?" The results of this question are reported in table 4.7. Less than 10 percent of consultants replied that the ideology of the client did not matter. The remaining responses were more or less evenly split between two categories. Just under half of these professionals claimed that a relative level of difference in ideology between client and firm shaped whether or not they took a job. Another large group claimed that it would only work for a client whose ideology meshed with its own.

The conventional wisdom in initiative campaign circles is that it is much easier to defeat an initiative than to pass one.[2] Indeed, most initiatives do fail (Magleby 1994). Decision theory suggests that voters are biased toward "no" campaigns that appeal to maintaining the status quo (Bowler and Donovan 1998), and our open-ended interviews with professionals confirmed that "no" campaigns are easier. Despite this, table 4.7 illustrates that only 14 percent of the consultants responding to our survey reported they preferred working on the "no" side, and only 23 percent preferred working on the "yes" side. Sixty-three percent responded that their preferred side depends on either the issue or the client, suggesting that most consultants are not looking for "no" campaigns, where they might find easy victories.

As for the sort of campaigns they preferred to work on, a majority of our respondents (59 percent) found it easier to work on initiative campaigns than on candidate campaigns. Only 14 percent said they found candidate campaigns easier—which may reflect some self-selection in our population, since these consultants were identified from lists of professionals known to work on initiatives. Some may have, in effect, made a career choice to work on initiatives more than campaigns.

These responses suggest that the majority of consultants are not "guns for hire" to anyone for any purpose, but are engaged by politics and the causes they help fight. To be sure, there is evidence here consistent with the view of a few consultants as unprincipled mercenaries. But it would seem that these are in a minority and—taking this survey as a guide—a very small minority at that.

Even consultants on a particular side of the ideological divide will refuse to work on some issues for clients who might otherwise share their ideological credentials. A consultant known for work on behalf of initiatives supported by conservative groups and the Republican Party, for example, refused to take on work for the NRA (Dash 1997, 1). Another vet-

Table 4.7   What Campaigns Will Consultants Work For?

Does the political or ideological leaning of the client affect whether you accept the job or not?

Yes, we will only work for a client whose ideology meshes with that of the firm	48
No, as professionals we offer a service, and the client's ideology is its own affair	9
It depends on how different the views of the firm and the client are	42

Do you prefer working on campaigns to pass initiatives or to oppose them? (check only one)

I would rather work on passing proposals	23
I would rather work on opposing proposals	14
Neither, it depends on the issue	49
Neither, it depends on the client	14

In comparison to candidate campaigns do you find working on initiative campaigns:

A lot easier than candidate campaigns	26
Somewhat easier than candidate campaigns	33
About the same as candidate campaigns	19
Somewhat harder than candidate campaigns	9
A lot harder than candidate campaigns	5
Don't work on candidate campaigns	9

Source: Authors' survey of 45 campaign professionals, spring 1999.
Note: Cell entries are percentages.

eran of Republican-backed initiatives expressed reservations about working on antigay initiatives (Zimmerman 1997, 1). A third consultant observed that after working numerous initiatives in two specific policy areas (card clubs and park bonds), he faced the same opponents each time. "In all cases the other side were the Jarvis people. The reason is ideological . . . you kind of had sides divided up that fought against each other up and down the state. . . . Jarvis people are against anything that is going to have any taxation" (Remer 1997, 1).

The temptation to take anyone as a client, however, may be great. Some consultants receive fees based on a percentage of media buys from a campaign, putting those working on some California initiatives in a position to make more money than anyone else in the industry (Magleby and Patterson 2000, 18–19). There are a number of factors, however, that limit just how mercenary most consultants may be. First, consultants are shaping the political messages that will be communicated to voters. Their effectiveness at this requires, at least to some extent, that they share their clients' policy goals. Second, as professionals, their future prospects for long-term employment depend upon building a reputation among a network of politically active groups and individuals (future clients) who might hire them based on their past record of success and on the types of causes that they have embraced.

It is important to recall that most initiative campaign professionals also work in partisan politics, where their professional and social networks are built. Roughly 10 percent of our sample worked only on initiative campaigns. Thus, it could be ideologically repugnant, as well as professional suicide, for a consultant who was well known for working with Democratic candidates and the CTA, and on prolabor initiatives, to hire onto a campaign such as the antilabor "paycheck protection" initiative simply for the profit. Since proponents of that initiative hired from the ranks of known Republican professionals, such a scenario is highly unlikely. Unless a consultant is in a position to score a huge, final payday from an initiative (for examples, see Magleby and Patterson 2000, 19), he is unlikely to work simply for profit, since he will be unable to find work far and wide across the ideological spectrum.

Charges against Initiative Professionals: The Initiative Industrial Complex

The growing numbers and presence of campaign professionals have given rise to increasing concerns vividly expressed in the phrase the "initiative industrial complex" (Schrag 1998; Magleby and Patterson 1998). Consultants are seen not just as "guns for hire"—but as guns who create the demand for their own services by advocating their own proposals for legislation. As table 4.8, illustrates, our own surveys indicate that political elites and the mass public both look unfavorably upon modern initiative campaigns. Despite being overwhelmingly in favor of the initiative process, both groups claim that initiative campaigns are misleading, that campaigns are too expensive, and that special interests dominate the process. In the minds of many, then, special interests using the initiative industry are to blame for the problems of direct democracy.

In an insightful examination of the role of consultants in direct democracy, David Magleby and Kelly Patterson (1998) seized on one critical normative question related to this subject. "One important issue for democratic theory," they wrote, "is whether the process is driven as much or more by consultants than by citizens" (167). Schrag (1998, 16) echoes this fear, writing that "there is a large network of consulting and initiative marketing firms that do not merely work for groups seeking to pass ballot measures (or block them) but sometimes test market issues for their feasibility . . . and then shop for a group to back them."

Table 4.8   **Mass and Elite Views of Initiative Campaign Process**

Washington State Voters[a]	
Ads and campaigns are misleading	81.7
Campaigns are too expensive	76.0
Issues on ballot reflect concerns of:	
special interests	46.2
average voter	6.2
both	43.0
no opinion	4.7
Candidates for Political Office[b]	
Ads and campaigns are misleading	86.0
Initiative process is dominated by special interests:	
agree	71.0
disagree	22.9
no opinion	5.5

[a]Authors' poll of Washington voters conducted by Applied Research Northwest, spring 1999. Number of cases = 405.
[b]Authors' poll of candidates for legislative office in California, Oregon, and Washington, spring 1999. Number of cases = 307.

Campaign professionals, despite the self-serving bluster and self-promotion of some, simply cannot generate independent demands for their services by creating their own initiatives. We find no evidence of this occurring in California, or elsewhere. Indeed, the examples and citations used by each of the authors cited in the previous paragraph refer to a single individual, Kelly Kimball, and to one street-level petition circulator. Rather than being one of the consultants who handles voter communication, Kimball was the owner of a major petition management firm. His boastful statements have been repeated in political science literature (e.g., Magleby and Patterson 1998, 167), in law reviews (e.g., Garrett 1999), and by nationally syndicated journalists (e.g., Broder 1998; Schrag 1998, 16, 211). Given this exposure, his personal claims are filtering through the literature and shaping perceptions of the initiative process. They serve as the primary example of a consultant "driving the process" by coming up with "his own" initiative. Although there is evidence of questionable profit taking by direct-mail fund-raising firms that worked on behalf of initiative proponents (Schrag 1998), Kimball's example is the only one we can find of a consultant taking credit for being the source of an initiative.

Kimball's atypical claims, however, are probably overstated, if not factually inaccurate. The measure he claims to have "test marketed" and then "pitched" to sponsors was California's Proposition 37 of 1984, the initiative that launched California's state lottery. Kimball claimed that he was "looking for something we could make money on, and somebody who would fund it" (Price 1992, 545; Schrag 1998, 211). The eventual proponent of the initiative that Kimball claims to have thought up was Scientific Games, a New Jersey–based firm that manufactures, services, and administers lotto gaming devices.

Can campaign professionals themselves drive the use of initiatives simply to pad their own wallets? The answer, we think, is probably not, for several reasons. First, and most narrowly, we should discount Kimball's claim to efficacy. Public votes to legalize gambling were not at all uncommon prior to Proposition 37. State and local referendum votes on gambling were common in the 1970s (Fairbanks 1977; Meier and Morgan 1980). In the 1980s, furthermore, gaming industry firms such as Scientific Games, General Instrument Corp., and GTECH were actively pursuing the expansion of their business—sometimes via initiatives—into places that had not yet adopted state-run lotteries. Arizona adopted a state lottery in 1981, Colorado in 1983, and Missouri in 1984 (Berry and Berry 1990, 411–412). Several initiatives proposing a state lottery, including some with revenues dedicated to education, were filed in Washington long before Kimball supposedly "sold" his idea (I-356, 1978; I-372, 1980, I-380, 1980, I-442, 443 and 447, 1982). Washington subsequently adopted a state lottery in 1982. Oregon voters approved two initiatives authorizing their state's lottery in 1984.

In all likelihood, Proposition 37's proponents did not need Kelly Kimball's assistance to realize the size of the California market and the fact that the initiative could give them an end run around the legislature and governor. More likely, Kimball realized the wealthy industry's growing use of the initiative process and made his services available. In general, the argument that campaign consultants can conjure up business does rather gloss over the problem of who will be investing in such schemes. As we saw above, the chances of actually getting an initiative proposal passed into law are quite small (less than 10 percent of those titled, or 30 percent of those which qualify in California). While consultants may get paid whether an initiative succeeds or fails, potential contributors might be expected to take a keener interest in pass rates. The assumption of huckster consultants, then, depends on the existence of well-heeled dupes. And even if Kimball pulled this feat off once, it is far from clear how often we are likely to see something like the lottery initiative repeated. Even he acknowledged, "There are just too few issues out there like that" (Price 1988, 545).

Related to this, the growth in the number of firms available seems, currently at least, to be supported by a growing availability of revenue. In California, 1998 was somewhat exceptional for campaign expenditures, but it does give some idea of the amount of revenue available. The general election ballot measures saw spending over $196 million dollars on initiatives at the general election and a further $55 million in the primary. In addition, the gubernatorial race saw $72 million spent in the primary,[3] and the first six months of 1998 saw another $34 million spent on state legislative primary races (Jones 1998b). Admittedly, California is something of a high-spending exception, but 1998 saw nearly $6 million spent in Washington State on ten proposals, while more than $10 million was spent in Massachusetts on four proposals.[4] In such a situation it seems difficult to suppose that the initiative industrial complex actually needs to drum up more business.

Our survey of consultants included questions designed to measure covertly if they had opportunities to instigate their own initiative proposals. We asked, "Each ballot proposition campaign is different, but what are the two most common ways in which you are brought into a campaign?" The most frequent single response was that they were hired by an initiative proponent who contacted the consultant's firm (65 percent). The next most common response was that a client contacted their firm due to a referral from an interest group or campaign committee (37 percent). Thirty-five percent also listed opposition campaigns contacting their firm as a source of business. Consultants also get work via recommendations from other consultants already working a campaign (33 percent), and 7 percent reported business resulting from referrals from a political party or candidate. There is very little self-reported evidence that consultants seek out business by themselves. Only 16 percent of respondents answered that they contacted campaigners directly—and cross-tabulations of responses indicate that only two consultants who self-initiate contacts with clients were ever hired by a client prior to the signature-gathering phase of the campaign. Few if any, then, appear to be in a position to shop their own proposals around to potential clients.

This does not mean that the argument in favor of an initiative industry with a vested interest is not without consequence or necessarily false all of the time. It is just that its applicability may be quite restricted. The growing number of firms does—or should—put pressure on profit margins. Right now, we seem to be amid an upswing in expenditures, but if the supply of initiative proponents dries up then we can expect to see even more pressure on profits. Not only could such events lead to a shakeout in the industry, they could conceivably provide an environment where consultants may want to find the proposal first and the investor second. But, as we noted above, needing investors is quite different from having investors.

Magleby and Patterson (1998, 167) ask, "will the growth of the initiative industry depend upon consultants generating business for themselves as

Kimball did with the California lottery?" Our discussion here suggests not. We have emphasized the role of a third player who is perhaps more important than citizens and the initiative industry in accelerating the use of the initiative—the issue-advocacy groups that fuel demands for initiatives in the modern era.

Issue-advocacy groups (e.g., antitax lobbies, environmental associations, labor groups, religious conservatives, heath care advocates, political reformers, and many others) propose a large amount of the initiative measures in California. Many of these groups are highly professionalized and have an institutionalized presence in the state; others form episodically and quickly evaporate. They employ campaign professionals. Clearly, these advocacy groups are not spontaneous "grassroots" movements that reflect the Populist ideal (or myth). Nevertheless, many can lay claim to being policy entrepreneurs who attempt to work on behalf of fairly broad constituencies (Donovan et al. 1998). Economic interests (firms) are also driving demand for initiatives to protect themselves from perceived threats to their businesses, and they provide further demands for more initiatives. But these rather common, dominant sources of demand for initiatives create a policymaking process that looks much different than one where campaign professionals themselves shop their own policy proposals to potential supporters. As one consultant offered in an unprompted comment on the demand for his services, "It is driven primarily by whomever it is that is paying the bills . . . if the person paying the bills chooses to bring a consultant in to get involved [they do], if not, not" (Shepard interview, p. 1). Or, as another consultant put it, "All I really am is, I think, an important cog in the wheel, but just a cog in the wheel" (Remer 1997, 2).

We see these issue-advocacy groups and the campaign professionals they employ as natural extensions of the lobbying efforts of broad-based and narrow-based groups active in legislative settings and candidate races. As American politics has taken a turn away from traditional partisan contests, toward more issue-oriented concerns, these groups have proliferated in legislatures (Lowery and Gray 1993), and their influence in candidate contests has increased (Sabato 1981). One of the stark realities of the contemporary American political scene is that for these groups to have influence in a representative democracy, they must contribute cash to legislators or prospective legislators, with much of the public left assuming that some quid pro quo is in operation.

Direct democracy states, however, have an additional point of access to the political system. In addition to lobbying candidates and legislatures, issue-advocacy groups can lobby voters directly. This is done by drafting and qualifying initiative laws, attempting to build (or maintain) support for the proposed laws, and attempting to mobilize opposition to proposed laws. It is not all that different from what advocacy groups attempt to accomplish in a legislature, and it is not cheap. The expanded use of the initiative and the rise of the "initiative industrial complex" of campaign professionals are driven by demands from these groups.

Can Campaigns Tell Lies?

Whether or not campaigns lie is an important issue, since one of the more common charges laid against initiative campaign consultants is that they deliberately misrepresent issues and positions (see, e.g., Lawrence 1995, 75). It is implied that they are paid to lie on behalf of a campaign and that these lies are believed by voters. Absent the manipulative impact of consultants, then, a voter who would have voted for x, ends up voting for y. As is often the case with claims of this sort, it is easier to state than to substantiate. Although it would be foolish to claim that all political consultants are honest all the time, it is far from clear how large a problem outright lying can be in initiative campaigns. There are, in fact, reasons for thinking that the potential for campaigns to be dishonest is quite constrained.

Perhaps the biggest single constraint is that once voters know a deception is being attempted they are likely to react to that knowledge—and possibly quite negatively. If a voter finds out that claims made by a campaign are lies, then at a minimum voters would discount those claims. More critically, they may discount the credibility of the campaign caught in a lie. The question thus becomes, How do voters know they are being lied to? If they are sensitive to false claims, there is the potential that voters will sanction liars.

There are several ways lies might be exposed, thus discouraging many consultants from presenting misinformation in ads. One way voters can be made aware of false claims is for a rival campaign to expose the lies. Rival campaigns that lack the resources to broadcast counterclaims, however, must rely on the media to expose misinformation. If these vehicles fail, voters themselves might see through false claims. Consultants working on initiative campaigns have a high regard for voters' abilities to see deception, and believe that lying in advertisements will probably hurt a campaign. As one consultant put it, "what works is having an overall message that resonates with the voter in a way that is believable. Voters are tremendous shit detectors—they really can sense when things are not straight. Lots of stuff fails because the voters can see through it" (Remer interview, p. 4). Constant exposure to political commercials might also make viewers more jaded and savvy.

Disincentives for lying also increase when players seek to build an enduring presence—or credible reputation—in a political arena. As an example, political parties and major candidates have a rational incentive to be truthful in campaigns, since they stay on the political scene long enough to have some interest in maintaining a reputation for honesty. If everything associated with their efforts were clearly lies, the long-term value of their label or name as a voting cue would be diminished. Initiatives can often be one-shot affairs, where new groups, unknown individuals, and narrow economic interests contest an issue, then leave the arena forever. If players lack the need to create a reputation for credibility, initiatives can be fertile ground for deception.

But as initiative politics matures, many if not most ballot proposals are contested by issue-advocacy groups that seek to have an enduring presence in the process, as in California. This applies to both initiative proponents and opponents. One of the less well-studied aspects of initiative politics is the degree to which there are repeat players who have incentives to establish credibility with voters (and who would thus avoid seriously deceptive campaigns due to their long-term stake in initiative politics). The result of interest groups' repeated involvement in initiative campaigns is that they are both willing and able to discover and minimize underhanded campaign tactics used on their behalf.

After all, repeat players in initiative contests such as the Planning and Conservation League, the Jarvis and Gann organizations, Common Cause, and the League of Women Voters have valuable reputations to protect. If their reputation becomes tarnished by a campaign firm or their own duplicity, then they will have lost something of great value (credibility) that would be difficult to recover. It is hard to believe, then, that such groups would allow themselves to be repeatedly associated with underhanded tactics.[5] And even well-funded economic interests who rarely use the process see a danger in lying. The organizing manual from the Nevada casino-funded "No on 5" campaign in California, for example, advised campaigners against lying in public forums and media interviews, noting, "it'll come back to haunt you" (CAUG 1998, 13, 16).

The same logic that limits the ability for repeat initiative players to lie may also constrain the consulting industry, which typically exists to make money over several electoral cycles rather than just one. If a consultant lies and that lie is exposed in one contest, then anyone hiring that company in the future will be assuming a potential campaign liability. One of the implications of this argument is that it is in the interests of "honesty" that we see relatively few short-lived "mom and pop" operations. Presumably the bigger and more established campaign firms—Clint Riley excepted—have much more to lose from being exposed as a liability or for having a reputation as being dishonest.

A second constraint is that there may simply be very little need to lie. This seems especially true for consultants running the "no" campaign.

As we have noted elsewhere in this chapter, one of the most established empirical patterns in direct democracy is that most proposals fail. A related pattern is that it is extremely hard to find systematic evidence of campaign spending on the "yes" side of an issue leading to the issue passing. On the other hand, campaign spending on the "no" side does have a robust and statistically significant impact.

One way of understanding this is to consider that campaigners on the "no" side can raise a whole series of questions, facets, and interpretations surrounding a particular proposition until they find one that works. As noted above, raising questions of cost, complexity, and controversy often makes it possible to persuade voters that an initiative is simply too ill thought out to be passed. Lying thus seems unnecessary.

Despite these points, there are cases where we might expect to see deliberate acts of duplicity. For example, none of the constraints we have mentioned so far would apply to once-only proponents of an initiative where the consultants are a fly-by-night consulting firm. For a lie to work, however, it must be heard and believed, and the "truth" either not heard or not believed. It seems reasonable to suppose that voters will react badly to lies once they are exposed as such. But lies may not always be exposed. For this problem, reform devices such as establishing a "floor" for campaign spending would presumably be quite useful. Spending floors (minimal levels of funding or air time provided to one campaign if the other side spends beyond a certain threshold) could establish a more competitive environment where each campaign is in some position to expose any false claims of the other.

CONCLUSION

At the end of the twentieth century, the politics of direct democracy are highly professionalized. Campaign professionals have long been involved with initiatives, and it is probably safe to state that their involvement in the process has grown and become institutionalized. Although there are still some campaigns that might be seen as grassroots, a specialized industry of campaign professionals works on behalf of initiative proponents and opponents, just as with candidate campaigns. As growth in population made qualification of initiatives increasingly difficult and made modern campaigns dependent upon broadcast media for communications, professional campaigners assumed a larger role in direct democracy. This is particularly evident in California, but by no means limited to that state. Campaigns for both liberal and conservative issue-advocacy groups, corporate and economic interests, as well as consumer-oriented groups all make use of campaign professionals.

As the center of gravity of American politics has moved from parties toward interest groups, many of these groups have established an enduring presence as political actors. As they have matured, and as more advocate and lobbyist groups have formed, demands for initiatives have grown in states where these groups are allowed to lobby the people directly. With groups proposing more initiatives, there are increased demands for professional services by advocacy groups and by those whose interests are threatened by initiatives. Consultants and campaign professionals, then, are likely to be an enduring part of the politics of direct democracy.

Consultants, we are often told, thrive in this environment by manipulating images, tricking voters, and determining the outcomes of campaigns. And it is said by some that, lacking the anchor of party, citizens should be even more susceptible to the manipulative abilities of professional campaigns in direct democracy. But the efficacy of campaign professionals and assumptions about their mercenary nature in direct democracy are overstated. Many initiatives fail to wage effective, traditional campaigns, and voters and consultants both reveal that there are several important sources of information that affect voter decisions other than broadcast advertisements. Some campaigns do make heavy use of TV, but we question how much these ad campaigns can manipulate voters. The ads, moreover, actually contain hard information cues that might assist voters in reasoning about issues and discovering how an initiative affects their interests. If this is the case, competitive campaigns with high levels of spending could actually serve a positive function.

While this may sound overly Panglossian, we end with some caveats. First, to find that the role of the "initiative industrial complex" is fairly benign does not establish that direct democracy is played on a level playing field. Corporate and economic interests have greater ability to employ the professionals needed to wage modern campaigns. It does seem, however, that this gives them far more defensive than offensive advantages. Second, contemporary politics of the initiative do not resemble the Progressive idea of an open forum for outsider groups. Ballot access in most states requires professional assistance and substantial sums of money. This limits the potential for many spontaneous grassroots groups to use the process to shape policy and the public agenda. Despite all of this, it seems clear that initiatives continue to provide issue-advocacy groups who might have a weak legislative presence with the ability to affect public policy and agendas. Although no longer the realm of novices, amateurs, and pure grassroots movements, direct democracy still provides a distinct point of access to the political system for groups who might otherwise be of limited consequence.

The Initiative Campaign Business: A Consultant's Perspective

Gale Kaufman

Since 1997, my business has spent the bulk of its time working in support of and in opposition to California initiatives. Most recently I successfully worked as lead consultant to defeat a voucher initiative that qualified for the November 2000 ballot. Given my involvement with initiative campaigns, I was gratified to read the conclusions of Donovan and his colleagues. I am especially relieved to see a scholarly work that concludes that most consultants who work on initiatives do not work for just anyone who asks, that they do have an ideological bent, and that they are professional in their endeavors.

While I agree with the basic thrust of the chapter, I would like to add a number of broad points that I feel would assist in further understanding the current state of the initiative industry in California. I have participated in a sizable number of focus groups in anticipation of different initiatives, as well as during and after their completion. One thing is very clear; California voters feel strongly that they want the process left intact. While voters do not always understand every initiative, and believe that there are too many of them each election cycle, they would fight hard against any reform effort to change their ability to have initiatives on the ballot.

There is no question that the vast majority of California voters believe that the legislature is not the place for major social or economic change and feel better knowing that they can have their say. By and large, voters know that the signature gatherers in front of their grocery stores are being paid. While many voters voice concern about this, they rarely say that this should be stopped. They are uneasy about special-interest groups taking over the process and try hard to learn the true sponsor of an initiative, as well as who the opposition is.

The most striking misconception we find is that voters have no idea that the initiatives they vote on are written by lawyers hired by an interested party or special-interest group. Moreover, they do not realize that these initiatives are not already cleared by the attorney general for constitutionality. And they are of the misguided view that once they vote on something, it will automatically become law, and they are mad that many are overturned.

While voters may complain that a huge amount of money is spent, or that their airwaves are filled with commercials, or that the ballot handbook is confusing, the vast majority of those surveyed, if they bother to vote, believe that they are conscientious in their approach to initiatives. They read the pro and con arguments, they differentiate between those individuals and groups that are listed as endorsers, and make a judgment on the veracity of those who are allowed to sign these arguments and rebuttals.

While Donovan and his coauthors mention ballot handbooks, they miss an important point relating to handbooks. The budget information that Donovan and his colleagues analyze does not contain a section for the significant cost of focus group research conducted by consultants. Finding the right language for the arguments in the ballot handbook, determining who of the endorsees would have the most impact as signers, and arriving at the best approach for rebuttal take a good deal of time, effort, and money.

The study also mentions the title and summary of initiatives as well as the analysis by the Legislative Analyst's Office. For voters who read their ballot handbook, or just the short title of the initiative on their ballot, the actual language can be critical. During the March 2000 primary, I saw polling figures drop more than 20 percent for an initiative when the final title and fiscal summary were released and tested. The initiative (Proposition 26) dealt with changing the voter requirement for local school bonds from two-thirds to one-half. A fiscal analysis that said it "could" cost taxpayers was extremely difficult to overcome; even with a large campaign budget.

Donovan and his coauthors spend a good deal of time differentiating between the types of players who are most often responsible for placing or paying for an initiative to be put on the ballot. Their study mentions special-interest groups, labor, business groups, environmentalists, and the like. However, in California a good number of recent initiatives have either been funded or contemplated by single individuals who have the economic wherewithal to do so. The recent school voucher initiative is expected to qualify for the November 2000 ballot that was funded by a single individual, Silicon Valley millionaire Tim Draper.

Ron Unz is mentioned, but it is not mentioned that he was the single funding source for two recent initiatives—Proposition 227 (ending bilingual education), which passed, and Proposition 25 (campaign reform), which failed. Rob Reiner was a single-source supporter of a recent California initiative that took the popular concept of taxing tobacco and combined it with children's health. Donovan and his colleagues do not address how an actor/director with no apparent expertise in either taxation of tobacco or complex children's health issues was competent to develop this initiative. I have no idea who actually wrote this initiative, but it has always puzzled me that no one has asked the question.

I believe it is critical to look at this somewhat new group of individuals who believe that they are uniquely qualified to legislate on tremendously complex issues that impact the lives of millions of Californians. I do not know who actually wrote the Draper voucher initiative, but it is an important fact that it did not come from a group of educators or academicians who have studied this issue for the last twenty years. Yet had it passed, it would have dramatically changed the public schools in California. Much the same can be said of my other examples.

The Proposition 226 campaign, which Donovan et al. make only small mention of, is one that I am intimately familiar with. Trying to build off the success of Proposition 13 and several other issues that received their birth through passage of an initiative in California, a national group, headed by Grover Norquist and J. Patrick Rooney, decided that it would put a "Paycheck Protection" initiative on the California ballot. They believed that once passed in California it would be much easier to pass throughout the rest of the country.

They took an issue that did not have broad interest or broad appeal and thought it sounded innocuous enough to pass. And initial polling (over 70 percent "yes") would have encouraged them. Much has been written about the 226 campaign, especially the amount of money spent to defeat it. But in detailing initiative component parts, the chapter fails to mention one critical element to the "no" on 226 campaign—the organizing of a massive grassroots field campaign, primarily by union members, throughout the state.

Proposition 226 was tricky. When first read, it sounded good to union members. However, once they understood that it was designed to take them out of the political process entirely, they quickly mobilized. And there is no question that the precinct walking, the phone banks, and the massive get-out-the-vote effort in major areas of the state helped push the "no" side to victory.

Not every initiative is able to use a grassroots organizing effort as part of its campaign. For 226, the "yes" side never put it in its calculations, while the "no" side budgeted for grassroots organizing at the same time it set its media budget. Therefore, I would encourage more research into elements of initiative campaigns that establish direct contact with voters, such as those devoted to absentee ballot voters, get-out-the-vote programs, paid and volunteer phone banks, and other field elements.

Donovan and his colleagues briefly mention the impact of the media and news reporting on initiatives. For many initiative campaigns, the "earned media" effort is a major budget item. An inordinate amount of time and effort is spent trying to get newspaper, television, and radio coverage of your issue. Spending time briefing political reporters on the substance of the initiative (both pro and con), responding to statewide independent polls that come out infrequently throughout the campaign, and working for editorial board support require a sizable team to be successful.

Initiative consultants spend a tremendous amount of time and effort for an appallingly limited amount of print and airtime on the substance of our issues. This is not of our choosing, but it is the reason that we look at other avenues of direct contact with voters to pick up the slack.

Again using 226 as an example, I knew at the outset of the campaign that no one in the California press corps had any knowledge of Grover Norquist or J. Patrick Rooney. Yet they were the major players in this initiative campaign. The D.C. press corps, however, was familiar with them. Our campaign team spent a good deal of time and effort helping the California press corps and opinion leaders familiarize themselves with Norquist and Rooney and why they had selected California as their battleground. Without this effort, voters might have thought that disgruntled union members put the initiative on the ballot. This effort helped people put the initiative in context and "leveled the playing field" for the "no" side just a little.

I would like to commend Donovan, Bowler, and McCuan for their objective and relatively thorough assessment of the role political consultants play in initiative elections. While their chapter does not represent a complete picture of the initiative consulting industry, they do dispel several myths and half-truths regarding the role that initiative consultants play in the political process. As the initiative process in California continues to develop and the "initiative industrial complex" grows in other states, it is important that voters form a more thorough understanding of the consulting industry. The work of Donovan and his colleagues marks an important step in this direction.

Observations of Initiative Elections

Ron Faucheux

In recent years, scholars and students of the political process have increased their efforts to unmask myths and stereotypes as they relate to professional campaign consultants. This is surely a useful undertaking. Hollywood and the media have created an image of consultants as dark, sinister puppet masters who pull the strings of not just their clients—but the entire governmental process. As the Donovan et al. chapter illustrates, this view is enlarged beyond reality in most cases. Most campaign practitioners would laugh at that exaggerated characterization. The biggest complaint I hear from many of them is how their clients do not listen to their advice or share their views. So much for the puppet master theory.

Ballot issue elections are unlike candidate elections in many important ways. Because of the differences between the two, many election watchers and political operatives often have a hard time understanding the dynamics underlying initiative and referendum campaigns. Because there is a tendency to force upon issue elections a set of rules that would superficially seem to apply—but do not—strategic blunders are frequently made by even the most seasoned initiative consultants.

In candidate campaigns, voters must select among alternative names on the ballot. In an issue election—be it a bond issue, a school tax, a citizen-sponsored initiative, a state constitutional amendment, or a recall question—voters simply vote on a proposition: up or down, for or against, yes or no. Candidates with high negative ratings frequently get elected because their opponents are in even worse shape. But few ballot proposals with high negatives win voter concurrence, regardless of the actions of political consultants.

This is not to say that consultants do not play an important role in ballot campaigns. Public opinion for ballot measures is usually more volatile than it is in candidate races. The voter cues are different. Candidates introduce a human element—the strengths and weakness of a person—and provide a set of credentials and party labels to guide voters into separating the "good guys" from the "bad guys." But an issue measure is really just a set of words. Contrary and often complicated arguments as to what those words actually mean, and what their full implications may be, sway voters back and forth.

Initiative and referendum campaigns, once they are on the ballot, are essentially strategic message battles. *Consultants play a larger role in them because of their large role in message development and the making of critically important strategic decisions involving timing, intensity of activity, message sequence, voter mobilization, and persuasive media.* In a sense, a ballot issue campaign is similar to a criminal trial: each side presents its case, calls witnesses, and introduces evidence. One piece of testimony may swing the jury over to the prosecutor's cause, but a subsequent piece of testimony may quickly snap them back the other way.

What matters in a court case is not the jury's shifting opinions during opening arguments or witness cross-examinations; what matters is the vote at the end. The same is true in ballot measure campaigns. Because of this, it is easy for both political novices and experienced hands to misread polls.

For example, only three weeks before the June 1998 balloting, California's Proposition 226—the "paycheck protection" measure to require an employee's or union member's permission to withhold wages or union dues for political contributions—was leading by a twenty percentage-point margin. A few months earlier, it led by upwards of forty points. On judgment day, however, following a volley of opposition attacks, it lost by six points.

One rule of thumb widely known among initiative consultants is that ballot issues are generally easier to kill than to pass. To pass a proposition, you have to offer a compelling reason why the change is both needed and desired. To defeat one, usually all you have to do is raise doubt. In line with this, it is important when reading polls on upcoming ballot measures to keep your eye on the "no" vote. When the proportion of voters against a measure starts rising rapidly, even if the "for" still has an edge, it's a sign that the issue is in trouble.

Here is another rule of thumb among initiative consultants: at the start of an initiative's public campaign phase if there is organized opposition and the "yes" support ratio is less than 2 to 1 over the "no" vote (or if the "no" vote is over 30 percent regardless of the "yes" level of support), then the issue may be in trouble. If Candidate A leads Candidate B by 55 to 32 percent in the polls two weeks before election day, in most cases Candidate B would have a very difficult time closing the gap. But if the "yes" side of a proposition leads the "no" side by the same margin—especially if the "no" side is just gearing up its campaign—then all bets are off.

Given the complexity of issues campaigns, inexperienced consultants might actually do more harm than good. For example, proponents often err when they publicize the support of well-known politicians. That is usually a big mistake. When a politician is too closely identified with a proposition, there is an amalgamation of negatives from both the politician—even if he or she is popular—and from the issue itself. A good example is the 1994 attempt to pass a state lottery in Oklahoma. Scandal-plagued Democratic governor David Walters saw the lottery as an appealing issue to ride. But his support for the proposal gave the lottery's opponents a juicy target that they used to defeat it by a 3 to 2 ratio, effectively pulling the plug on Walters's gasping political career.

A second example is the "paycheck protection" measure in California. The visible support of Republican governor Pete Wilson gave opponents of the measure—particularly organized labor and public employees—a useful symbol to fight. Before the campaign was over, opponents had brought all of Wilson's enemies into their corner and torpedoed the proposition.

Issue campaigning, from a strategic sense, is the most challenging for a political professional. Timing, targeting, message discipline, and election-day mobilization are vital factors, often requiring counterintuitive tactics. Ironically, once an initiative makes the ballot, even one that was spawned by grassroots citizen activism, the ensuing campaign battleground is usually no place for amateurs—or professionals, for that matter—who don't understand the tricky nuances and hidden subtleties of the war they're fighting.

5

The Logic of Reform: Assessing Initiative Reform Strategies

Elisabeth R. Gerber

Whether one generally supports or opposes the use of initiatives, virtually all observers have ideas about how to improve the initiative process. Over the last two decades, an abundance of proposals to reform the initiative process have been suggested or instituted in a number of states. Some of these attempts at reform are quite modest in scope, dealing with such apparently mundane issues as the numbering of propositions or the formatting of the ballot pamphlet. Others call for a complete overhaul of a state's direct legislation institutions. Together, these reforms seek to change virtually every aspect of the initiative process, from who can propose initiatives and how signatures are gathered, to how ballots are organized, how campaigns are run, how information is disclosed, how state legislatures participate, how initiatives are amended, and how courts behave.

As different as these many individual reform attempts appear, they share a common logic. Reformers believe that current direct legislation institutions lead to a particular set of outcomes (or at least make some outcomes more likely); that these outcomes diverge from the reformers' view of some "ideal"; and that changing some aspects of direct legislation institutions would lead to different, more preferred outcomes. In some cases, this logic is made clear as reformers identify problems with the initiative process and propose clear (institutional) solutions to those problems. In other cases, the logic is more vague. In any case, reformers view institutional change as the key to achieving more preferred outcomes.

In this chapter, I seek to reveal the logic underlying some of the major recent proposals to reform the initiative process. I argue that most recent reforms are designed, either explicitly or implicitly, to address one or more of the following common criticisms of the initiative process:[1]

1. There is too much money/interest-group influence in the process.
2. Voters are incompetent.
3. Laws are poorly written.
4. Initiatives infringe upon minority rights.

To understand the thinking that underlies each of these, consider the second criticism. Some critics believe that because there are few restrictions on content or format, direct legislation propositions tend to be long, complex, and technical. These long and complex measures are too much for voters to comprehend. As a result, voters are unable to make competent decisions in the voting booth and their aggregate decisions may not reflect the "informed" decisions of a fully competent electorate. A proposed solution to the problem of incompetent voters is to limit the length of propositions and/or require their language to be simple and readily accessible. Voters, then, would have a better chance of understanding the propositions and making "good" decisions.

The problem with most reform proposals is that while they may be designed to address what their proponents perceive as real problems with the initiative process, they typically lack sound empirical foundations. Specifically, reform proposals are rarely based on sound empirical evidence of either the existence of a problem (i.e., whether initiative outcomes in fact fail to reflect the informed decisions of fully competent voters) or of the impact of direct legislation institutions on outcomes (i.e., whether uninformed decisions are caused by long or complex propositions). Such empirical foundations are critical to knowing whether proposed reforms will solve the problems they are intended to address. They also allow us to predict, more generally, what the consequences of the proposed reforms might be.

Unlike the reformers, political scientists have much to say about how the initiative process works and, to some extent, about how direct legislation institutions affect political outcomes. A number of recent studies have analyzed the initiative process, providing empirical evidence to help us answer questions such as: How much influence do interest groups have? What is the role of money? Are voters competent? Are laws poorly written? How do legislatures respond? How do minorities fare? The purpose of this chapter is to bring this empirical evidence to bear upon an assessment of recent reform proposals.

CRITICISM 1: TOO MUCH MONEY/TOO MUCH INTEREST-GROUP INFLUENCE

Perhaps the most common criticism of the initiative process is that there is too much money involved. And, indeed, critics apparently have much to complain about. In California alone, proponents and opponents of nine direct legislation measures spent over $54 million in the 1998 primary election and are estimated to have spent more than $200 million on twelve measures in the general election (California Secretary of State 1998c). This spending represents the continuation of a trend toward more and more expensive direct legislation campaigns that began in the mid-1980s (California Commission 1992). As a comparison, in the same year, all general election candidates for the U.S. House of Representatives together spent $88 million, while candidates for the U.S. Senate spent $49 million (Federal Election Commission 1998). Certainly, claim the critics, this money must be having some effect on direct legislation outcomes.

Closely related to, but analytically distinct from, the concern about money is the more general concern about interest-group influence in the initiative process. Most modern observers interpret the Populist and Progressive vision for the initiative process as a way for grassroots movements to pass laws without the participation or agreement of state legislators, political parties, or organized interest groups.[2] In modern times, however, the initiative process seems to bear little resemblance to this vision. It is practically impossible for unorganized citizen movements to mobilize the vast resources required to run a successful statewide initiative campaign.[3] Interest groups play a key role in virtually every successful initiative campaign. Their role is critical in every phase of the initiative process, from drafting initiatives, to qualifying them for the ballot, to financing and running campaigns, to defending the legislation after the election. Organized interest groups provide a vast array of resources, including manpower, expertise, and perhaps most important, money.

Of course, interest groups and money are not synonymous. Many interest groups that participate in the initiative process are mass membership citizen organizations that lack the ability to mobilize monetary resources. These groups often have severely limited budgets. They depend, instead, on their large numbers and organizational resources as their main source of political power. In fact, a vast majority of campaign contributions to direct legislation campaigns come not from organized interests groups, but from single businesses and individual citizens. One recent study estimates that these two categories of contributors accounted for nearly 72 percent of contributions to initiative and referendum campaigns in eight states in the late 1980s and early 1990s (Elisabeth Gerber 1999). Still, there is an important sense in which interest groups and money are linked. Many of the largest and most important players in the initiative process are interest groups. Because they are already organized, interest groups may have an advantage in mobilizing resources—monetary and other—which individual businesses and citizens do not enjoy. Their ability to coordinate and target these resources may provide an advantage in influencing the course of direct legislation.

While money in politics is a general concern, three major factors make the initiative process especially vulnerable to the influence of interest groups and their money. First, due to several U.S. Supreme Court decisions, contributions to direct legislation campaigns are constitutionally unlimited, allowing groups with money to spend as much as they wish to try to influence direct legislation outcomes. In its landmark decision in *Buckley v. Valeo*, 424 U.S. 1 (1976), the Court established basic principles with regard to the regulation of campaign financing. Although the decision considered the legality of the 1974 Amendments to the Federal Election Campaign Act and therefore strictly applied only to federal elections, many of the arguments made in *Buckley* laid the foundation for future Court decisions that directly or indirectly addressed campaign financing in direct legislation campaigns. In *Buckley*, the Court upheld limits on contributions to candidate campaigns. The Court argued that contributions to candidates were given to secure a political quid pro quo. Unlimited contributions could lead to corruption on the part of elected officials, whose campaign debts would lead them to compromise their principles in order to secure such contributions. Limits on contributions would therefore serve to reduce corruption, or at least the appearance of corruption, resulting from overreliance on large individual contributors. Thus, the Court ruled that the state's interest in reducing corruption justified the abridgment of contributors' First Amendment rights. However, the Court struck down all forms of expenditure limits on the grounds that they impose direct and substantial restraints on the quantity of political speech without the benefit of reducing corruption.

With respect to spending limits in direct legislation campaigns, such expenditures are subject to the same reasoning that led the Court to invalidate limits on spending in candidate campaigns in *Buckley*. These expenditures are considered expressions of speech protected by the First Amendment. With respect to contribution limits, however, the Supreme Court views candidate campaigns and direct legislation campaigns differently. In *First National Bank of Boston v. Bellotti*, 435 U.S. 765 (1978), the Court established the right of corporations to make contributions to and expenditures on behalf of ballot measure campaigns. In its majority decision, the Court argued that contrary to prohibitions on contributions to candidate campaigns, where the potential for actual or perceived corruption associated with campaign contributions is great, the same corruptive potential does not exist in direct legislation. Following this line of argument, the Court in *Citizens against Rent Control v. City of Berkeley*, 454 U.S. 290 (1981) reaffirmed prior decisions by further invalidating any limits on contributions to direct legislation campaign committees. Again, the Court deemed there was no potential for corruption, that is, no quid pro quo associated with these contributions that would justify the curtailment of contributors' First Amendment rights.

A second factor that opens the initiative process to the influence of interest-group money is that many direct legislation propositions are complex, technical, and unfamiliar to voters. Voters therefore tend to have very little prior information about, or understanding of, the propositions they are asked to evaluate. Few actors besides organized interest groups themselves are likely to have such substantive information. As a result, voters who desire information about the content of propositions have few alternatives but to rely on interest groups for that information. When interest groups can influence the channels of political communication, they may be able to use their informational advantages to mislead voters.[4]

A third factor is that many of the shortcuts and low information cues that voters rely on when they lack information in candidate elections are absent in direct legislation elections. Perhaps the most important missing cue is partisanship. In candidate elections, voters can infer a great deal about a candidate's policy positions and likely voting behavior simply by learning his or her partisanship (Popkin 1991). In such cases, it may be both convenient and rational to vote on the basis of party. In direct legislation elections, by contrast, partisan cues are generally absent. Although partisan candidates and officials may endorse particular initiatives and referendums, political parties rarely do. Therefore, party cues—so important to voters in other settings—are absent or ambiguous in direct legislation campaigns. Candidates also have past histories from which voters may learn about a candidate's likely future actions (Fiorina 1979). New policy initiatives have no such history, making the voters' problems all the more complicated. The absence of useful cues makes direct legislation voters especially reliant on substantive information disseminated by interest groups during the campaign.[5]

Proposed Reforms

Many recent reform proposals aim to limit the role and influence of interest groups and their money in the initiative process. In describing these reforms, it is useful to note that money enters the initiative process at three key points. First, during the drafting and qualifying stages, interest groups pay political consultants to help them write their propositions and obtain signatures for ballot qualification. Second, during the campaign stage, proponents and opponents of a measure establish campaign committees and spend financial and nonfinancial resources to promote their side. Third, during the postelection stage, proponents and opponents finance legal challenges to successful initiatives and lobby state legislators to amend initiative legislation. Proposed reforms seek to limit money and its influence at each of these three stages.

Drafting and Qualifying Stages

At the drafting and qualifying stages, proponents of initiative legislation can draw upon internal expertise and manpower to draft and qualify their propositions, or they can expend monetary resources to hire consultants to draft and qualify their measures. The use of consultants and paid signature gatherers has been one of the favorite targets of initiative reformers. Indeed, since one of the primary justifications for the signature requirement is to measure popular support for a proposition, many argue that this purpose is defeated when a proponent can simply pay professional petition circulators who care little about the initiative legislation (Garrett 1999). Furthermore, given the tactics of paid signature gatherers, who have little incentive to engage potential signers and fully explain the proposed legislation, it is unclear even whether the people who sign their petitions necessarily support the initiative (Collins and Oesterle 1995).

Despite these concerns, the U.S. Supreme Court has upheld the use of paid signature gatherers. In *Meyer v. Grant,* 486 U.S. 414 (1988), the Court struck down a Colorado law prohibiting payment of petition circulators. In its decision, the Court argued that prohibiting such payment "restricts political expression in two ways: First, it limits the number of voices who will convey [the proponents'] message and the hours they can speak and, therefore, limits the size of the audience they can reach. Second, it makes it less likely that [the proponents] will garner the number of signatures necessary to place the matter on the ballot, thus limiting their ability to make the matter the focus of statewide discussion." Since the forms of expression limited by the prohibition on paid signature gatherers take place in an "area in which the importance of First Amendment protections is 'at its zenith,' " they require an equally compelling justification by the state, which the Court concluded was not present.

Despite the Court's decision in *Meyer,* numerous attempts have been made to restrict the use, if not the existence, of paid signature gatherers. Colorado legislation passed in the wake of *Meyer* attempted to regulate paid circulators in a number of ways. One provision required petition circulators to wear nametags that identified them as paid or volunteer. This provision—identification of the circulator's status—was based on the assumption that citizens would be less likely to sign petitions if they knew the circulators were professionals rather than volunteers (Garrett 1999). By providing citizens with information that would dissuade them from signing petitions, paid circulators would have more difficulty obtaining their signatures and the advantage of the proponents who paid them would be reduced. However, in its decision in *Buckley v. American Constitutional Law Foundation*, 119 S. Ct. 636 (1999), the Court struck down these requirements, ruling that the state lacked sufficient justification to warrant restricting the potential for political speech in this manner.

A second approach to reducing the impact of paid signature gatherers is to increase the length of the circulation period. Circulation periods currently range from several months (e.g., 150 days in California) to two years. A number of reform proposals recommend lengthening the circulation period (see Collins and Oesterle 1995; California Commission 1992). The argument behind this reform proposal is that by lengthening the period during which proponents can obtain the required number of signatures, groups who rely on volunteers will be under less pressure to also use paid signature gatherers. Groups who rely on professional circulators will have less of an advantage over their volunteer counterparts. Some observers (Dubois and Feeney 1992) argue that this reform is likely to have little impact.

A third approach to reducing the impact of paid signature gatherers is to employ a two-tiered signature requirement (Lowenstein and Stern 1989; California Commission 1992). Under this proposal, states would have two separate signature requirements, one (higher than the current threshold) for signatures gathered by paid circulators and a second lower one for signatures gathered by volunteers. The intent of this reform is to provide initiative sponsors with an incentive to rely on volunteers. The proponents argue that this will result in some groups who now rely on paid circulators being priced off the ballot. Other groups who now cannot mobilize enough volunteers will be able to meet the lower threshold. The state of Nebraska is currently considering such a proposal (Boellstorff 1995).

A fourth proposed reform is to allow alternative means for gathering signatures. The California Secretary of State is currently considering allowing initiative sponsors to obtain signatures over the Internet (California Secretary of State 1998b). This reform would reduce the impact of paid signature gatherers by providing groups with a low-cost alternative to human signature gatherers. Opponents of this reform argue that signers with Internet access are unrepresentative of the general public, and that the Internet medium discourages debate and public discourse (Garrett 1999).

A fifth proposed reform is to eliminate the signature requirement altogether, relying instead on a simple cash payment to the state (referred to as the "Cynic's Choice" in California Commission [1992, 168–169]) or a lottery system to determine which initiatives will make it to the ballot (California Commission 1992; Garrett 1999). Some argue that a lottery should be preceded by a state-run public opinion poll to assess the level and intensity of popular support (Garrett 1999).

A sixth reform proposal is to adopt some form of public financing. This could be in the form of state subsidization of the cost of signature collection, especially when signatures are collected primarily through electronic means (Garrett 1999). One could also envision more traditional forms of public financing, such as direct payments to ballot measure committees, perhaps tied to voluntary expenditure restrictions.

Campaign Stage

As explained at the beginning of this section, the U.S. Supreme Court has ruled that contributions to and spending on direct legislation campaigns is constitutionally unlimited. Since these decisions invalidate attempts to limit the amount of campaign contributions and spending at the campaign stage, most reform attempts in this area focus instead on limiting the influence of money. The primary way reformers seek to limit the influence of money in campaigns is through disclosing the sources of contributions. Most states require contributors to ballot measure campaigns to form campaign committees. These committees are then required to file detailed periodic reports documenting the contributions they receive and the expenditures they make. Some states require committees to report all campaign activities; others require disclosure of contributions only over some amount (Dubois and Feeney 1992).

While campaign committee disclosure reports are publicly available, they are rarely easily accessible. Thus, additional attempts to disclose the sources of campaign contributions include requirements to state the main financial supporter of a ballot measure on paid campaign advertisements (California Commission 1992). California's Proposition 105 required that the primary source of campaign contributions (not simply their committee's name) be identified on all print, radio, and television advertisements. However, the state supreme court struck down the measure on the grounds that it violated the state's single-subject law. Other states such as Michigan and Oklahoma also require initiative campaigns to disclose their primary sources of support.

Another reform intended to improve the disclosure process is to require on-line filing of disclosure statements (California Secretary of State 1998b). Since final summaries of campaign finance activities are now only available months after the election, they are of little use to voters who are trying to discover the supporters and opponents of a measure. Internet technology makes instantaneous on-line access a real possibility.

Postelection Stage

After the election, proponents and opponents continue to battle over initiative legislation. Most successful initiatives are now challenged in state or federal courts. Millions of dollars are spent in these legal challenges, and observers are concerned that wealthy interest groups are able to thwart the will of the majority by dominating the legal process (Holman and Stern 1998). In addition, state legislatures have the power to amend initiative legislation in most states, although often only after some waiting period or by a supermajority vote (Dubois and Feeney 1992). Initiative proponents and opponents spend substantial resources to influence postelection legislative decisions regarding successful initiatives.

One reform proposal designed to limit the potential for interest-group influence over (postelection) judicial review is made by Holman and Stern (1998). They advocate replacing a single judge with a three-judge panel to hear challenges to initiative legislation. Increasing the number of judges would arguably reduce the ability of interest groups to influence legislation by influencing or corrupting a single judge.

Many reforms have been proposed to reduce interest-group influence over postelection legislative amendments. These reforms include proposals to limit campaign contributions to state legislators (for recent examples, see California's Propositions 208 and 212). State legislators respond to interest-group pressure because they desire something the interest groups have—technical information, political information, constituency support, organizational resources, or money. Restrictions on campaign contributions or other transfers of resources from interest groups to elected representatives may limit their influence in all phases of the legislative process, including the postelection amendment stage.

Empirical Evidence

All of these proposed reforms assume that interest groups influence direct legislation outcomes with their money and other resources, and that limiting the amount and influence of money would change outcomes in a significant and favorable way. What is the evidence on this front? First, I consider evidence regarding the role of money at the qualifying stage.

Qualifying Stage

It is clear that money is sufficient to qualify a measure for the ballot (see Garrett 1999). Campaign consultants in most direct legislation states will provide professionals to circulate petitions. Proponents pay per signature an average of $.30 to $1.50, and consultants guarantee the required number of signatures, plus up to 10 percent extra to compensate for error or fraud. Although there is no solid data on this topic, it appears from anecdotal evidence that professional petition circulators can qualify just about any measure, no matter how narrow, obscure, extreme, or obnoxious, for a price. In a large state like California, that price is between $1 million and $2 million.

Not all proponents have access to a million dollars to qualify their measure. Those who lack sufficient monetary resources rely either entirely or partially on volunteers. Other proponents are priced off the ballot altogether. Further, even proponents who appear to represent broad-based, grassroots citizen interests tend to rely on organized interest groups to offset the steep cost of qualifying and later campaigning for their initiatives. "Citizen" groups such as Common Cause relied on paid circulators to qualify their recent initiatives (California Secretary of State 1996). In a recent study, Daniel Smith (1998) found that behind the allegedly "Populist" tax reform movements in several states, and their associated tax limitation initiatives, were highly professional campaign organizations and substantial corporate or economic interest-group backing. While I disagree with Smith's ultimate conclusion that involvement by organized interest groups necessarily implies that the tax reform movement was not a truly Populist movement, I agree that his case studies highlight the importance of organized interest groups and their resources in the initiative process.[6]

Given the great advantage that money provides at the qualifying stage, we would expect the set of measures that make it to the ballot to reflect this bias toward wealthy interest groups. Surprisingly, however, the bias, if one exists at all, is not overwhelming.[7] Examining ballots in a number of states, we find that some measures are supported by narrow economic interests with vast financial resources, but a surprisingly large number are supported by broad-based citizen groups. For example, of the eighty-seven initiatives that qualified for the ballot in eight states between 1988 and 1992, twenty-nine received majority support from economic interests, forty-four from citizen interests, and fourteen from other contributors (Elisabeth Gerber 1999).[8] There are at least two explanations for the lack of bias toward wealthy economic interest groups. One is that groups that have the money to qualify their measures with paid signature gatherers can also use those resources for other purposes, and so don't bother pursuing their interests through the initiative process. A second possible explanation is that groups know that qualification is just the first step in a long and costly process. Many additional resources will be required to run a successful campaign and pass an initiative, and the group might not have (or choose to spend) those resources.

Still, even if groups know that the probability of passing an initiative is slim, it might still benefit them to qualify their measure for the ballot. Garrett (1999) argues that qualifying a measure can have indirect effects, most importantly by placing the issue on the legislative agenda. She notes that there are always many groups competing for a place on the political agenda, too many for all to receive consideration from legislative policymakers. Groups have many ways of attracting legislator attention to their issues—playing off critical events, making campaign contributions, engaging in traditional lobbying, mobilizing grassroots pressure, and organizing an initiative petition drive. A petition drive may have advantages over these other methods of affecting the legislative agenda, since it both signals the level of interest-group preferences and mobilizes broad-based public support.[9] Thus, groups with sufficient monetary resources to qualify an initiative gain an advantage in influencing the legislative agenda, and ultimately policy outcomes, even if their measure enjoys little support from the broader public.

Campaign Stage

Whereas money is sufficient to qualify a measure for the ballot, recent research indicates that it is far from sufficient to pass initiative legislation. A number of studies have addressed the role of money in the initiative process, particularly at the campaign stage. The basic finding of this research is that while some amount of money is necessary for getting initiatives passed, allowing proponents to purchase advertisements, mass mailings, and other forms of campaign information, groups with vast financial resources are regularly stymied at the ballot box. Something important is lacking from their expensive campaigns.

A recent study by Elisabeth Gerber (1999) provides insight into why money is insufficient to guarantee success at the polls. Gerber distinguishes between several forms of influence that groups might try to pursue through the direct legislation process. Influence can be direct, in which the effect on policy results directly from an initiative or referendum, or indirect, in which a group uses direct legislation to affect policy in some other arena (i.e., the legislative process). Influence can also modify or preserve the status quo policy. Thus, the four forms of influence are direct modifying (e.g., passing new initiatives), direct preserving (e.g., blocking initiatives), indirect modifying (e.g., pressuring state legislators to pass new laws), and indirect preserving (i.e., pressuring state legislators to block new laws).

Gerber's basic argument is that each form of influence requires different resources. To achieve direct preserving influence (blocking initiatives), opponents of an initiative require monetary resources or personnel resources (manpower, volunteers, or expertise) to campaign against a measure. Often, a large campaign directed against a ballot measure is sufficient to turn voters against it. Lowenstein (1982) and Owens and Wade (1986) each show that when opponents waged "big no" campaigns, defined as campaigns in which opponents outspent proponents by at least 2 to 1 and spent at least $250,000 (adjusted for inflation in the Owens and Wade study), the measures they targeted were defeated approximately 90 percent of the time. While neither study provides a microlevel model to explain why voters respond to "big no" campaigns, this ability to defeat measures by spending large sums on an opposition campaign probably derives from voter risk aversion. When opponents spend enough to create doubt in the minds of voters, voters may prefer to stick with the status quo policy—flawed though it may be—rather than risk moving to a new policy that just might have very bad consequences.

To achieve direct modifying influence (passing new initiatives), by contrast, groups require both monetary and personnel resources. This is due to the types of information and cues that voters use when deciding how to vote on ballot measures. Studies by Lupia (1994) and Bowler and Donovan (1998) illustrate how voters overcome vast informational shortcomings in initiative campaigns. One of the main findings of both studies is that voters rely heavily upon endorsements to link their own interests to a position on an initiative. When "citizens like them" support an initiative, voters are more likely to support the measure; when narrow, wealthy economic interests are known to support a measure, voters see less in common with the endorsers and are less likely to support a measure. Therefore, to mobilize voter support, groups must have broad-based citizen constituencies with whom regular voters affiliate. Money alone does not buy this affiliation.

Finally, to achieve indirect modifying or indirect preserving influence, groups require either monetary or personnel resources. Groups with monetary resources can use (unsuccessful) initiatives to provide legislators with a costly signal about their preferences on a given issue. If legislators value the groups' support or desire their resources in the future, they may pass or block legislation on the group's behalf.[10] Groups with personnel resources can credibly threaten to pass an adverse initiative if the legislature does not act. Legislators may prefer to pass moderate compromise legislation themselves rather than relinquish agenda control to initiative proponents.[11] In either case, groups need not expend the full amount of resources required to achieve direct modifying or direct preserving influence.

Given the different resources required to achieve each form of influence, we expect different types of groups to pursue them. Specifically, economic interest groups with vast financial resources tend to lack the personnel resources required to achieve direct modifying influence.[12] We therefore expect them to expend most of their direct legislation resources on achieving direct preserving or indirect influence. Citizen interest groups can more easily mobilize personnel resources; for them, the difficulty comes in mobilizing monetary resources. When they are successful in extracting monetary resources from their citizen membership, we expect citizen groups to pursue direct modifying influence more often.

These expectations are borne out in the data. Analyzing the detailed disclosure reports for all ballot measure campaign committees in eight states between 1988 and 1992, Elisabeth Gerber (1999) finds that 74 percent of contributions from citizen interests are made to support initiatives and referendums, while only 32 percent from economic interests are made to support ballot measures (94). This difference is consistent with the expectation that citizen interests will try to pass new laws by initiative and economic interests will try to defeat proposed initiative legislation. In the same study, Gerber also finds that these differences in interest-group activity translate into important differences in outcomes. Initiatives that receive majority support from citizen interests pass at a much higher rate (50 percent) than those that receive majority support from economic interests (31 percent), and the set of successful initiatives reflects greater citizen group support (47 percent of total contributions) than economic group support (37 percent, with 16 percent from other contributors). In other words, Gerber's analysis shows that economic groups with primarily monetary resources tend not to pursue direct modifying influence, and their interests are not strongly reflected in the initiatives that pass.[13]

Postelection Stage

What is the role of money at the postelection stage? For analytic purposes, it is useful to separately consider two aspects of the postelection stage: judicial review and legislative amendments. To the author's knowledge, there are no empirical studies of the role of money in influencing court decisions. Clearly, some money is necessary to successfully defend or challenge initiative legislation. Since state officials are charged with defending initiative legislation once it passes and becomes law, the state effectively subsidizes the cost of the proponent's defense, thereby reducing their financial burden.

The other aspect of the postelection stage regards legislative amendments. Here, the important question is whether groups can use financial resources to influence whether state legislators amend initiative legislation. There is a vast empirical literature on the role of money in legislative politics at both the congressional and state legislative levels (see Richard Smith 1995 for a review of the literature on interest-group influence in Congress; see Gray and Lowrey 1996 and Thomas and Hrebenar 1996 for work on interest-group influence in state legislatures). While specific findings are mixed, the main conclusion from this body of research is that the effect of money, typically in the form of campaign contributions, is important but limited. Many studies show that contributions cannot "buy votes" and, in fact, are not intended to. More likely, they are intended to buy access. Access then allows interest groups to influence the legislative agenda, make the groups' positions heard, and otherwise affect the content of legislation. This research also indicates that while money is important in obtaining access to the legislative process, so might be other resources that legislators value (promises to deliver votes, in kind contributions, etc.).

To summarize, the literature on the role of interest groups in the initiative process identifies when and how groups can use their monetary and other resources to achieve various forms of influence. In the qualifying stage, money plays an important role in determining what laws qualify for the ballot and hence what issues voters ultimately decide. However, there are other ways that groups with limited financial resources can qualify their measures, and, in fact, the set of issues that qualify for the statewide ballot in most states reflects a mix of support from economic and citizen interest groups. In the campaign stage, money plays a more limited role. Groups can use money to block initiatives they oppose or to pressure state legislators; however, they need much more than money to pass initiative legislation. Finally, in the postelection stage, groups can use either monetary or personnel resources to defend or challenge initiative legislation, and to lobby legislators to pursue or block amendments to initiative legislation.

Assessment

This empirical research has important implications for prospects for reforming the initiative process. The research suggests that money may be most influential at the agenda-setting stage. To a large extent, money affects what gets on the ballot. If reformers wish to open the initiative process to interest groups that lack the resources to qualify their initiatives under current institutions, proposals such as extending the qualification period or instituting a two-tiered system may help level the playing field. The effects of such efforts will be severely limited, however, if those groups are subsequently unable to mobilize the resources required to run a successful initiative campaign.

Money may also help groups pressure legislators to pass or block amendments to initiative legislation, or even to pursue legislation in policy areas where initiatives fail. To limit this sort of influence, reformers ought to look not to the initiative process itself, but to regulating the role of money in state legislative politics. A number of states already have limits on campaign contributions to state legislative candidates, on the model of congressional campaign finance laws. Strengthening the role of political parties in state legislative elections, perhaps through public financing of party activities, is one way of reducing the reliance of individual candidates on wealthy economic groups.

CRITICISM 2: INCOMPETENT VOTERS

A second common criticism of the initiative process is that voters are not competent to decide complex matters of public policy. As evidence, critics often point to the low levels of information that voters report having about the details of initiative legislation immediately before elections. For example, the Field Poll periodically surveys California voters about their positions on upcoming statewide initiatives. In its survey immediately preceding the November 1998 general election, between 30 and 60 percent of likely voters in its sample reported not being aware of three of the four major upcoming initiatives (DiCamillo and Field 1997).[14] Granted, numerous factors probably depress self-reported levels of information—length of time before the election, fear of being asked follow-up questions that probe the respondent's factual knowledge, and apathy or disinterest in the survey. Nevertheless, anecdotal evidence of this same lack of voter information abounds.

Some of the same features that make the initiative process especially vulnerable to interest-group influence also exacerbate the information problems that voters face. First, initiative legislation is often technical and complex. Initiatives cover a multitude of issues regulating social, economic, and political behavior. Some initiatives are written in complex legal language and are difficult to discern on their face;[15] others appear quite simple but have vast implications that are difficult for even policy experts to comprehend.[16] Voters, who typically have very little experience with the policies they are evaluating, decide these issues directly. By contrast, voters in candidate elections choose representatives who decide for them. These representatives either have expertise themselves or can rely on professional staffs and other policy experts. Second, many of the important cues that voters rely on in candidate elections are absent in direct legislation elections. Most important, party cues, which are so important in guiding voter decisions in candidate elections, are either absent altogether or are difficult to infer. Other characteristics that aid voters in candidate elections but that are missing in direct legislation elections include candidate incumbency, experience, and personal characteristics.

Proposed Reforms

A number of reform proposals seek to make initiatives easier to understand. Several of these reforms are based on the assumption that voter incompetence derives from the complexity of the initiatives themselves. For example, several proposals seek to limit word length or require initiative language to be below some specified reading level (California Commission 1992; Collins and Oesterle 1995). A number of states already have such restrictions in place (Dubois and Feeney 1992). Other proposals seek to lower voter informational demands by limiting the number of initiatives on the ballot (California Commission 1992; Dubois and Feeney 1992; Gais and Benjamin 1995) or by grouping together on the ballot multiple measures dealing with a single issue (Dubois and Feeney 1992). These reforms assume that with fewer initiatives or distinct issues on the ballot, voters can devote more of their time and energy to each individual measure. Still others seek to institute or more vigorously enforce a single-subject law (Collins and Oesterle 1995). Single-subject laws reduce complexity by limiting the number of subjects that can be contained in a single measure.

A second set of reform proposals seeks to enhance voter competence by changing the campaign environment. As with the reforms discussed above, these changes attempt to ease the voter's informational burden. Unlike the above reforms, however, they do so by providing information that voters can use to better understand initiative propositions. One such reform requires public hearings on all qualified initiatives (California Commission 1992). These hearings would provide a mechanism for political and technical experts to directly disseminate information to voters, opinion leaders, and policymakers. They would also provide the media with low-cost access to such information. Along similar lines, Gais and Benjamin (1995) call for a standing constitutional commission that is empowered to call hearings if the legislature fails to, and Tornquist (1998) advocates a citizens initiative review committee to assess all qualified initiatives and provide an impartial review to the public. A number of states already allow or require public hearings on qualified initiatives (Dubois and Feeney 1992).

A second reform that aims to enhance the voter's informational environment is to improve the content and availability of the ballot pamphlet. A number of states now mail an official voter guide (also known as a voter handbook or ballot pamphlet), which describes the propositions in detail, to registered voters in the state. Reformers in other states propose the same (Cronin 1989). However, the quality of the information contained in these pamphlets varies widely. In the late 1980s, California reorganized its ballot pamphlet to include a summary of signed arguments for and against each proposition at the beginning of the pamphlet. This improvement seems to have increased voter reliance on the pamphlet. In 1982, only 27 percent of Californians reported using the ballot pamphlet as a source of information about ballot measures (Magleby 1984, 133). In 1990, a majority of California voters reported using the ballot pamphlet, including 62 percent of highly educated voters (Bowler and Donovan 1998, 57). Reform proposals recommend further improvements (California Commission 1992, Dubois and Feeney 1992).

A third reform that improves the voter's information environment is to require better disclosure of campaign activities. All initiative states except Nevada require campaign committees to disclose some of their campaign activities, including by-name disclosure of contributions or expenditures above some amount. Nineteen states require all campaign committees to register with state election officials, while fourteen require individual contributors to separately file (Dubois and Feeney 1992). Voters may use this information to determine the sources of support and opposition for a proposition. Reformers propose more stringent reporting requirements, including lower thresholds and more covered activities. Along these lines, California secretary of state Bill Jones's proposal to require on-line disclosure would make information about campaign activities immediately available to voters during the campaign, rather than several months after the election (California Secretary of State 1998b).

It is one thing to require committees and individuals to disclose their campaign activities; it is another to disseminate that information to voters. In many states, information on campaign activities is publicly available but not easily accessible. Voters must rely on interest groups or the media to wade through the raw disclosure reports. Naturally, they are less likely to provide this information on low-salience measures. This problem of disseminating information on campaign activities has generated a number of reform proposals. Twenty states require initiative advertisements to identify the sponsors of the ads. Some, such as California, provide detailed requirements such as the size and color of print for these disclosure statements on mass mailings. Numerous reform proposals recommend more extensive requirements for identifying an advertisement's sponsors (California Proposition 105; California Commission 1992; Dubois and Feeney 1992).

Empirical Evidence

Since the behavioral revolution began in the 1950s, political scientists have studied whether regular citizens are competent to make political decisions in a modern democracy and, more recently, in direct democracy. A number of studies have argued that despite low levels of detailed information about specific political issues, regular citizens are capable of making informed political decisions. Key (1966), and later Fiorina (1979) and others, argued that voters use readily available indicators of performance, such as retrospective evaluations of the economy, to reward or punish incumbent politicians. Popkin (1991) generalized this argument to contend that voters rationally employ simple cues about candidates, most importantly partisanship, to infer the candidates' policy positions. Indeed, according to Popkin, obtaining detailed policy-specific information is irrational—busy voters with extreme informational demands can do just as well with easily accessible information such as party.

To what extent do these conclusions about low-information voter rationality apply to direct legislation voters? Despite their low levels of reported substantive information, are direct legislation voters able to make informed decisions about initiatives? A number of empirical studies have considered voter rationality in direct legislation elections. In his study of voting on the 1988 California insurance initiatives, Lupia (1994) conducted an exit poll to assess what voters knew and how they voted on the five initiatives. Information demands in this election were especially severe, for several reasons. First, each of the five insurance initiatives was a long, technical, and complex piece of economic regulation legislation—together they totaled more than thirty thousand words. Given the complexity of the measures, most experts were unaware of important provisions in the initiatives; one would expect that voters would be even less informed. Second, the campaigns for and against the several measures deliberately attempted to mislead and confuse voters. Trial lawyers and the insurance industry placed four of the measures on the ballot to compete with a proconsumer measure opposed by both industry groups. Statements by important actors in the campaigns suggest that one of the primary motivations was to lead voters to vote "no" by swamping them with confusing and contradictory information. The campaign committees formed by the industry groups to support and oppose the various measures also adopted misleading names (e.g., Californians against Unfair Rate Increases) that masked the true identities of the sponsors.

Lupia found that, despite these severe informational demands, when voters possessed just one key piece of information—which measures were supported and opposed by the insurance industry—they were able to link their personal economic self-interests to the measures and behave as if they possessed detailed substantive information. In other words, voters used key endorsements to successfully overcome their informational shortcomings.

Building upon Lupia's basic logic, Bowler and Donovan (1998) examine in detail the various ways direct legislation voters cope with their informational demands. They argue that voters can employ at least three strategies: abstaining or voting "no"; using low-cost information sources; and relying on elite endorsements. Bowler and Donovan find significant empirical support for each of these strategies. Under the first strategy, voters who lack sufficient information to make informed decisions simply stay home altogether, skip the measures they are unsure about, or vote "no." In all three cases, voters avoid supporting measures about which they lack information, letting more-informed voters decide on their behalf. Under the second strategy, voters obtain information from the ballot pamphlet, newspaper editorials, television ads, and friends and neighbors. These information sources may provide less than complete details about the ballot propositions, but they may provide enough information to allow voters to make reasonable decisions. Similarly, under the third strategy, voters rely on elite endorsements. These endorsements allow voters to link their preferences, and hence their policy positions, to the known preferences or interests of the endorsers.

Analyzing thirty-six California statewide initiatives, Gerber and Lupia (1996) find that when spending by both the proponents and the opponents of a measure is high, election outcomes more closely reflect their estimates of "informed votes," as inferred from the preferences of well-informed survey respondents.[17] When spending is one-sided or absent altogether, voters lack information about the identity and intensity of a measure's supporters and opponents, and initiative outcomes diverge from estimated "informed votes." Gerber and Lupia attribute these differences to the nature of information available in each competitive scenario: in two-sided competitive races, each side has an incentive to reveal the identity, and hence the interests, of the other side. In one-sided campaigns, campaigners can provide false or misleading information without an adversary to expose them. In low-spending campaigns, no such information is available to voters.

Assessment

Empirical research shows that voters who participate in direct legislation elections can and do overcome their informational shortcomings and make good decisions. They are best able to do so when they have easy access to valuable low-cost information sources. This implies that to enhance voter competence, states should strive to provide all voters with useful information. This includes ballot pamphlets that contain summaries of the measures and identification of (or preferably signed arguments by) the measure's supporters and opponents. Such efforts seem to have paid off in California, where voters now rely heavily on the redesigned ballot pamphlets. It also includes ready access to disclosure reports in a format that facilitates usage by voters. Empirical research also shows that voters make better decisions when campaigns are more competitive. Reforms that aim to limit or restrict campaign activity and money make matters worse for voters, as they distort this important information about how intensely groups support and oppose a given measure. Likewise, public funding similarly masks the intensity of interest-group preferences. Instead, more extensive and easily accessible disclosure of campaign activities would allow voters to better discern the interests of an initiative's supporters and opponents and hence to link their own interests to positions on the initiative.

CRITICISM 3: POORLY WRITTEN LAWS

A third common criticism of the initiative process is that it produces poorly written laws. Critics contend that in the traditional legislative process, professional lawmakers draft legislation with the input of knowledgeable staff and interest-group experts. Bills go through numerous iterations before a final version is produced, and numerous policy actors have opportunities to influence the language of the bill. By contrast, initiative legislation is written by "outsiders"—interest-group officials, activists, or regular citizens who may lack lawmaking experience and expertise—and is not subject to the same level of scrutiny as traditional legislation.

Critics contend that the drafting of initiative legislation by nonprofessionals leads to poorly written initiatives in three different senses. First, they argue that initiative legislation is prone to technical errors, contradictions, lack of clarity, and confusing or ambiguous language (see, e.g., Magleby 1984; Cronin 1989). These errors result from mistakes made by nonprofessionals in writing the legislation.

Second, critics argue that initiative legislation tends to have many unintended consequences (Dubois and Feeney 1992; Schrag 1998). These unintended consequences result from two factors. One factor is that the nonprofessionals who draft initiative legislation simply lack the experience to anticipate the far-reaching effects of their measures. A second factor is that the initiative process excludes the input of interested parties who might be better able to anticipate consequences. Both factors mean that policy actors who might be better able to anticipate an initiative's ultimate consequences are excluded from the drafting phase of the initiative process.[18]

Third, critics argue that initiative laws fail to reflect underlying citizen preferences. Initiative proponents are not required to balance the many complex dimensions of citizen preferences. Rather, they must simply offer voters an alternative that a majority prefers to the status quo policy (Ferejohn 1995; Johnston and Lupia 1999). In other words, by allowing initiative proponents monopoly agenda-setting power, the process forces voters to choose between the lesser of two evils (Romer and Rosenthal 1978; Lupia 1992).

Of course, all of these criticisms are made relative to the legislative process. In other words, critics contend that the initiative process leads to poorly written legislation relative to the legislative process. Whether or not this is true is a question for empirical investigation.

Proposed Reforms

Reforms have been proposed to address each of the three potential problems with the language of initiatives. Reforms intended to reduce technical errors or ambiguity in language include provisions for assistance from state election officials during drafting (California Commission

1992; Dubois and Feeney 1992; Collins and Oesterle 1995; Martin 1997). A number of states already make public resources and employees available for these purposes (Dubois and Feeney 1992). These public resources and expertise may be especially valuable to citizen interest groups that lack the financial resources to hire professional campaign consultants. Along similar lines, some states require public hearings in which interested parties can review initiative legislation and offer suggestions for clarifications and improvements (Dubois and Feeney 1992).[19]

Reforms intended to reduce or mitigate unintended consequences include several forms of preelection review (administrative, legislative, or judicial) and postelection legislative amendments and judicial review. Prior to the election, administrative, legislative, or judicial branch officials can review, analyze, and comment on qualified initiatives to help proponents and voters understand the likely consequences of the legislation.[20] Many states currently allow voluntary preelection review or require review but do not allow proponents to amend their propositions in response (Dubois and Feeney 1992). Reforms would widen these preelection review powers (see Michael 1983, Michael Farrell 1985, and Martin 1997 on judicial review; see California Commission 1992, Citizen's Commission 1994, Collins and Oesterle 1995, Elisabeth Gerber 1995, and Tornquist 1998 on legislative review; and see Dubois and Feeney 1992 on administrative review).

After the election, legislators can amend initiative legislation to address consequences that are revealed after the initiative's implementation. All states except California currently allow some form of postelection legislative amendments, sometimes requiring a supermajority vote or waiting period. A number of reform proposals include provisions to allow easier postelection legislative amendments (California Commission 1992; Dubois and Feeney 1992; Citizen's Commission 1994; Elisabeth Gerber 1995; California Constitution Revision Commission 1996). Some require a legislative supermajority vote or waiting period.

Reforms to reduce the monopoly agenda-setting power of interest-group proponents include greater involvement by legislators in the initiative process, perhaps through the indirect initiative (California Commission 1992; Citizen's Commission 1994; Elisabeth Gerber 1995; Gais and Benjamin 1995; Collins and Oesterle 1995). Nine states currently allow some form of the indirect initiative. In these states, the legislature is required to consider all qualified initiatives prior to the election. If the legislature passes the measure itself, the proposition is removed from the ballot either automatically or upon the sponsor's request. If the legislature does not pass the measure, the proposition is placed on the ballot as a regular initiative, sometimes requiring additional signatures for ballot qualification. This reform tends to be very appealing to political elites who desire a greater role in the initiative process. However, voters tend to be reluctant to provide the legislature—which they distrust even more than they distrust their fellow citizens—with significant power over initiative legislation (DiCamillo and Field 1997).

A second proposed reform that reduces an interest-group proponent's monopoly agenda power involves allowing the legislature to propose a compromise bill to appear on the ballot with the initiative. Voters would then be given a wider range of policy options—the initiative, the legislature's compromise, and the status quo—to choose from. This practice is currently used at the national level in Switzerland. Ferejohn (1995) also recommends a similar reform.

Empirical Evidence

Unfortunately, there is little empirical research on whether initiative legislation is, in fact, poorly written. We do observe that most successful initiatives are challenged in state or federal courts, and many are invalidated in part or whole. It is also important to note, however, that many measures passed by state legislatures are also challenged in the courts and are overturned, or are amended by the legislature within several years. Some, but clearly not all, legislative amendments are due to errors in drafting; presumably, some, but not all, court challenges to initiative legislation are also due to errors in drafting. There is no reason to expect that initiatives would have fewer errors than regular legislation.

Assessment

Progressive reformers made initiatives difficult to amend precisely because their purpose was to bypass state legislators in order to pass legislation opposed by the legislators or their financial constituents. This means that, to the extent that critics are correct in asserting that initiative legislation is prone to drafting errors and unintended consequences, the ability to fix such errors is severely limited. In some states, legislators must wait three to five years after a statutory initiative's passage before it can amend the legislation. In other states, legislative amendments to statutory initiatives require a supermajority vote. In all initiative states except Delaware, if the initiative is passed in the form of a constitutional amendment, the legislature must also obtain a majority popular vote for any subsequent amendments. This popular vote requirement applies to all initiatives, statutory and constitutional, in California.

Reforms that make it easier for legislatures to amend initiative legislation would reduce the impact of drafting errors by allowing amendments after the initiative is implemented and its consequences are observed. However, these reforms are likely to be met with harsh criticism from direct legislation advocates who resist empowering the legislature vis-à-vis voters. Reforms that involve legislative, administrative, or judicial branch actors in the drafting stage of the initiative process may be more feasible. Preelection review allows input from experts and professionals in government who have more experience drafting legislation. From an efficiency perspective, preelection involvement may be less efficient than postelection amendments, since the actors must anticipate the consequences of an initiative's passage. From a feasibility standpoint, however, preelection involvement may be less offensive to reformers and direct legislation advocates, since the initiative's sponsors retain final agenda control and can simply ignore the reviewers' recommendations.

CRITICISM 4: DISREGARD FOR MINORITY RIGHTS

A fourth major criticism of the initiative process is that it exposes minorities to potentially severe rights violations.[21] Direct legislation is, by definition, a form of lawmaking by majority rule. A majority interest can propose, qualify, and pass legislation without any regard to the interests, preferences, or demands of others. In some cases, these "others" are important groups in society with substantial numbers (but less than a majority) and important claims on societal resources. In other cases, they are "minorities at risk," groups that society deems worthy of protection. Since the initiative process involves decision making by simple majority rule, affected minorities have few ways of protecting their interests from hostile majorities but to try to defeat the initiative or, if unsuccessful, to take their case to the courts. By contrast, representative government is designed to provide minorities with many opportunities to influence policy. They have formal opportunities to participate in deciding what issues will be considered and how bills will be drafted. Most important, minorities have numerous veto points at which they can protect their interests by blocking detrimental legislation (Shepsle and Weingast 1987). No such veto points exist in the initiative process.

Concerns about the antiminority biases of direct legislation date to the earliest days of American democracy. In the founding period, few intellectuals advocated large-scale direct democracy, and most dismissed any but the most limited forms of citizen participation in government. Perhaps the most forceful (and influential) articulation of this latter view is found in Madison's *Federalist 10*. Madison warns of the potential for tyranny of the majority and makes the case for a republican government to protect the interests of minority factions. The opposing view was well represented by Jefferson, who advocated a more participatory government, perhaps including small-scale self-governing communities. However, even Jefferson's vision excluded anything so radical as statewide direct legislation.

In recent years, concerns about the antiminority bias of the initiative process have heightened. Initiatives are now frequently used to decide social and moral issues with direct implications for racial, ethnic, and social minorities. Indeed, as observers such as Schrag (1998) contend, the politics of immigration reform, affirmative action, gay rights, and bilingual education, embodied in statewide initiatives in several states, have been the most important state-level political battles of the 1990s. Many believe that minorities suffer under the will of the majority, who are quick to sacrifice the rights and policies minorities have achieved through the traditional legislative process.

Proposed Reforms

A number of reforms have been proposed that would allow policy minorities more participation in drafting initiative legislation. Most important, mandatory public hearings would provide a forum for minorities to make known their positions on prospective initiatives (California Commission 1992; Gais and Benjamin 1995). Of course, the value of public hearings in protecting minority rights depends on whether or not initiative sponsors choose to incorporate other perspectives into their propositions. In some cases, initiative sponsors might accommodate minorities whose positions they had previously not considered. In other cases, initiative sponsors might accommodate minorities to preempt legal action that is threatened during the hearings. In still other cases, however, where a sponsor has interests that are directly antithetical to a minority, there is little reason to believe that the sponsor will be more accommodating after hearing the minority's appeal.

Other reforms would better allow minorities to protect their interests through the legal system. Of course, these reforms would be limited to providing a way to protect a minority's constitutionally granted rights and not other policy advantages that they may have gained through the legislative process. Two forms of judicial review enhance the protection of minority rights. The first is preelection judicial review (see Michael 1983; Michael Farrell 1985; Martin 1997). Under this reform, courts rule on the constitutionality of initiative legislation before it goes to the ballot. If the measure is ruled unconstitutional, it is either removed from the ballot or left on the ballot with a comment regarding its constitutionality. Proponents argue that in addition to protecting minorities against clear cases of rights violations, this reform would lead to substantial cost savings if unconstitutional measures are removed from the ballot and costly postelection legal battles are avoided. Opponents argue that it is extremely difficult for the courts to decide such matters as rights violations until a law is implemented and its consequences are felt.

The second form of judicial review that would enhance the protection of minority rights is a more activist postelection judicial review. Most important successful initiatives are now challenged in state or federal courts. Judges already rule often in favor of minorities, overturning many of the initiatives they consider. Holman and Stern (1998) encourage judges to more actively police and protect minority rights, and they advocate a three-judge panel to hear such cases. Beyond these recommendations, however, it is not clear that specific institutional reforms would lead to better protection of minorities.

Empirical Evidence

A number of recent articles consider the consequences of direct legislation for minority rights. Several analyze the success of antiminority initiatives and referendums in various jurisdictions. Gamble (1997) analyzes a number of antiminority initiatives and referendums in American states and cities. Finding that 78 percent of the antiminority measures in her sample passed, she concludes that direct legislation significantly curtails minority rights achieved through the legislative process. Donovan and Bowler (1998) question this result. They demonstrate that, at least at the state level, an analysis based on a more complete dataset of measures on the civil rights of gays and lesbians contradicts part of Gamble's findings. They find a passage rate of only 18 percent for the statewide antigay and antilesbian measures in their sample. Since this passage rate is lower than for other initiatives, they argue that the antiminority potential of the initiative process is quite limited. Finally, Frey and Goette (1998) show that, in Switzerland, comparatively few measures restricting minority rights have passed in popular votes. They observe passage rates of 20 percent (for national level), 62 percent (for cantonal level), and 23 percent (for local level) for antiminority measures.

Gerber and Hug (1999) argue that focusing only on direct effects can bias our inferences about the consequences of the initiative process in two ways. If the threat of initiatives makes legislators more responsive to antiminority views in the population, then analyzing only direct effects will understate the antiminority potential of the initiative process. If votes on antiminority initiatives lead legislators (at the same or different levels of government) to compensate affected minorities by passing more protective legislation, then analyzing only direct effects will overstate the antiminority potential of the initiative process.

The second limitation of Gamble (1997), Donovan and Bowler (1998), and Frey and Goette (1998) is that they fail to account for differences in voter preferences across states. Indeed, the patterns they reveal could be caused by differences in preferences that happen to correlate with the existence of the initiative.

Building on these two points, Gerber and Hug (1999) analyze the relationship between institutions, voter preferences, and policy for ten policies dealing with protections against discrimination for gays and lesbians. They find that the critical factor in determining policy is not simply whether a state has direct legislation institutions. Rather, direct legislation simply aggregates the preferences of the majority. On some policies the majority has preferences that involve restricting the rights of minorities. In these cases, direct legislation states have more antiminority policies than non–direct legislation states. On other policies, the majority prefers policies that enhance the rights of minorities (such as hate crime laws), and direct legislation states have fewer antiminority policies than non–direct legislation states. In other words, it is not simply direct legislation institutions that may bias policy against minority rights, but rather direct legislation institutions in the hands of an antiminority majority.

To summarize, the empirical evidence on the alleged antiminority bias of direct legislation institutions in general, and of the initiative process in particular, is mixed. Some studies conclude that voters use direct legislation to strip minorities of the advances they have made through the legislative process. Others claim that the direct effects of initiatives on minorities are quite limited. Still others claim that the total effects of direct legislation—both direct and indirect—are conditional upon the majority's preferences. In the end, it is clear that to fully appreciate the ultimate impact of direct legislation on policy, we must account for both direct and indirect effects.

Assessment

Considered on their own, there are clearly some direct antiminority effects of direct legislation. Donovan and Bowler (1998) argue that since the passage rates of antiminority initiatives are lower than for initiatives in other policy areas, concerns over these effects are misplaced. However, I would argue (and do so in Gerber and Hug 1999) that if any antiminority initiatives are passing, then some minority groups are being adversely affected by the initiatives process (whether or not legislatures compensate these groups is a separate question, and the empirical evidence suggests that legislatures reinforce, rather than offset, antiminority preferences). Reforms that may help reduce the potential for antiminority bias in direct legislation measures are public hearings. Public hearings may help to inform citizens of the potential harms of antiminority initiatives. To the extent that antiminority preferences come from ignorance rather than malice, providing such information may reduce support for antiminority initiatives.

The empirical evidence also shows that indirect effects may be important. Therefore, one way to offset the direct antiminority effects of the initiative process is to institute reforms that make legislatures more responsive to vulnerable minorities. One approach is to more extensively involve the legislature in conceiving and drafting initiative legislation, perhaps through mandatory, preelection legislative review. A second approach is to encourage more independent legislative involvement in policy areas that initiative proponents pursue, perhaps through requiring legislatures to debate and vote on qualified propositions as in the indirect initiative.

MULTIPLE EFFECTS, EXTERNALITIES, AND INTERACTIONS

It is convenient to organize the discussion of proposed reforms as responses to specific perceived problems with the initiative process. However, as is evident from the discussion above, we really should not consider these problems and their proposed solutions in isolation. Some of the reforms have multiple effects and are proposed by reformers to address multiple problems. Some are proposed to address one or more problems, but in so doing, exacerbate other problems with the process or create new ones. Others, if enacted simultaneously, interact with one another and may produce unpredictable results.

A single reform might address more than one problem. Indeed, different reformers concerned with very different aspects of the initiative process have proposed a number of the same reforms discussed above. A prime example is the case of public hearings. Public hearings are proposed as a way of increasing voter competence (by increasing the quality and quantity of information available to the public), reducing the possibility of poorly written laws (by facilitating participation by experts and interested parties), and enhancing involvement by the legislature (by involving them in the hearings). We might think of these multiple effects as "positive externalities"—additional benefits associated with a given reform.

Not all externalities are positive, however, and not all effects of a given reform are necessarily positive. A reform that is designed to solve one problem with the initiative process might, in fact, exacerbate another problem. Perhaps the strongest example of negative externalities arises in the context of campaign finance reform. Campaign finance reform has been advocated as a way to reduce the role of money and interest groups in the process. We noted above that the empirical evidence casts serious doubt on whether this reform is likely to achieve its stated purpose, since the effects of money are quite limited. Worse, it is likely to create new problems for voters. Limiting campaign contributions distorts the information available to voters regarding the strength and intensity of preferences of an initiative's supporters and opponents. In other words, by attempting to reduce the amount of money in the initiative process, reformers advocating campaign finance reform remove or weaken an important electoral cue and make the problem of voter incompetence more severe.

A second example of a reform that may produce negative externalities is restricting competing measures. Proponents argue that restricting competing measures enhances voter competence by making their choice simpler (i.e., voting "yes" or "no" on a single issue). While there is little or no empirical evidence that voters make bad decisions because their choices are too complex, simplifying the task that voters face may nevertheless have some positive effects, such as enhancing voters' feelings of efficacy and increasing voter turnout. The downside, however, is that restricting competing initiatives limits the opportunities for legislative involvement in the direct legislation process. Legislatures are often the proponents of competing measures. Thus, in the 1990 California general election, the state legislature placed four referendums on the ballot in response to initiatives it opposed. The referendums were widely viewed as moderate alternatives to the extreme interest-group measures.[22] Likewise, in Switzerland, most popular initiatives are accompanied on the ballot by a legislative alternative, and often the original initiatives are ultimately removed from the ballot before the election (Butler and Ranney 1994). Placing competing measures on the ballot provides an opportunity for legislatures to respond to interest-group initiatives and creates an incentive to actively participate in the direct legislation process. Restricting legislatures' ability to propose competing measures removes these opportunities and incentives, and effectively sidelines them from the policy process.[23]

A final consideration is the extent that multiple reforms interact. Consider what would happen if a jurisdiction simultaneously enacted reforms requiring more extensive disclosure and public funding. Disclosure is intended to provide the public with information about campaign activities. If those activities are financed or subsidized by the state (or county or city), however, then the information conveyed in the disclosure reports is ambiguous at best. Presumably, reformers would anticipate this interaction and choose one reform or the other. Consider also what the consequence would be of simultaneously increasing the length of circulation period and limiting the number of propositions. If increasing the length of the circulation period has its intended effect of increasing the number of (grassroots) initiatives that qualify for the ballot, additional reforms would be necessary to select among those that qualify.

It is not surprising that reform proposals have multiple effects, externalities, and interactions. Many of the criticisms of the process are closely linked, emphasizing different aspects of a single complex process. What this discussion makes clear is that it is critical to recognize the tradeoffs involved in any reform proposal. We cannot consider possible weaknesses with the process in isolation, nor can we expect to improve all or even several aspects of the process at the same time. Improvements on one dimension might necessarily involve impediments on another, and reformers need to be aware of these tradeoffs.

CONCLUSION

The empirical evidence fails to support the criticism that there is too much money or too much interest-group influence in the initiative process. Economic interest groups with vast financial resources are severely limited in their ability to use the initiative process. Most of their activities are defensive—aimed at defeating initiatives they oppose—and the set of initiatives that passes does not reflect their interests or support. To the extent that interest groups can use their monetary resources to gain an advantage in the initiative process, it is through their superior ability to qualify initiatives. The U.S. Supreme Court has found most attempts to directly limit this ability to be unconstitutional. Therefore, any attempts to reduce the relative advantage of wealthy economic interest groups to gain ballot access must be made through empowering citizen interests. Reform proposals such as increasing the length of the circulation period or instituting a two-tiered signature requirement achieve this goal. The cost of empowering citizen interests, however, is that the total number of measures to qualify for the ballot may very well increase, perhaps creating greater informational burdens on voters.

This minor informational concern aside, there is little empirical evidence that voters are incompetent to decide policy via the initiative process. At least when campaigns are vigorous and information is available about a measure's supporters and opponents, voters are able to figure out a measure's likely impact and vote as they would if they were better informed. Reforms that simplify voters' informational problems may have some benefits, such as increasing voter participation and feelings of efficacy, but they are not likely to change outcomes dramatically.

These considerations tie into my view of the effects of the initiative process on minorities. The empirical results presented in this chapter show that the effect is conditional upon the preferences of the majority. Sometimes majorities have preferences that are detrimental to minorities, and sometimes they do not. The problem is that, in the short term at least, we cannot ensure that the former will not occur. In Madison's spirit, it is therefore necessary to control the effects, rather than the causes, of these antiminority tendencies. Policy minorities tend to have better access via the legislative process. The same sorts of reforms that increase legislative flexibility and accountability may therefore help to protect minorities. These include more legislative involvement in drafting direct legislation and easier postelection legislative amendment of initiatives.

Finally, I address some normative considerations. Throughout this chapter, I have tried to report the empirical evidence from an objective, "positive" perspective. I have also tried to assess the proposed reforms in light of the empirical evidence without bringing in any particular normative judgment. Of course, all observers have their own normative perspectives that filter into and color their perceptions of evidence and their conclusions about the proposals. Indeed, one can quite legitimately object to the initiative process even if it is not broken, simply because one disagrees with the types of interests that are able to use the process or the types of policies that result. If this is the case, it is important to be clear that these are one's objections based on normative considerations and not allegations that the process is broken.

Prospects of Reforming the Initiative Process

M. Dane Waters

William Jennings Bryan stated the importance of direct democracy best in 1920, when he said, "We have the initiative and referendum in Nebraska; do not disturb them. If defects are discovered, correct them and perfect the machinery. Make it possible for the people to have what they want. We are the world's teacher in democracy; the world looks to us for an example. We cannot ask others to trust the people unless we are ourselves willing to trust them." This statement is as true today as it was eighty years ago.

In recent years the initiative process has become one of the most important mechanisms for altering and influencing public policy at the local, state, and even national level. In the last two years alone, utilizing the initiative process, citizens were heard on affirmative action, educational reform, term limits, tax reform, campaign finance reform, drug policy, and the environment.

Once the initiative process was established, many of the initiative states provided that these powers, reserved for the people, would be "self-executing." In other initiative states, the legislature was entrusted with creating procedures by which the people could exercise the initiative. Citizen concern about the legislature's efforts to limit initiative rights was the primary reason that, in some initiative states, the legislature is specifically instructed to enact laws designed only to facilitate, not hinder, the initiative process.

However, while the citizenry adopted the initiative to ensure citizen government, in most initiative states the legislature has enacted legislation that restricts rather than facilitates the use of initiatives. The legislatures' regulation of the initiative and referendum has often violated the citizenry's First Amendment rights as articulated by U.S. Supreme Court in *Meyer v. Grant*, 486 U.S. 414 (1988). Furthermore, the restrictions imposed on the initiative process are typically not imposed on other methods of bringing political change, including lobbying, legislating, or running for political office.

States do have a compelling interest in ensuring that all elections, including those on initiatives, are conducted in a nonfraudulent manner. However, if state legislatures wish to regulate lawmaking by the people, they should impose the same restrictions on their own legislative process that they place on the people's. For example, why should lobbyists, who seek to have the legislature enact new laws or propose amendments to the state constitution, have no voter registration or residency requirements imposed on them when signature collectors for initiatives do? The intent of legislatively imposed limitations on the citizenry in the initiative process seems dubious in the absence of voter fraud associated with this process.

A variety of legislation passed in various states demonstrates how the legislatures have reacted to the use of the initiative process. Many argue that the regulation of initiatives appears based on the self-interest of legislators rather than on an interest in protecting a process in which citizens act as an independent branch of government. Control of the people acting as a distinct branch has more to do with raw political power than fraud.

Many, if not most, of the regulations on the initiative process were enacted or proposed during the recent wave of term limit, tax limitation, and campaign finance initiatives enacted by the citizenry. However, legislatures have always vigilantly inhibited the people's right to the initiative and referendum. Regulation of these powers by legislatures has typically been a direct response to the people's use of the initiative and referendum.

Numerous issues regarding the initiative process need to be addressed, including the role of money in the process, the competence of voters when making decisions on initiatives, and the effect of the process on minority rights. Numerous books addressing these issues have been written by leading academics and these books address these topics far better than I can in a few pages. However, many of the concerns over initiatives appear to be unfounded, especially those regarding the effect of special interests.

Professor Liz Gerber discusses the influence of money in the initiative process. She surveyed 168 different direct legislation campaigns in eight states and found that "economic interest groups are limited in their ability to use the initiative process and that by contrast, citizen groups with broad-based support and important organization resources can much more effectively use direct legislation to pass new laws."

Additional research by political scientists Shaun Bowler and Todd Donovan (1998) found that while 40 percent of all initiatives on the Californian ballot from 1986 to 1996 passed, only 14 percent of initiatives pushed by special interests passed. They concluded, "our data reveals that these are indeed the hardest initiatives to market in California, and that money spent by proponents in this arena is largely wasted." Likewise, Howard Ernst's recent research (1999) of initiatives across the country (1994–1995) found that narrow interests with a financial stake in initiatives operate at a severe electoral disadvantage.

Many people, including me, are predisposed to believe that money influences elections—and this is why the vast majority of Americans want campaign finance reform—but when it comes to initiative campaigns, no proof exists for the influence of money. But even granting for a moment that money does influence the initiative process, why should the process be abandoned? If the influence of money justifies abolishing a legislative process, then the normal legislative process controlled by state and federal lawmakers should be abolished as well.

The initiative process is not a perfect lawmaking process—just as the traditional lawmaking process is not perfect. But the true motivations of lawmakers in passing new regulations must be scrutinized. These new regulations are only increasing the cost of undertaking an initiative. If legislators truly want to address the concerns raised about the process, they should consider increasing circulation periods so that the need for paying signature gatherers is diminished; establishing a requirement that public hearings on initiatives be held before the election so voters can be better informed; establishing more comprehensive financial disclosure requirements so the citizens know who is behind a measure; establishing a procedure where the state can help initiative proponents draft initiative language so the citizens can take advantage of their "expertise"; and creating the indirect initiative process so legislators have the opportunity to adopt or amend initiatives before they are voted on by the people.

It is hard to predict the future of the initiative process. The true struggle is in protecting the process from unnecessary and frivolous attempts by elected officials to "reform" it. Unfortunately, elected officials have chosen to regulate and reform in a vacuum. Far too often the citizens have no choice but to resort to litigation to stop these unconstitutional "reforms," which represent an unnecessary drain on the people's and the state's limited resources. Many argue, and I agree, that a moratorium on new regulation be imposed until a comprehensive review of the process can take place so that elected officials can intelligently address legitimate issues. Additionally, it is imperative that no new regulation be adopted without the input of the citizens who are most affected by these proposed changes.

Our founding fathers dealt in theory, but we now must deal in reality—for in reality representative government is not always representative. It's full of imperfections that allow legislators to pass bad laws and ignore important reforms. The truth is that representative government and the initiative process are perfect checks against each other. They're perfect complements—two imperfect systems of governance, each designed to help the people, and together constructed to balance the weaknesses of one with the strengths of the other.

An Alligator in the Bathtub: Assessing Initiative Reform Proposals

Peter Schrag

No one doubts that it's tough to devise any effective reforms of the initiative process. As Elisabeth Gerber reminds us, the combination of obstacles created by the courts and the devotion of voters, who when it comes to major policy decisions appear (according to the polls) to have far more confidence in direct democracy than they do in the governor and legislature, makes any significant change difficult.

But having followed the plebiscitary trail for some twenty-five years, I'm not nearly as sanguine about its effects on our politics as she appears to be, and thus not quite as dispassionate about the need for reform. To begin with, the concern is not merely with the consequences, intended or unintended, of individual measures, but with their cumulative impact—shrinking the discretion, responsiveness, and accountability of state and local elected officials, and increasing the impenetrability of the governmental process, and thus the alienation of voters. It's not just that many measures reduce that discretion: by definition almost all do. In California, the initiative has become not just an occasional remedy to legislative excess or inaction but a major component—if not *the* major component—of the policymaking process.

In California more than 40 percent of the state budget is driven by one measure, Proposition 98, which decrees minimum funding for schools and which has been faithfully followed. On the one major occasion when it was not, the teachers union sued and won a settlement that gave the schools virtually everything they asked. Something similar occurred when the legislature and governor attempted to raid tobacco tax funds generated and earmarked under another initiative, Proposition 99. The beneficiaries of the tax sued and won.

For a time, local governments found various legal devices to soften the blow of California's tax-cutting Proposition 13, but subsequent initiatives fairly well closed those loopholes. More telling still, in 1987, when the state approached the spending limits enacted through yet another initiative, there were technical devices open to the governor and legislature to circumvent the limits. The governor, notwithstanding the pressing needs of schools and other local agencies, chose instead to refund $1 billion to the taxpayers. It was that decision that led the state's school lobby to draft (and ultimately pass) Proposition 98. Thus initiative leads to initiative.

Tax-cutting measures, passed by initiative voters in California, have drained the power of local government and have hopelessly confounded government accountability. The result is that voters understand less and less about how the system works. Most believe that their property taxes support local services, when in fact the property tax has for most practical purposes become a state tax that's then redistributed by the legislature and governor as they see fit. Local government, which has only the most marginal ability to raise its own revenues, gets the blame for things that are often beyond its control.

As for the process itself, it's by now widely recognized that in large initiative states, the only people who get to play at all are those who can raise the large sums—in California, $1 million plus—to hire the consultants and buy the signatures needed to qualify a measure for the ballot. Two of California's recent hot-button issues, Proposition 187 (immigration) and Proposition 209 (race preferences), would never have qualified without money generated by parties and politicians seeking to use those issues for partisan purposes; Proposition 22, a recent "definition of marriage" initiative, would probably not have qualified without the deep pockets and organized help of two major religious organizations. Major gambling interests spent a total of $90 million in 1998 and in the 2000 primary to prove they were poor Indians and persuade voters to pass slot-machine gaming laws that will soon make California a rival to Nevada in casino gambling. In 2000, the insurance industry spent $50 million plus to qualify and then defeat two referendums seeking to overturn legislation, which had been pushed by the trial lawyers, broadening the ability of accident victims to sue another motorist's insurer. Because of the peculiarities of the state's constitutional provisions, a "no" vote on these measures was a vote to overturn the legislation. And since voters who think they are being forced to choose sides in a fight they don't understand between two big special interests will generally vote "no," the insurers won an easy victory. Confusion worked for them.

Finally, we come to the issue of minority rights, which of course concerns minorities who lack both the muscle and money to defend those rights, not the insurance industry, the tobacco industry, the Democratic Party, the Republican Party, the big public employee unions, or the trial lawyers. While the federal courts have given reasonable scrutiny to possible constitutional violations, the initiative is by its nature a majoritarian process. Minorities without resources rarely, if ever, prevail, or indeed get to the table at all. More particularly, as Gerber acknowledges, they rarely have a voice to plead for compromises modifying measures, as they do in the conventional political process. The result is a tendency to address problems—real and perceived—with sledgehammer solutions.

Having said all that, I concede that the possibilities of major reform are limited. Clearly the most important reform is to require more disclosure by the parties and funders of ballot measures at all stages of the process. The 1998 *Buckley* decision left unanswered the question of whether petition collectors could be forced to identify themselves as being paid if they were not otherwise required to identify themselves. But given the fact that voters often take cues from who supports or opposes a ballot measure, better (and faster) disclosure, both in the ballot measure and on-line, would help. I'd also go a step further than Gerber in trying to redemocratize the process. I would submit to voters a whole new process—call it the citizens' initiative—that would reduce the number of signatures required or lengthen the time allowed to collect them, provided they were all collected by volunteers. There is no certainty the courts would approve such an additional system either, but it's worth trying. If such citizen measures were identified as such—if the volunteers identified themselves as such—voters might become more sensitive to the money considerations in the existing system. If that were combined with more effective legislative review both before and after a measure gets to the ballot, perhaps some of the unintended consequences on the governmental process could be prevented. One of the crucial differences between the representative governmental process and the initiative is that in places like California, every initiative error is cast in stone. It can only be corrected through another vote of the people.

Finally, I submit that if the courts began to give ballot measures strict scrutiny for compliance with the single-subject rule and with constitutional prohibitions against constitutional revisions (as opposed to amendments), as they to do in Florida (where all measures go to the supreme court before they even qualify), both the confusion and the rush to the ballot might be tempered. There are critics, such as Craig Holman and Robert Stern (1998), who contend that the courts have meddled in the process too much. I'd go rather with former California Supreme Court justice Otto Kaus, who complained that adjudicating hot-button ballot measures was a little like having an alligator in the bathtub. State courts, where judges periodically have to face the electorate, have been too deferential in my view. In California, a lot of initiatives go to court, but very few get struck down. If more did, the whole process might again be what it was intended to be—a citizen's remedy for legislative failure in a representative democracy.

6

A Call for Change: Making the Best of Initiative Politics

Larry J. Sabato, Howard R. Ernst, and Bruce A. Larson

Deliberative democracy and popular governance are perhaps best considered distant cousins, and throughout the history of the United States they have seldom been on speaking terms. America's founders were acutely aware of the pressure to satisfy these competing forces. On the one hand, the founders recognized the necessity to create an energized, stable, and deliberative national government, curing the irrefutable ills of the Articles of Confederation.[1] On the other hand, in the name of protecting liberty and individual rights, the founders agreed that the national government needed to be legitimized through popular means.[2]

Endeavoring to create a system that was both insulated from public passions (i.e., deliberative and energized) and legitimized by the principle of citizen control (i.e., democratic), the founders were ultimately forced to stress one of these rival aspirations over the other. In the end, they concluded that "the majority who rule [not the people themselves] . . . are the safest guardians of both the public good and private rights."[3] In sum, they resolved that democratic liberties were too precious to be left to the unchecked passions of the American people.

With this in mind, the founders devised a three-pronged strategy to extricate direct citizen influence from the political arena. First, with only the exception of the House of Representatives, all national officeholders (the president, senators, and Supreme Court justices) were to be chosen by representatives of the people, not the citizens themselves.[4] Second, these officeholders were given lengthy terms of office, further insulating their decisions from the public will.[5] Third, the framers believed that the size and diversity of the new nation would further forestall the formation of a majority interest, hence, further diluting citizen influence.[6]

179

The nation's constitutional arrangement, however, did not resolve the tensions that arise from popular sovereignty's contentious relationship with deliberative democracy. On the contrary, the founders' reluctance to adopt more democratically modeled mechanisms, like those found in many of the state constitutions at that time,[7] in favor of a severely limited form of democracy, set the stage for future change.

As discussed earlier in this book, one of the strongest pushes to move American politics away from its modestly democratic roots toward more direct democracy occurred in the late 1800s. Initially, the movement was led by a group of farmers who were growing frustrated in their attempts to resist the pressures of industrialization.[8] Hoping to protect their livelihood, farmers worked to secure laws that would protect their interests. Having failed to secure the relief they sought through the existing political system, farm organizations, in particular the Farmers' Alliance, soon became convinced that narrow-material interests had come to control government officials and the nation's two leading political parties (Cronin 1989, 44). From this crisis, and the inability of the ordinary political mechanisms to address the problem, grew the People's Party (or Populist Party) in America.[9]

By the early 1880s, the platform of the People's Party called for the implementation of directed democracy in order to help free the political system from the control of narrow-material interests (McKenna 1974, 94). The movement to pass statewide direct democracy in the United States was born from this effort.[10] Describing the situation, political scientist Thomas Cronin writes:

> For most populists these direct democracy devices were a means of temporarily bypassing their legislatures and enacting needed laws on behalf of the downtrodden farmer. . . . Direct democracy became especially appealing as populists saw legislature after legislature defeat the proposals a majority of their members favored. A majority of the people, they believed, could not be corruptly influenced. (Cronin 1989, 45)

By the early 1900s, the call for statewide direct democracy had grown and was being championed by a wide array of groups. Progressives, women's suffragists, prohibitionists, and other disenfranchised groups joined the push for more direct citizen control of government.[11] What the pro-direct democracy groups held in common was the belief that the political process had come to be controlled by the narrow interests of a moneyed few and that implementation of more direct forms of democracy was needed to help correct this injustice (Elisabeth Gerber 1999, 4). In a 1912 article, Progressive thinker Jonathan Bourne argued, "The citizens of every state have seen legislature after legislature enact laws for the special advantage of a few and refuse to enact laws for the welfare of the many" (Bourne 1912, 3). Arguing along similar lines, direct democracy supporter Delos Wilcox claimed:

The constant, unremitting application of corrupt influence to control the action of legislative bodies comes to be expected, almost tolerated. . . . That politics should be a school of corruption is enough to make the angels weep. . . . What plague can equal this plague of political leprosy? (Wilcox 1912, 50–51)

As discussed earlier (see chapter 1), nearly all the states have since adopted some form of statewide direct democracy and hundreds of important political decisions have been made directly by the voters in these states. The fact that statewide direct democracy has moved the political system away from the insulated and deliberative function that the founders envisioned is unquestionable. While many scholars lament this change, preferring a political model more in line with the founders' original plan, arguing against the system on these grounds is futile.

If nothing else, the growing literature regarding the initiative process suggests that the system is not likely to be eliminated in the near future. The system continues to be employed with growing frequency and no state that has adopted direct democracy methods has ever abandoned them later. Skepticism regarding the "normal" political process and distrust of elected officials in general assures the initiative process a place in American politics for the foreseeable future. A recent poll of California residents revealed that nearly two-thirds of the people in this high-use initiative state approved of the process (*San Francisco Chronicle*, November 11, 1999). Knowing this, the question of whether or not the system should be eliminated becomes less important than the question of how best to improve the system: or more accurately, how best to improve the systems, since no two states are governed by the same initiative laws.

CHARTING THE COURSE OF REFORM:
SPENDING LIMITS VS. CAMPAIGN SUBSIDIES

At some point the disparate volumes of two competing discussants may become so great that the more vocal of the speakers entirely drowns out the message of the opposing discussant, leaving only one audible message and no true interplay of ideas. The solution to such a predicament, if a fair exchange of ideas is the desired outcome, is likely to take one of two forms. Either the louder of the two voices may be lowered to a reasonable level, allowing the competing message to be heard, or the more diminutive voice can be raised to a volume that enables it to be heard alongside its more vocal counterpart.

Essentially, these two strategies, or some combination of them, are the basic approaches offered by those desiring to offset the potentially deleterious effects of one-sided information flows and to assure a fair interchange of ideas. One group of reformers (discussed in detail below) proposes setting limits on the amount a campaign can spend on behalf of its cause, thereby reducing the volume of the high-spending side's message. Another camp seeks to provide insufficiently funded campaigns with some sort of campaign subsidy by which to magnify the otherwise inaudible public message of underfunded campaigns. Of course, these reform strategies need not be viewed as mutually exclusive. It is quite possible for a reform proposal, as many have, to aim at both setting limits on campaign spending and providing subsidies for insufficiently funded campaigns.

SPENDING LIMITS CONSIDERED

Since at least the late 1970s, scholars and legal experts have argued in favor of enacting campaign limits for initiative elections (Hart and Shore 1979; Lowenstein 1982; Ertukel 1985; Lagasse 1995). Each of the studies supporting spending limits follows a similar line of reasoning. In short, the prolimit argument stipulates that unlimited spending by moneyed interests leads to an unfair electoral advantage for the moneyed side. The message of the moneyed interests, the proponents argue, drowns out the message of the competing side, making democratic deliberation impossible and resulting in electoral bias, if not outright corruption, in the political process. In other words, the unchecked right of moneyed interests to project their message at any volume unfairly impedes the successful dissemination of a countermessage. The prolimits side argues that the First Amendment rights of less-affluent interests are violated as a consequence.

As discussed earlier by Gerber (see chapter 5) and Smith (see chapter 3), the courts have consistently reached a different conclusion. In case after case, the courts have established and reestablished the right to unrestricted campaign spending in initiative politics, most notably in *Buckley v. American Constitutional Law Foundation*, 119 S.Ct. 636 (1999), *Meyer v. Grant*, 486 U.S. 414 (1988), *Federal Election Commission v. Massachusetts Citizens for Life*, 479 U.S. 238 (1986), *Citizens against Rent Control v. City of Berkeley*, 454 U.S. 290 (1981), and *Buckley v. Valeo*, 424 U.S. 1 (1976). The courts have equated campaign spending in initiative politics with political speech. The argument goes, to limit an interest's spending is to infringe upon that interest's First Amendment right to free political speech.[12] As the Supreme Court clearly stated in the *Bellotti* decision, unless it can be proven that "advocacy threatens imminently to undermine democratic processes, thereby denigrating rather than serving the First Amendment interests," the Court is unlikely to lessen its scrutiny of state-imposed spending limits.

Despite the Court's commitment to defend unlimited expenditures in initiative campaigns, attempts to impose limits have preoccupied the efforts of many of those endorsing initiative campaign finance reform. The would-be reformers contend that if enough evidence is amassed to illustrate a bias toward moneyed interests in initiative politics, the Court would be obligated to reverse its earlier decisions (see Hart and Shore 1979; Ertukel 1985). Over the course of the last two decades, however, no such evidence has been revealed, and, if the findings of recent initiative studies are valid (e.g., Bowler and Donovan 1998; Ernst 1999; Elisabeth Gerber 1999), no such evidence is likely to appear. These studies suggest that the spending advantage of narrow-material interests is often offset in initiative politics by the public's general predisposition against these very interests (Bowler and Donovan 1998; Ernst 1999), and business interests often operate in the initiative process at a nonmonetary resource disadvantage (Elisabeth Gerber 1999). Consequently, the overwhelming evidence that the Court would require to be convinced of a clear and direct bias in favor of moneyed interests is not likely to be unearthed. Knowing this, it becomes increasingly important to judge if similar results as those sought through spending limits are likely to be achieved by other, less problematic, reform methods.

CAMPAIGN SUBSIDIES CONSIDERED

While somewhat less prevalent than proposing spending limits, there are a growing number of scholars who suggest that campaign subsidies hold the potential to cure the ills of one-sided initiative campaigns (Lowenstein 1982; Easley 1983; Polashuk 1993; Calhoun 1995; Ernst 1999). While the general idea for subsidies remains more or less constant in these studies, the actual subsidy proposals come in several forms. Some proposals call for public spending to be given directly to underfunded initiative campaigns. Other subsidy suggestions include tax incentives for media outlets to provide free airtime to needy campaigns. Several proposals suggest requiring media outlets to provide limited amounts of unpaid or discounted airtime to underfunded initiative campaigns in exchange for use of public airwaves, a privilege media outlets currently enjoy at no cost. What each of the subsidy proposals holds in common is their desire to make it easier for underfunded campaigns to compete against moneyed interests.

Unlike its reaction to spending limits, the Supreme Court has not resisted the idea of public campaign subsidies directed at improving public debate. Most notable, the *Buckley* decision affirmed the government's right to take action that "facilitates and enlarges public discussion and participation in the electoral process" (*Buckley v. Valeo*, 424 U.S. 1 [1976]). The Court applied this principle to uphold public financing of presidential campaigns and fairness regulation of the media. Simply stated, the Court has ruled that attempts to equalize public debate, or at least combat gross inequalities among discussants, are better pursued by bolstering the disadvantaged side's message than by attempting to mute part of the moneyed interest's message.

Another factor contributes to the attractiveness of pursuing campaign subsidies over campaign limits as a viable reform method. As two relatively recent studies (Polashuk 1993; Lagasse 1995) make clear, the structural means by which subsidies could be enacted are not new to the world of politics in this country. That is, Congress, through the Fairness Act,[13] has in the past required broadcasters to operate in the public interest in exchange for their broadcasting licenses. As stated in the 1989 Senate *Fairness Report*, the Federal Communications Commission once required broadcasters "to provide coverage of vitally important controversial issues of interest in the community . . . and to provide a reasonable opportunity for the presentation of contrasting viewpoints on such issues" (reprinted in Polashuk 1993, 392). While the Fairness Act has been all but abandoned in recent years, returning to this constitutionally upheld approach may prove more politically acceptable than enacting an altogether new reform strategy, certainly more acceptable than trying to enact spending limits.

In addition, campaign subsidies may actually help to reduce runaway spending in the initiative process. For example, if a moneyed interest is not likely to increase its overall spending advantage (i.e., increase its percent of total spending) by committing additional resources to a campaign, the campaign may very well choose to spend less money in the election than it would have otherwise spent. There is little reason to increase spending if doing so simultaneously increases the competition's spending. Any additional spending by the high-spending side would not increase its spending advantage and, consequently, is unlikely to increase that side's electoral fortunes. Looked at this way, the subsidy approach may have the benefit of controlling spending costs, as well as producing elections that more closely mirror the public will.

It is also important to note that subsidies, in a way that spending limits alone are unlikely to achieve, hold the potential to open the initiative process. That is, interests that are currently locked out of the process due to the high cost of successfully competing are likely to gain increased access to the initiative as a result of subsidies. As Ernst illustrates (see chapter 1), it is uncommon for interests that are not narrow and material to propose legislation against narrow-material interests. For example, in the 1994–1995 campaigns, these head-to-head matchups occurred in only eight out of seventy-five elections (less than 11 percent). Historically, the occurrence rate is equally low for these types of elections (see chapter 1). From this perspective, the initiative process to date has fallen well short of the Populist ideal from which the process was born. Quite simply, the process does not generally serve as a safeguard against narrow moneyed interests, as the Populists intended, because interests that are not narrow and material are rarely able to use the system to their advantage against narrow-material interests.

With subsidies, however, this phenomenon could possibly change. By making the system more accessible for interests that are not narrow and material (i.e., reducing the disparities in spending between narrow-material interests and interests that are not narrow and material), subsidies could potentially change the very nature of the initiative process in the United States. That is, subsidies are likely to increase the use of the system for interests that are not narrow and material against interests that are narrow-material. This is the case because these interests would be better able to compete against narrow-material interests and compete at a lower cost with subsidies in place. In this way, subsidies might not only make the system more accurately reflect the public will and reduce overall spending, but they might have the additional benefit of unleashing the latent energies of broad-based interests that have previously been excluded from the system. In doing so, subsidies hold the potential to move the initiative process toward the ideal upon which the system was created.

A REFORM PROPOSAL

The reform suggestions that follow are made under the assumption that the initiative process is here to stay. With this in mind, we suggest that the best way to improve the system is to take steps to assure that initiative elections accurately reflect the will of an informed citizenry. The underlying assumption of the reform measures suggested here is that efforts that are likely to increase public levels of information and, consequently, improve the public's ability to make informed decisions are the preferred means of reform. Moreover, the reform suggestions discussed below are limited to practical suggestions, that is, suggestions that could be enacted at a relatively low cost and are likely to withstand court scrutiny.

Improving Financial Disclosure Rules

The inability to accurately and easily track monetary backers in initiative campaigns poses a challenge to initiative politics in many states (Elisabeth Gerber 1999). For people to make informed decisions regarding initiative campaigns it is essential that the media and the general public have access to accurate information regarding the groups and people that contribute to initiative campaigns. The chief remedy for this problem is to increase the amount of "sunshine" that illuminates the financing of initiative campaigns.

Several steps can be taken toward this end. First, groups or individuals desiring to contribute to or spend money on behalf of an initiative campaign should be required in all states to form a campaign committee with the state's Secretary of State Office or to work through an existing campaign committee. All campaign committees should be required to clearly identify the side of the particular initiative that they favor and to list the primary sources of their funds.[14] Each individual committee should be limited to contributing to no more than one initiative campaign. Moreover, all financial disclosures should be required by law to be submitted to the Secretary of State Office in a timely manner. Ideally, the information would be reported through some form of electronic disclosure. Filing reports electronically could vastly reduce the amount of time required for states to disclose campaign finance information to the media and the general public. Currently, campaign finance data for initiative campaigns is not available in most states until months after initiative elections, when it is no longer of any use to voters.[15]

While Massachusetts is an example of a state that has rules in place similar to those outlined here, many states currently do not have similar controls. For example, the state of Florida collects campaign contribution information in such a way that it is next to impossible to infer meaningful information from that state's records. In a state like this, it is extremely hard, and impossible in some cases, to determine any campaign finance information other than the most basic (i.e., how much money was spent on each side of each initiative). Even this information is slow to be disclosed, making campaign spending more of a postelection issue than an election-day concern.

Support Public Dialogue

In far too many cases, one side of an initiative is able to spend a substantial amount of money spreading its campaign message, while the opposing side has little or no resources at its disposal to effectively promote its cause. While recent studies (Bowler and Donovan 1998; Ernst 1999; Elisabeth Gerber 1999) have found that the problem may be less overwhelming than earlier initiative literature claims, the issue is still a serious one and needs to be addressed. Several reform options could be pursued that would most likely reduce the deleterious impact of one-sided information flows in initiative politics.

As discussed earlier, modest campaign subsidies and free airtime for underfunded campaigns would likely help remedy this situation (Lowenstein 1982; Easley 1983; Polashuk 1993; Calhoun 1995; Ernst 1999). A scheme as simple as a "20/80" subsidy proposal might be all that is necessary to assure a fair interplay of ideas in the initiative process. The 20/80 subsidy assures that no campaign falls below 20 percent of the total spending in an initiative election. Consequently, no message can be entirely drowned out by a well-financed opponent. By assuring that no side entirely dominates the information received by the general public, the system would more likely reflect the unbiased will of the citizens.[16]

It should be noted that we are sensitive to the argument that Professor Gerber makes in this book (see chapter 5) against campaign subsidies for initiative campaigns. Gerber makes the case that subsidies may remove or weaken an important cue that voters use when making decisions regarding initiative campaigns. She argues that voters use information regarding who finances a campaign and how much a campaign is financed to help them make informed decisions and that campaign subsidies may distort this information. We also believe that cues are important to voters when making electoral decisions. However, we hold that a modest campaign subsidy would not disrupt the available cues, but actually improve them. The 20/80 subsidy would provide severely underfunded campaigns with the tools necessary to disseminate the very cues that Gerber desires to protect—cues that are not likely to be circulated in elections with extreme one-sided information flows (Gerber and Lupia 1996). Hence, the proper way to look at the 20/80 subsidy is not as a threat to cues but as a necessary vehicle for disseminating them.

The 20/80 subsidy proposal is by no means the only method that may help to improve the flow of information in the system. In fact, most plans that are likely to increase the amount and quality of information available to the general public are worth considering. For instance, initiative debates and public hearings might help to inform the general public. These activities would not only influence those in attendance, but they would be reported in the mainstream press, further disseminating initiative information. Moreover, improving the quality and availability of state-produced voter guides (discussed in detail below) may also reduce information costs to campaigns and voters alike. The common theme of the ideas discussed here is that relatively inexpensive efforts could be taken to improve the information available to the general public.

Improve Voter Guides

The quality and availability of state-published voter guides in initiative states vary tremendously. California has perhaps the nation's most complete and widely circulated guide and should serve as a model for other states.[17] California's voter guide is sent to every registered voter in the state. In addition to its statewide circulation, another attractive feature of California's guide is that it is also available over the World Wide Web at <http://ss.ca.gov/VoterGuide>, providing schools and newsrooms across the state with up-to-date information regarding initiative campaigns. Moreover, the Web-based voter guide contains financial information concerning each initiative campaign. The California guide contains an independent legislative analysis completed by the Secretary of State Office. This analysis summarizes the initiative in easy-to-understand language and provides information regarding the probable fiscal impact of each initiative on the state economy. The guide even supplies a list of groups that endorse each side of each initiative, easing the burden of forming voting heuristics for the general public. Lastly, the California guide provides arguments in favor and against each initiative as written by the competing campaigns.

While an excellent start, even the California voter guide could be improved. For example, the information within the guide could easily be made into an educational videocassette. In video form, it is possible that the information would be more interesting to the general public than the printed format, which can span over fifty pages. People might be more attentive to a well-produced video presentation than a traditional voter guide that forces people to take time and energy to read through several pages of often difficult information. Producing the information in this inexpensive format would enable the state to regularly broadcast the guide on public access and, possibly, network television. Moreover, the video guide could also be sent to schools, retirement communities, public libraries, and other places that provide educational information to large numbers of people.

With the voting guide as its centerpiece, secretary of state offices could also more actively engage in voter awareness efforts. School programs could be created to promote issue awareness among high school and college age voters.[18] Community forums, organized by secretary of state offices, could be held in which the voting guide is discussed and the competing interests have the opportunity to openly and candidly debate the issues, as well as an opportunity to answer questions from the audience.

As mentioned earlier, the news media would most likely cover such events, and, consequently, initiative information would be further disseminated throughout the state. In short, active efforts by secretary of state offices, coordinated with existing education programs, could make it easier for the general public to become informed than currently is the case.

Fix the Ballot

Reforming the ballot itself may also help to assure that people have a fighting chance to make informed decisions in initiative politics. Toward this end, the number of initiatives appearing on ballots could be limited. As some scholars have argued (Dubois and Feeney 1992; Bowler and Donovan 1998), ballots that call on people to read through a dozen or more initiatives likely require people to give more time and energy than they are willing to provide. Limiting the number of issues on the ballot would help assure that voters do not feel overwhelmed by the number of choices that they face on election day.

Second, each initiative should be summarized by the Secretary of State Office in one easily understandable paragraph that appears on the ballot. It might be advisable, as one study suggests (Collins and Oesterle 1995), to limit word use to a specified reading level so as not to discourage voters with limited educational backgrounds from participating. In any case, the title of the ballot should be such that the substance of the initiative is easily recognizable. Moreover, the instructions should clearly indicate whether a "yes" vote brings about a policy change or simply confirms the status quo.

Lastly, there should be limits to the number of initiatives that are allowed to cover similar issues on the same ballot (see Dubois and Feeney 1992). Having four or five versions of an initiative on a single ballot undoubtedly increases the difficulty of making an informed decision and should be avoided whenever possible. Secretary of state offices should be given the authority to combine like initiatives into a single ballot measure or to cap the number of similar initiatives at a certain level.[19] Likewise, the number of issues a single initiative can cover should also be limited (Collins and Oesterle 1995). A measure that deals with a wide array of issues is inherently complex and should be avoided. States with "single issue" rules, like California, avoid this problem.[20] All states should adopt and enforce similar measures.

CONCLUSION

I am persuaded myself that the good sense of the people will always be found to be the best army. They may be led astray for a moment, but soon will correct themselves. To punish their errors too severely would be to suppress the only safeguard for the public liberty. The way to prevent these irregular interpositions of the people is to give them full information.[21]

—Thomas Jefferson

The proper role of citizen participation in the political process has proven to be an enduring and rich source of controversy. In a small way, the disagreements and conflicts that are found among the authors of this book mirror this nation's founding controversy. As we were at the time of the nation's founding, and we undoubtedly have been throughout the history of the country, we remain a nation torn between the competing desires for both a responsive and a responsible government. In short, we desire a government that reflects the will of the people, yet is able to produce policies that are somehow superior to the unfiltered passions of citizenry—an illusive goal indeed.

As Jefferson states and our reform plan suggests, the key to bridging the gap between responsive and responsible government in the initiative process is supplying the public with the necessary information that can achieve this end. Full disclosure, increased sunshine, ensuring competing campaign information, and education efforts are all designed to promote the dissemination and flow of information. Information is by no means a cure-all for the shortcomings of the initiative process, but to proceed in the absence of adequate information is certainly a recipe for disaster.

Few among either champions or detractors of the initiative process would argue that the quality and quantity of information currently provided to initiative voters are sufficient for voters to make the difficult decisions that they are often called on to make. If the system continues to be used, as all indications suggest, then it should be empowered with the resources that allow it to operate responsibly. While the price of an informed electorate may appear high to some, it pales in comparison to the potential cost of public policy decisions made by an ill-informed populace.

Response to "A Call for Change"

Kenneth Mulligan

In chapter 6, Sabato, Ernst, and Larson discuss proposed reforms of the initiative process intended to improve the quality and quantity of information available to voters, but they do not address the problems these reforms are intended to rectify. In this response, I discuss the supposed problems and proposed solutions, with particular attention to Sabato, Ernst, and Larson's most far-reaching proposal— taxpayer financing of poorly funded initiative campaigns. While some of their reforms are sensible, modest, and likely to generate little controversy, the existing research provides little support for the theory that economic interests exercise disproportionate influence in initiative elections; thus the reforms advocated by the authors involving taxpayer financing of initiative campaigns are unwarranted.

Political researchers who study the initiative process generally agree that the lack of candidate and partisan vote cues, the complexity of the issues on the ballot, and the limits of voter knowledge and interest make for more difficult voting choices on initiatives than on political candidates. The difficulty of voting choices in initiative elections highlights the importance of the information sources available to voters when deciding how to vote on ballot propositions. Directly or indirectly, the reforms advocated by Sabato and his colleagues would address the content, quality, or amount of these sources of information.

One potentially valuable source of information for voters is the identities of initiative sponsors and campaign contributors. Knowing who is behind an initiative can help citizens to make better-informed voting choices (Lupia 1994). Weak disclosure laws in some states make it difficult to determine who are the proponents and opponents of initiatives. Requiring campaign committees to report the sources of their funding during the course of the campaign, as Sabato, Ernst, and Larson suggest, would provide the media and the public greater opportunity to scrutinize the supporters and opponents of initiative proposals.

A potentially consequential area for reform is the state voter pamphlet. As of 1992, fourteen of the twenty-four states that have either or both the direct or indirect initiative sent voter pamphlets to registered voters in the state (California Commission 1992). Political polls suggest that many voters rely on the pamphlets as a primary source of information when deciding how to vote on ballot issues (Bowler and Donovan 1998; Benedict 1975; Cronin 1989; California Commission 1992). This is surprising when one considers the relative complexity of the pamphlets. One study applied three readability formulas to four states' pamphlets between 1970 and 1979 and found them to be written at the college to postgraduate level (Magleby 1984). A state election official described his state's pamphlet as "fifty or sixty pages of absolutely impenetrable prose" (quoted in Wolfinger 1978). The complexity of the voter pamphlets suggests that voters' stated reliance on them may be inflated by social desirability bias (Magleby 1984). The proposal by Sabato and his colleagues to make voter pamphlets easier to read and more informative would be an important and measured step in improving the initiative process.

A similarly useful reform they offer is public debates of ballot propositions. Held across the state at various times during the campaign, reported in the media, and broadcast on public and perhaps private television, these forums could do as much as any of the reforms they discuss to educate voters on ballot issues.

Also, their proposal to encourage more readable ballot language could ease the cognitive burden of citizens in the voting booth. Studies suggest that initiative ballot titles and summaries are subject to the same complexities of wording and format as the voter pamphlets (Magleby 1984) and can lead to confusion in the voting booth (Gafke and Leuthold 1979; Bowler, Donovan, and Happ 1992). Their advocacy of simpler initiative ballot language could limit the potential for confusion and make for easier and more reliable voting choices.

The authors' most far-reaching proposals would limit campaign spending or subsidize poorly funded initiative campaigns with taxpayer dollars. They recognize that the U.S. Supreme Court consistently has ruled that restrictions on initiative campaign contributions and spending violate the First Amendment protection of political speech. Thus they wisely focus on taxpayer subsidies, which they suggest would achieve results similar to contribution limits without violating the First Amendment. They suggest that taxpayer funding of poorly funded initiative campaigns would enhance public debate and generate electoral outcomes that more accurately "reflect the unbiased will of the citizens." Taxpayer subsidies would bring the initiative process more in line with its Populist roots by encouraging citizens' groups that are reflective of the public will to use initiatives against economic "narrow-material" interests.

This proposal is problematic for at least two general reasons. First, it could have any number of negative unintended consequences. In addition to helping the citizens' groups that Sabato and his colleagues prefer, taxpayer financing might just as well put the state in the distasteful position of having to fund fringe elements against relatively better-funded mainstream minority groups. To be sure, voters may be inclined to oppose measures proposed by fringe groups, and the courts have been vigilant in protecting minority rights in initiative lawmaking. Yet it is worth considering that the subsidy proposal could have the consequence of providing taxpayer dollars to interests that might be better left to their own devices. Equally important, there is no systematic evidence that the citizens' groups that the authors hope would benefit from their subsidy proposal reflect the public will.

In addition, they suggest that taxpayer financing could "reduce runaway spending in the initiative process," but it could just as easily increase it. They note that it would be irrational for a well-funded initiative campaign to spend lavishly in full knowledge that doing so will automatically increase funding of the weaker side. Yet political candidates, though not publicly funded, routinely engage in similar escalating spending races. Leaving nothing to chance, the well-funded side of an initiative contest may decide to spend even more. We might also consider that opening up the process with taxpayer subsidies would likely increase the number of propositions on the ballot. This would contravene another of their reform proposals—to limit the number of propositions on state ballots.

Second, the evidence does not support the notion that poorly funded citizens' groups face an unfair electoral disadvantage in initiative elections when paired against better-funded business groups. Among the most noted observations of initiative politics is that well-financed corporate interests are not especially effective in "buying" initiative outcomes, but they are very effective in maintaining the status quo by defeating measures they oppose (Ernst 1999; Elisabeth Gerber 1999). But the available evidence, though inconclusive, suggests that the correlation between opposition spending and "no" voting is more complicated than that. Some recent empirical studies show a significant effect of opposition spending on "no" voting (e.g., Magleby 1994; Banducci 1998), while others show a modest or no effect (e.g., Owens and Wade 1986; Thomas 1991; Tobin 1997; Mulligan 1997). Studies that incorporate individual-level survey data show a weak or nonexistent effect of opposition media spending on "no" voting intentions (Bowler and Donovan 1998). Other recent research suggests that economic interests actually face an inherent electoral disadvantage at the polls (Elisabeth Gerber 1999; Ernst 1999), a disadvantage they are able to overcome in part when on the opposing side, because of voters' tendencies to oppose complex ballot propositions (Ernst 1999).

Although hardly conclusive, the available evidence suggests that business interests face an inherent electoral disadvantage in initiative campaigns, but that they are usually able to overcome this disadvantage (when on the opposing side) with the help of voters' tendencies toward risk aversion (see, e.g., Kahnemann and Tversky

1984; Quattrone and Tversky 1988) and the tendency of voters to be more persuaded by negative information than positive information (Cobb and Kuklinski 1997; Lau 1985; Fisk 1980; Kanouse and Hanson 1986). In this regard, voting "no" in initiative elections may be a baseline voting tendency, akin to voting for the incumbent in candidate elections (Magleby 1984). If so, then it is no more apparent why the state should subsidize poorly funded initiative campaigns than it should subsidize poorly funded minor party candidates for political office.

To their credit, Sabato, Ernst, and Larson recognize that "no such evidence has been revealed" in relation to whether economic interests exercise undue influence in the initiative process sufficient to convince the Supreme Court that contribution limits should be constitutionally permissible. Given this, the inconclusive results of studies of the effects of campaign spending in initiative elections, and the plausible alternative explanations for the apparent effectiveness of opposition spending, it is difficult to see why the political deck should be stacked in favor of poorly funded interest groups through taxpayer subsidies.

Notes

INTRODUCTION

1. Four types of ballot initiatives exist: direct statutory, direct constitutional, indirect statutory, and indirect constitutional. Of the twenty-four direct democracy states, most use *direct* initiatives and allow for the consideration of both statutory and constitutional measures. A small number of states use *indirect* statutory and/or constitutional initiatives. The difference between direct and indirect initiatives is that indirect initiatives must be submitted to the legislature prior to being placed on the ballot. The legislature may then typically respond in one of three ways: (1) adopt the measure, (2) place the measure on the ballot for voter approval, or (3) revise the law and place the revised version on the ballot for voter approval. With both direct and indirect initiatives, representative government is largely sidestepped.

2. Every state but Alabama requires voters to approve state constitutional amendments. In addition, twenty-six states allow state legislatures to submit legislation to voters for approval (Council of State Governments 2000).

3. For an excellent analysis of the impact of Proposition 13 on both California and the United States more generally, see Schrag (1998) and Daniel Smith (1998).

CHAPTER 1

1. The following states proposed legislation in 1999 that would establish the legislative initiative or referendum: Alabama, Connecticut, Delaware, Georgia, Hawaii, Iowa, Louisiana, Minnesota, New Jersey, New York, Pennsylvania, Rhode Island, and Texas.

2. Initiative descriptions and election results were collected from the Congressional Research Service (Graham 1978) for the years 1898–1976. Descriptions for initiatives after 1976 were collected from McGuigan (1985); Public Affairs Research Institute of New Jersey (1992); Public Affairs Research Institute of New Jersey (1996); and Schmidt (1989). Of the 1,726 statewide initiatives that occurred over this period (1898–1995), 79 were excluded from the analysis because of insufficient information for classification purposes. Moreover, descriptions were not available for the years 1978–1980, further reducing the number of classified initiatives by 107 cases.

3. As with this study, Bowler et al. (1997) distinguish between narrow-material groups and other groups by the types of benefits that the groups seek (6). Both studies classify narrow-material campaigns as those that seek material benefits that are distributed in a concentrated way.

4. Studies that attempt more specific classification schemas have run into exclusivity problems. For example, studies that attempt to differentiate between tax issues and education issues (see Butler and Ranney 1994) face inevitable exclusivity problems. These studies are not able to classify an initiative that proposes a tax increase for school construction into a single category. This is only one example of the exclusivity problems that researchers inevitably face when attempting to implement highly differentiated category schemas. The category schema implemented here avoids these problems by using only broad categories that are necessarily mutually exclusive. See Bowler et al. (1997) for a project that implements a category schema similar to the one in this essay.

5. The discussion of frequency of usage in this section makes use of all cases between 1977 and 1996. However, due to lack of available information, discussion of changes in type only run though 1995 and omit the years 1978 to 1980.

6. The years 1978 to 1980 and 1996 are omitted from this analysis due to insufficient descriptive information.

CHAPTER 2

1. Twenty-two states adopted the initiative or referendum (or both) between 1898 and 1918 (Cronin 1989, 51).

2. The term "Populist" was first used in the early 1890s as an epithet against the People's Party and its members, but party adherents gradually came to accept it (Hicks 1931, 238).

3. The state constitutions of Colorado and Nevada were amended to prevent judicial invalidation of initiatives: Colorado Constitution Article 6, sec. 1 (1913), and Nevada Constitution Article 19, sec. 2 (1904). Colorado's prohibition is no longer in effect; the Nevada prohibition remains on the books, but Nevada's courts have not recognized it as preventing them from reviewing the constitutionality of direct legislation. *Caine v. Robbins*, 61 Nev. 416 (1942).

4. *U.S. v. Carolene Products*, 304 U.S. 144 (1938).

5. *Citizens Against Rent Control/Coalition for Fair Housing v. City of Berkeley*, 475 U.S. 260, 261 (1986).

6. See oral argument in *Reitman v. Mulkey*, 387 U.S. 369 (1967).

7. 387 U.S. 369 (1967).

8. 402 U.S. 137 (1971).

9. 393 U.S. 385 (1969).

10. 517 U.S. 620 (1996).

11. Id. at 647.

12. *Coalition for Economic Equity et al. v. Wilson et al.*, 122 F.3d 692, 699 (9th Cir. 1992). The affirmative vote for Proposition 209 in fact was 5,268,462.

13. *Legislature v. Deukmejian,* 34 Cal.3d 658, 683 (1983) (preelection invalidation of a redistricting initiative), Richardson, J., dissenting.

14. *Amador Valley Joint Union High School District v. State Board of Equalization,* 22 Cal.3d 208 (1978) (upholding Proposition 13 property tax reduction and limitation).

15. *Legislature et al. v. Eu et al.,* 54 Cal. 3d 492 (1991) (upholding Proposition 140 state term limits and legislative cutbacks).

16. 32 Cal.3d 236 (1982).

17. Id. at 265–266 (internal quotations and citations omitted.)

18. Id. at 298.

19. *Coalition for Economic Equity et al. v. Wilson et al.,* 946 F. Supp. 1480, 1489 (USDC N.D. Cal. 1996).

20. Since state court judges (unlike federal judges) must face voters in retention elections, there is at least the potential that state judges will be less inclined than federal court judges to invalidate high-profile, voter-approved initiatives. Based on this dynamic, Holman and Stern (1998) argue that attorneys challenging initiatives may have an incentive to bypass state courts and instead file suit in federal court. Although throughout the four-decade period more initiatives were challenged in state court than in federal court, in one state (California) there was a significant shift toward filing such challenges in federal court. During the 1980s, only one of thirteen cases challenging California voter-approved initiatives was filed in federal court, whereas in the 1990s seven of sixteen such suits were filed in federal court. For a time, this strategy seemed highly effective. During the mid-1990s, federal district judges struck down a series of controversial California initiatives (e.g., initiatives restricting the rights of illegal immigrants, banning affirmative action, and imposing state term limits). Several of these decisions, however, were later reversed on appeal. By the end of the period, California initiatives were invalidated in whole or in part at only a slightly higher percentage in federal court than state court. The results were similar in Oregon and Colorado. Overall, for the three states over the period, roughly twice as many initiatives were challenged in state court than in federal court (forty-six versus twenty-four), but initiatives challenged in federal court were somewhat more likely to be invalidated in whole or in part than those challenged in state court (60 percent versus 50 percent) (Miller 1999).

Box: *Time to Walk the Talk*

1. James Wilson, *The Works of James Wilson,* ed. Robert Green McCloskey, Cambridge: Belknap Press of Harvard University Press, 1967, vol. 1, p. 405.

2. Alexander Meiklejohn, *Political Freedom—The Constitutional Powers of the People,* New York: Harper, 1960, p. 18.

CHAPTER 3

1. Figures for ballot measure spending are slightly understated, as they do not include independent expenditures or expenditures made by educational committees.

2. It is questionable, though, whether all noncorporate contributions that Gerber lumps together under the category of "citizen interest" should be treated alike. Likewise, Braunstein's study has some research design defects. Although his analysis shows that committees sponsoring ballot measures that receive most of their contributions from organizations (corporations, businesses, nonprofit organizations, and other entities) do rather poorly at the polls, there is much variation among these organizations in their financial and human resources. Unfortunately, because both models subsume dissimilar actors in their analytic categories and exclude relatively small contributions to issue committees, the studies focusing on campaign contributions and ballot outcomes have not definitively established whether grassroots or Populist citizen interests and ordinary individuals really are more successful than vested economic interests (be they individual or corporate) in using the process.

3. 435 U.S. 765 (1978).

4. In *Buckley*, 424 U.S. 1 (1976), which considered the constitutionality of contribution and expenditure limits in the 1974 Amendments to the Federal Election and Campaign Act (FECA), the Court's reasoning led it to uphold the law's limits on campaign contributions to federal candidates and invalidate limits on campaign expenditures by federal candidates. Consistent with the Court's logic in *Buckley*, the Court in *Citizens against Rent Control v. City of Berkeley*, 454 U.S. 290 (1981) also struck down a city ordinance limiting campaign *contributions* to ballot campaigns.

5. See id. at 789, 792–793, 795.

6. See 454 U.S. 290 (1981).

7. See id.

8. See id. at 190–191.

9. 479 U.S. 238 (1986).

10. See *U.S. Code*, vol. 2 sec. 441b (1982).

11. See id. at 257.

12. See id. at 257.

13. 494 U.S. 652 (1990).

14. See *Austin*, 494 U.S. at 654–655. As a nonprofit corporation, the Chamber of Commerce argued that the statute should be held unconstitutional under *MCFL* because the state's interest in curbing the unfair advantages of corporations was not compelling when applied to nonprofit, ideological organizations. See id. at 661. The Court rejected this argument, concluding that the Chamber of Commerce was more related to a business corporation than an advocacy corporation. See id. at 662.

15. But see Winkler (1998, 148–154), which argues that the *Bellotti* Court may have been wrong in concluding that ballot measure spending cannot corrupt candidates, because candidates who adopt ballot issues as part of their campaign may feel indebted to groups that make large independent expenditures that are aligned with the candidate's views.

16. See *Austin*, 494 U.S. at 659; *MCFL*, 479 U.S. at 257.

17. See id. at 7.

CHAPTER 4

1. Propositions 136 and 137, for example, were circulated by the Jarvis Association and had low reported signature costs but more than $3.5 million in consulting fees.

2. As an illustration of this, at least three consultants indicated they would advise that a client on the "yes" side of a campaign was in grave trouble if early polls showed "only" 55 to 60 percent support for an initiative.

3. A figure skewed upwards by Al Checchi's $38 million; the previous gubernatorial primary saw just $28 million spent.

4. Neither of these, we should note, were record highs for these states. In 1992, Massachusetts saw $16 million spent, including $9.1 million on a single initiative on nuclear power. In Washington, more than $6 million was spent on a single stadium initiative in 1997.

5. One might even argue that amateurs engaged in their first campaign for an issue they care very much about are the ones most likely to bend the truth and, in their enthusiasm, disregard acceptable campaign practice.

CHAPTER 5

1. Another common criticism leveled at initiative politics is that the process undermines representative government. This argument strikes at the very nature and function of the initiative process and is not easily addressed through reform proposals. In this book, Cain and Miller explore this critique in great detail. For these reasons, reforms aimed at this critique of the initiative process are not included in this chapter.

2. For an alternative view of the Progressive movement, see Deverell and Sitton (1994).

3. I use the term "successful" to refer to initiative campaigns that ultimately result in the policy change desired by the campaigners. Depending on the campaigners' goals, this can include campaigns that result in the passage of a new initiative, the blockage of an initiative, or a favorable response by other policy actors. I describe each of these forms of influence in Elisabeth Gerber (1999) and below.

4. Lupia (1997) and Lupia and McCubbins (1998) explore both the opportunities for, and limitations of, such deceptions.

5. Voters in direct legislation elections may use other cues not available in candidate elections. Research by Lupia (1994) shows that voters who know the interests of groups involved in direct legislation campaigns can use this information to infer how to vote. For example, Lupia found that voters who were able to identify which of the five insurance initiatives on the 1988 California ballot were endorsed by the insurance industry were more likely to cast votes that were in their economic self-interest.

6. An alternative interpretation is that a modern Populist movement can and must rely to some extent on organized interest groups. What defines a modern

movement as "Populist" is the types of organizations that are involved (citizen versus economic) and the types of interests that are promoted (broad-based versus narrow).

7. To accurately assess the extent of bias, one must compare the current ballot to the hypothetical ballot that would occur in the absence of a financial advantage.

8. "Economic interests" include economic interest groups, professional groups, and businesses. "Citizen interests" include citizen interest groups, labor unions, and individuals. "Other contributors" include political parties and candidates for elected office.

9. Garrett (1999) notes that groups who rely on professional circulators may be able to exaggerate public support for their measures.

10. Legislators may respond to interest groups, even if their policies are not majority preferred. Indeed, it is quite likely that many laws passed by state legislatures would fail to obtain majority voter support, especially when they deal with political, economic, or social regulations that affect narrow constituencies.

11. There are at least two reasons legislators may respond to an interest group's credible threat. First, if a law passes by initiative, legislators cannot claim any credit for the policy. Second, if a law passes by initiative, legislators are limited in their ability to act in that policy area in the future.

12. Elisabeth Gerber (1999) defines economic interest groups as those whose members are businesses or organizational representatives. Citizen interest groups are defined as those whose members are autonomous individuals. Note that the critical distinction lies in a group's membership composition. Citizen interest groups may pursue policies with economic consequences, and economic interest groups may be involved in issues of only limited economic importance. The importance of membership composition is that it directly affects a group's ability to mobilize and dedicate political resources.

13. See Ernst (1999) for another recent study that comes to similar conclusions.

14. The one initiative on which voters did report high levels of awareness was Proposition 5, the Indian gaming initiative. By late October, an estimated $71 million had been spent on the Proposition 5 campaign (Sweeney 1998).

15. Several observers have suggested that proponents may deliberately write their initiatives in complex language to deceive voters (e.g., Cronin 1989, 208).

16. An example of the former is California Proposition 104, an auto insurance initiative in 1988 that contained more than 29,200 words and a multitude of technical provisions (Dubois and Feeney 1992). An example of the latter is California Proposition 209, the anti-affirmative action "California Civil Rights Initiative." Only 369 words in length, this measure had vast implications for public university admissions, hiring, and contracting policy.

17. Gerber and Lupia employ a heteroscedastic logit model which weights the preferences of informed voters more heavily and the preferences of uninformed voters less heavily.

18. Of course, many interests are excluded from drafting regular legislation as well. The point is that there are fewer formal opportunities for interest-group input in the initiative process.

19. For these hearings to be an effective means for improving initiative legisla-

tion, proponents must be allowed the opportunity to amend their propositions prior to the election. However, some states, such as California, that require public hearings for qualified initiatives do not allow such amendments, since they change the legislation that originally qualified.

20. Such preelection review may also help proponents clarify language and otherwise improve the drafting of initiative legislation.

21. In this section, the term "minorities" refers to any groups that are less than a majority of the total population. These policy minorities include but are not limited to racial and ethnic minority groups.

22. Some observers have argued that these moderate referendums were intended as "killer initiatives," placed on the ballot with the intention of drawing support away from the extreme initiative but with little real support from the legislature. See Dubin et al. (1992).

23. Furthermore, restricting competing initiatives distorts the policy agenda. It ensures that the choice presented to voters is between only two stark policy alternatives, rather than several from which voters can select the most preferred (see Ferejohn 1995).

CHAPTER 6

1. The writings of John Jay, Alexander Hamilton, and James Madison in the *Federalist* provide the best discussion of this point. In particular, see *Federalist 10, 23, 35, 51, 57, 64, 68,* and *71.*

2. See *Federalist 39.*

3. See James Madison's writing reproduced in Madison (1973, 88).

4. *Federalist 61.*

5. *Federalist 62 and 71.*

6. *Federalist 10.*

7. For a more complete discussion of this topic, see Thach (1923).

8. Cronin (1989, 44) estimates that from the 1880s to the early 1890s the foreclosure rate for farms in several counties in Kansas approached 90 percent.

9. See Green (1978) for a work that links farmers' discontent to the growth of Populism.

10. See Cree (1892) and Sullivan (1893) for two works published at this time arguing in favor of direct democracy as a means of reducing the influence of business interests.

11. See Magleby (1984) for a thorough discussion of the Progressive movement's involvement in promoting direct democracy.

12. For a full treatment of this line of thought, see Mueller and Parrinello (1981).

13. See Radio Act of 1927; Communications Act of 1934; Federal Communications Commission 1985 *Fairness Report;* Fairness in Broadcasting Act of 1987; and Fairness in Broadcasting Act of 1989.

14. Michigan, Massachusetts, and Oklahoma currently require initiative campaigns to disclose their primary sources of support, not just the committee names.

California's Proposition 105 enacted similar requirements but was struck down by that state's supreme court on the grounds that it violated the state's single-subject law (Elisabeth Gerber 1999).

15. See the California secretary of state's "Voluntary On-Line Campaign Disclosure Project" at <http:reform.ss.ca.gov> for an example of how the Internet might be implemented to better disclose campaign contribution information.

16. A proposal such as the 20/80 subsidy would require improvements in the disclosure rules similar to those discussed above. This is because the subsidy would only have an impact if resources were allocated in a timely manner, something that would require up-to-date campaign spending information.

17. Other states with excellent voter guides include Washington State and Massachusetts.

18. The Center for Governmental Studies at the University of Virginia is currently implementing a program called the Youth Leadership Initiative that could be used as a model for future voter awareness campaigns at the college and pre-college levels. For more about this program see <www.uva/govstudies>.

19. Nine states currently impose content restrictions that could be used toward this end.

20. For example, California law requires that each initiative cover only one general issue. Four initiative states—Arkansas, Maine, Mississippi, and South Dakota—are currently without single-subject laws (Dubois and Feeney 1992).

21. Reproduced from Jefferson's 1787 letter to St. John de Crevecoeur, printed in Merril Peterson (1984).

Bibliography

Adamany, David. 1977. "Money, Politics, and Democracy: A Review Essay." *American Political Science Review* 71 (March): 298–304.

Allswang, John. 1991. *California Initiatives and Referendums*. Los Angeles: Edmund G. "Pat" Brown Institute of Public Affairs.

Alvarez, R. Michael. 1997. *Information and Elections*. Ann Arbor: University of Michigan Press.

American Bar Association. 1992. "The Challenge of Direct Democracy in a Republic: Report and Recommendations of the Task Force for Initiatives and Referenda." *American Journal of Political Science* 42: 1343–1348.

"American Indians Raise the Stakes." 1999. *Campaigns and Elections*, May 11.

Ammons, David. 1999. "Signatures May Be Enough to Slash Tax on Car Tabs: Initiative Could Be on November Ballot after Petition Collects 450,000 Names." Associated Press. July 6.

Ansolabehere, Stephen, Roy Behr, and Shanto Iyengar. 1993. *The Media Game: American Politics in the Television Age*. New York: Macmillan.

Ansolabehere, Stephen, and Shanto Iyengar. 1995. *Going Negative: How Attack Ads Shrink and Polarize the Electorate*. New York: Free Press.

Arnold, Rick. 1999. Comments presented at the conference "Maturity or Malaise: The Growing Use of Referendums across Liberal-Democratic Societies," in May at Queen's University, Kingston, Ontario.

Bagatelos, Peter. 1996. Interview by Todd Donovan, September.

Banducci, Susan. 1998. "Direct Legislation: When Is It Used and When Does It Pass?" In *Citizens as Legislators: Direct Democracy in the United States*, edited by S. Bowler, T. Donovan, and C. Tolbert. Columbus: Ohio State University Press.

Bartels, Larry M. 1996. "Uniformed Votes: Information Effects in Presidential Elections." *American Journal of Political Science* 40: 194–230.

Beard, Charles A. 1912. "Introduction." In *Documents on the Statewide Initiative, Referendum and Recall*, edited by Charles A. Beard and Birle E. Schultz. New York: MacMillan Company.

Beard, Charles A., and Birle E. Schultz. 1912. *Documents on the Statewide Initiative, Referendum, and Recall*. New York: Macmillan Company.

Beiler, David. "The 1990 Campaign Scorecard." *Campaigns & Elections* 12: 26–33.

Bell, Derrick, Jr. 1978. "The Referendum: Democracy's Barrier to Racial Equality." *Washington Law Review* 54: 1.

Bender, Earl. 1999. Comments presented at the conference "Maturity or Malaise: The Growing Use of Referendums across Liberal-Democratic Societies," in May at Queen's University, Kingston, Ontario.

Benedict, Robert C. 1975. "Some Aspects of the Direct Legislation Process in Washington State: Theory and Practice, 1914–1973." Ph.D. diss., University of Washington.

Bennett, W. Lance. 1996. *The Governing Crisis: Media, Money, and Marketing in American Elections.* New York: St. Martin's.

Berelson, Bernard. 1952. "Democratic Theory and Public Opinion." *Public Opinion Quarterly* 16: 313–330.

Berry, Frances Stokes, and William D. Berry. 1990. "State Lottery Adoptions as Policy Innovations: An Event History Analysis." *American Political Science Review* 84: 395–416.

Berry, Jeffrey M. 1977. *Lobbying for the People.* Princeton: Princeton University Press.

Bickel, Alexander. 1962. *The Least Dangerous Branch: The Supreme Court at the Bar of Politics.* Indianapolis: Bobbs-Merrill.

Billings, Erin. 1998. "Big Bucks Couldn't Sway State Voters." *Missoulian*, December 6 <missoulian.com/archives>.

Billington, Ray. 1949. *Westward Expansion.* New York: Macmillan.

Blumenthal, Sidney. 1994. "The Candidate." *New Yorker*, October 10.

Boellstorff, Leslie. 1995. "Legislature Advances Proposals on Petitions." *Omaha World-Herald*, April 4.

Booth, William. 1999. "Maverick Millionaire Tries to Force the GOP's Hand: Initiative Drive Mixes Campaign Reform, Redistricting Threat." *Washington Post*, June 1, p. A03.

Bourne, Jonathan. 1912. "Functions of the Initiative, Referendum, and Recall." *Annals of the American Academy of Political and Social Science* 43: 3–16.

Bowler, Shaun, and Donovan, Todd. 1994a. "Economic Conditions and Voting on Ballot Propositions." *American Politics Quarterly* 22 (January): 27–40.

———. 1994b. "Information and Opinion Change on Ballot Propositions." *Political Behavior* 16: 411–433.

———, eds. 1998. *Demanding Choices: Opinion Voting and Direct Democracy.* Ann Arbor: University of Michigan Press.

Bowler, Shaun, Todd Donovan, and Ken Fernandez. 1996. "The Growth of the Political Marketing Industry and the California Initiative Process." *European Journal of Marketing* 30: 173–185.

Bowler, Shaun, Todd Donovan, and Trudi Happ. 1992. "Ballot Propositions and Information Costs: Direct Democracy and the Fatigued Voter." *Western Political Quarterly* 45: 559–568.

Bowler, Shaun, Todd Donovan, and Dave McCuan. 1997. "Grassroots Democracy & California's Political Warriors: Campaign Professionals & the Initiative Process." Paper presented at the annual meeting of the American Political Science Association, Washington, D.C.

Bowler, Shaun, Todd Donovan, and Joseph Snipp. 1993. "Local Sources of Information and Voter Choice in State Elections." *American Politics Quarterly* 21: 473–489.

Bowler, Shaun, Todd Donovan, and Caroline Tolbert, eds. 1998. *Citizens as Legislators: Direct Democracy in the United States.* Columbus: Ohio State University Press.

Braunstein, Richard. 1999. "Big Money and Ballot Issues: Do Voters Care Where the Money Comes From?" Paper presented at the Western Political Science Association meeting, Seattle.

Brestoff, Nick. 1975. "The California Initiative Process: A Suggestion for Reform." *Southern California Law Review* 48: 922–948.

Brians, Craig Leonard, and Martin P. Wattenberg. 1996. "Campaign Issue Knowledge and Salience: Comparing Reception from TV Commercials, TV News and Newspapers." *American Journal of Political Science* 40: 172–193.

Broder, David. 1972. *The Party's Over: The Failure of Politics in America.* New York: Harper and Row.

———. 1998. "Ballot Battle: Collecting Signatures for a Price." *Washington Post,* April 12, p. A01.

———. 2000. *Democracy Derailed: Initiative Campaigns and the Power of Money.* New York: Harcout.

Brune, Tom, and Barbara A. Serrano. 1997. "Signature Gatherers: Their Race Become Issues in Init. 2000 Effort." *Seattle Times.* December 12.

Buck, Claudia. 1998. "Tribal Gaming: Indians Spend Bundles to Win Oodles." *California Journal* 29: 44–47.

Butler, David, and Austin Ranney, eds. 1978. *Referendums: A Comparative Study of Practice and Theory.* Washington, D.C.: American Enterprise Institute for Public Policy Research.

———. 1994. *Referendums around the World: The Growing Use of Direct Democracy.* Washington, D.C.: American Enterprise Institute for Public Policy Research.

Calhoun, Emile. 1995. "Initiative Petition Reforms and the First Amendment." *University of Colorado Law Review* 66: 129–141.

California Commission on Campaign Finance. 1992. *Democracy by Initiative: Shaping California's Fourth Branch of Government.* Los Angeles: Center for Responsive Government.

California Constitution Revision Commission. 1996. "Final Report and Recommendations to the Governor and the Legislature." Sacramento: California Constitution Revision Commission.

California Journal. 1988. "Propositions." 19 (Dec): 15–17.

———. 1990a. "Instant Initiative Qualification." 21 (Feb): 77.

———. 1990b. "Tax Props." 21 (Dec): 586.

———. 1992. Goddard Clausen/1st Tuesday advertisement, Woodward & McDowell advertisement, in *Roster of Government Annual Edition.*

———. 1996a. "June 1996 Ballot Book." 27 (May). Special insert.

———. 1996b. "November 1996 Ballot Book." 27 (Sept). Special insert.

———. 1998. "November 1998 Ballot Propositions." 29 (Sept): 32–43.

California Legislative Analyst's Office. 1990. *The California Budget Process: Problems and Options for Change.* Sacramento. *California Opinion Index.* San Francisco: Field Institute.

California Secretary of State. 1996. "Financing California's Statewide Ballot Mea-

sures: 1996 Primary and General Elections." Sacramento: California Secretary of State.
————. 1998a. "Analysis by Legislative Analyst for Proposition 227." *California Voter Guide* <http:Primary98.ss.ca.gov/VoterGuide/Proposition/22227analysis.htm>.
————. 1998b. "California Digital Signature Regulations" <http://www.ss.ca.gov/digsig/regulations.htm>.
————. 1998c. "Financing California's Statewide Ballot Measures: Campaign Receipts and Expenditures through June 30, 1998. Sacramento.
Camobreco, John F. 1998. "Preferences, Fiscal Policies, and the Initiative Process." *Journal of Politics* 60: 819–829.
Campbell, Angus, et al. 1960. *The American Voter*. New York: Wiley.
Chavez, Linda. 1998. *The Color Bind: California's Battle to End Affirmative Action*. Berkeley: University of California Press.
Citizens Commission on Ballot Initiatives. 1994. "Report and Recommendations." Sacramento.
Citrin, Jack. 1996. "Who's the Boss? Direct Democracy and Popular Control of Government." In *Broken Contract: Changing Relationships between Americans and Their Government*, edited by S. Craig. Boulder, Colo.: Westview.
City Club of Denver. 1927. "Direct Legislation in Colorado." Denver: Eames Brothers.
Coalition against Unregulated Gambling (CAUG). 1998. *No on Proposition 5 Six Step Organizing Manual*. Sacramento: Coalition against Unregulated Gambling.
Cobb, Michael D., and James H. Kuklinski. 1997. "Changing Minds: Political Arguments and the Political Persuasion." *American Journal of Political Science* 41: 88–121.
Collins, Richard B., and Dale Oesterle. 1995. "Structuring the Ballot Initiative: Procedures That Do and Don't Work." *University of Colorado Law Review* 66: 47–127.
Common Cause. 1999. "National Parties Raise $193 Million in Soft Money during 1997/1998 Election Cycle" <commoncause.org/publications/020399.htm>.
Converse, Philip. 1964. "The Nature of Belief Systems in Mass Publics." In *Ideology and Discontent*, edited by David E. Apter. New York: Free Press.
Cordes, Henry. 1999. "Initiative 414 Spending Set Record." *Omaha World-Herald*, January 7.
Cottrell, E. 1939. "Twenty-Five Years of Direct Legislation in California." *Public Opinion Quarterly* 31: 30–45.
Council of State Governments. 2000. *The Book of States, 2000–2001*. Lexington, Ky.: Council of State Governments.
Craig, Stephen. 1996. "The Angry Voter: Politics and Popular Discontent in the 1990s." In *Broken Contract: Changing Relationships between Americans and Their Government*, edited by S. Craig. Boulder, Colo.: Westview.
Cree, Nathan. 1892. *Direct Legislation by the People*. Chicago: McClurg.
Cronin, Thomas E. 1989. *Direct Democracy: The Politics of Initiatives, Referendum, and Recall*. Cambridge, Mass.: Harvard University Press.
Crouch, Winston, and Dean McHenry. 1949. *California Government*. Berkeley: University of California Press.

———. 1950. *The Initiative and Referendum in California*. Los Angeles: Haynes Foundation.

Cushman, Robert. 1916. "Recent Experience with the Initiative and Referendum." *American Political Science Review* 10: 532–539.

Dash, Hal. 1997. Interview by Todd Donovan.

Deverell, William, and Tom Sitton. 1994. *California Progressivism Revisited*. Berkeley: University of California Press.

DiCamillo, Mark, and Mervin Field. 1997. "Statewide Ballot Proposition Elections." *California Opinion Index*. San Francisco: Field Institute.

Domhoff, William. 1998. *Who Rules America? Power and Politics in the Year 2000*. Mountain View, Calif.: Mayfield.

Donovan, Todd, and Shaun Bowler. 1998. "Direct Democracy and Minority Rights: An Extension." *American Journal of Political Science* 43: 1020–1025.

Donovan, Todd, Shaun Bowler, David McCuan, and Ken Fernandez. 1998. "Contending Players and Strategies: Opposition Advantages in Initiative Elections." In *Citizens as Legislators: Direct Democracy in the United States*, edited by Shaun Bowler, Todd Donovan, and Caroline Tolbert, 133–152. Columbus: Ohio State University Press.

Donovan, Todd, Jim Wenzel, and Shaun Bowler. 1999. "Direct Democracy and Gay Rights Initiatives after *Romer*." In *Politics of Gay Rights*, edited by C. Rimmerman, K. Wald, and Clyde Wilcox. Chicago: University of Chicago Press.

Downs, Anthony. 1957. *An Economic Theory of Democracy*. New York: Harper and Row.

Dreyfuss, Robert. 1998. "Reform Beyond the Beltway: States as Laboratories of Clean Money." *American Prospect* (May–June).

Dubin, Jeffrey A., D. Roderick Kiewiet, and Charles Noussair. 1992. "Voting on Growth Control Measures: Preferences and Strategies." *Economics and Politics* 4: 191–213.

Dubois, P., Floyd Feeney, and E. Constantini. 1991. *The California Ballot Pamphlet: A Survey of Voters*. Report for the Secretary of State of California. Sacramento.

Dubois, Philip, and Floyd Feeney. 1992. *Improving the California Initiative Process*. Berkeley: California Policy Seminar.

Dusha, Carla Lazzareschi. 1975. "The Koupal's Petition Factory." *California Journal* 8: 83.

Easley, Allen K. 1983. "Buying Back the First Amendment: Regulation of Disproportionate Corporate Spending in Ballot Issue Campaigns." *Georgia Law Review* 17: 675–758.

Eaton, Allen. 1912. *The Oregon System*. Chicago: McClurg.

Elazar, Daniel. 1970. *Cities of the Prairie*. New York: Basic.

———. 1984. *American Federalism: A View from the States*. 3d ed. New York: Harper and Row.

Erickson, Robert. 1990. "Economic Conditions and the Congressional Vote: A Review of the Macrolevel Evidence." *American Journal of Political Science* 34: 373–399.

Ernst, Howard R. 1999. "The Pulse of Democracy: Understanding the Determinants of Initiative Elections." Ph.D. diss., University of Virginia.

Ertukel, A. D., ed. 1985. "Debating Initiative Reform: A Summary of the Second Annual Symposium on Elections at the Center for the Study of Law and Politics." *Journal of Law and Politics* 2: 313–334.

Eule, Julian N. 1990. "Judicial Review of Direct Democracy." *Yale Law Journal* 99: 1503.

Fairbanks, David. 1977. "Religious Forces and 'Morality' Politics in the American States." *Western Political Quarterly* 30: 411–417.

Fallows, James. 1996. *Breaking the News: How the Media Undermine American Democracy.* New York: Pantheon.

Farrell, David. 1997. "Political Consultancy Overseas: The Internationalization of Campaign Consultancy." Paper presented at the American Political Science Association meeting, Washington, D.C.

Farrell, Michael J. 1985. "The Judiciary and Popular Democracy: Should Courts Review Ballot Measures Prior to Elections?" *Fordham Law Review* 53: 919.

Federal Election Commission. 1998. <http://www.fec.gov/press/cany-e98.htm>.

Ferejohn, John. 1995. "Reforming the Initiative Process." In *Constitutional Reform in California,* edited by Bruce E. Cain and Roger G. Noll. Berkeley, Calif.: Institute of Governmental Studies Press.

Field Institute. 1998. "The Field Poll" #1909, October 31. San Francisco: Field Institute.

Finkel, Steven E. 1993. "Reexamining the 'Minimal Effects' Model in Recent Presidential Campaigns." *Journal of Politics* 55 (February): 1–21.

Fiorina, Morris. 1979. *Retrospective Voting in American National Elections.* New Haven: Yale University Press.

Fisk, Susan T. 1980. "Attention and Weight in Person Perception: The Impact of Negative and Extreme Behavior." *Journal of Personality and Social Psychology* 38: 889–906.

Flannigan, William, and Nancy Zingale. 1996. *Political Behavior of the American Electorate.* Washington, D.C.: Congressional Quarterly Press.

Fountaine, Lisa. 1988. "Lousy Lawmaking: Questioning the Desirability and Constitutionality of Legislating by Initiative." *Southern California Law Review* 61: 733–776.

Frey, Bruno S., and Lorenz Goette. 1998. "Does the Popular Vote Destroy Civil Rights?" *American Journal of Political Science* 42: 1343–1348.

Gafke, Roger, and David Leuthold. 1979. "The Effects on Voters of Misleading, Confusing, and Difficult Ballot Titles." *Public Opinion Quarterly* 43: 394–410.

Gais, Thomas, and Gerald Benjamin. 1995. "Public Discontent and the Decline of Deliberation." *Temple Law Review* 42: 1343–1348.

Gamble, Barbara. 1997. "Putting Civil Rights to a Popular Vote." *American Journal of Political Science* 41: 245–269.

Garrett, Elizabeth. 1997. "Perspective on Direct Democracy: Who Directs Direct Democracy?" *University of Chicago Law School Roundtable* 4: 17–36.

———. 1999. "Money, Agenda Setting, and Direct Democracy." *Texas Law Review* 77: 1845–1890.

Garrison, Michael. 1989. "Corporate Political Speech, Campaign Spending, and

First Amendment Doctrine." *American Business Law Journal* 27 (summer): 163–213.

Gatke, Roger, and David Leuthold. 1979. "The Effects on Voters of Misleading, Confusing, and Difficult Ballot Titles." *Public Opinion Quarterly* 43: 394–401.

Gerber, Alan. 1998. "Estimating the Effects of Campaign Spending on Senate Election Outcomes Using Instrumental Variables." *American Political Science Review* 92 (June): 401–411.

Gerber, Elisabeth R. 1995. "Reforming the California Initiative Process: A Proposal to Increase Flexibility and Legislative Accountability." In *Constitutional Reform in California*, edited by Bruce E. Cain and Roger G. Noll. Berkeley: Institute of Governmental Studies Press.

———. 1996. "Legislative Response to the Threat of Popular Initiatives." *American Journal of Political Science* 40: 99–128.

———. 1998. "Interest Group Influence in the California Initiative Process" <ppic.org/publications/briefs.html>.

———. 1999. *The Populist Paradox: Interest Group Influence and the Promise of Direct Legislation.* Princeton, N.J.: Princeton University Press.

Gerber, Elisabeth R., and Simon Hug. 1999. "Minority Rights and Direct Legislation: Theory, Methods, and Evidence." Working paper, University of California, San Diego.

Gerber, Elisabeth R., and Arthur Lupia. 1996. "The Benefits of Expensive Campaigns." Working paper, University of California, San Diego.

Gilmore, Susan. 1995. "Gay-rights Leaders Fight Back—Hands Off Washington Circulates Own Petition." *Seattle Times*, July 4, p. B1.

Goldberg, Carey. 1998. "2 States Consider Boldly Revamping Campaign Finance." *New York Times*, October 19.

Graham, Virginia. 1978. *A Compilation of Statewide Initiative Proposals Appearing on Ballots Through 1976.* Washington, D.C.: Congressional Research Service, Library of Congress.

Gray, Virginia, and Herbert Jacob. 1996. *Politics in the American States: A Comparative Analysis.* Washington, D.C.: Congressional Quarterly Press.

Gray, Virginia, and David Lowrey. 1996. *The Population Ecology of Interest Representation.* Ann Arbor: University of Michigan Press.

Green, James R. 1978. *Grass Roots Socialism: Radical Movements in the Southwest, 1895–1943.* Baton Rouge: Louisiana State University Press.

Grodin, Joseph R. 1988. "Developing a Consensus of Constraint: A Judge's Perspective on Judicial Retention Elections." *Southern California Law Review* 61: 1969.

Grofman, Bernard, and Scott Feld. 1988. "Rousseau's General Will: A Condorcetian Perspective." *American Political Science Review* 82: 567–576.

Hadwiger, David. 1992. "Money, Turnout and Ballot Measure Success in California Cities." *Western Political Quarterly* 45: 539–547.

Hahn, Harlan, and Sheldon Kamieniecki. 1987. *Referendum Voting: Social Status and Policy Preferences.* Westport, Conn.: Greenwood Press.

Hamilton, Alexander, John Jay, and James Madison. 1938. *The Federalist Papers.* Edited by Sherman F. Mittel. Washington, D.C.: National Home Library Foundation.

Hamilton, Edward. 1982. "California's Sloppy Ballot Measures." *Los Angeles Times*, August 11.

Hart, Gary, and William Shore. 1979. "Corporate Spending on State and Local Referendums: *First National Bank of Boston v. Bellotti.*" *Case Western Reserve Law Review* 29: 808–829.

Heard, Alexander. 1960. *The Costs of Democracy.* Chapel Hill: University of North Carolina Press.

Hicks, John D. 1931. *The Populist Revolt.* Minneapolis: University of Minnesota Press.

Hofstadter, Richard. 1955. *The Age of Reform.* New York: Random House.

Hofstetter, C. Richard, Cliff Zukin, and Terry Buss. 1978. "Political Imagery and Information in an Age of Television." *Journalism Quarterly* 55: 562–569.

Holbrook, Thomas. 1996. *Do Campaigns Matter?* Thousand Oaks, Calif.: Sage.

Holman, Craig, and Robert Stern. 1998. "Judicial Review of Ballot Initiatives: The Changing Role of State and Federal Courts." *Loyola of Los Angeles Law Review* 31: 1239–1266.

Hubbard, Burt. 1998. "Ballot Measure Funds Set Record." *Rocky Mountain News*, December 4.

Hudson, William. 1995. *American Democracy in Peril: Seven Challenges to America's Future.* Chatham, N.J.: Chatham House.

Initiative and Referendum Institute. 1998. "Revised Overview of Statewide Initiatives, Popular Referendum and Legislative Referendum on the 1998 Election Ballot" <iandrinstute.org/updates/ud!5htm>.

———. 1999. "1999 Initiative and Referendum Legislative" <http://www/iandrinstitute.org/legislation/default.htm>.

Jamieson, Kathleen Hall. 1992. *Dirty Politics: Deception, Distraction, and Democracy.* New York: Oxford University Press.

Ji, Chang-Ho. 1999. "California's Direct Democracy 1976–1998: Predictors, Outcomes, and Issues." Paper presented at the Western Political Science Association meeting, Seattle.

Johnson, Claudius. 1944. "The Adoption of the Initiative and Referendum in Washington." *Pacific Northwest Quarterly* 35: 291–304.

Johnston, Richard, and Arthur Lupia. 1999. "Are Voters to Blame: Voter Competence, Elite Manipulation, and the Unseen Dynamics of Public Referendums." Working paper, University of California, San Diego.

Jones, Bill. 1998a. *Financing California's Statewide Ballot Measures: 1996 Primary and General Elections.* Sacramento, Calif.: Office of the Secretary of State.

———. 1998b. *A History of the California Initiative Process.* Sacramento, Calif.: Office of the Secretary of State.

Joslyn, Richard. 1987. "Liberal Campaign Rhetoric in 1984." In *Campaigns in the News*, edited by Jans Pons Vermeer. New York: Greenwood.

———. 1980. "The Content of Political Spot Ads." *Journalism Quarterly* 57: 90.

Kahnemann, David, and Amos Tversky. 1984. "Choices, Values, and Frames." *American Psychologist* 39: 341–350.

Kanouse, David, and L. Hanson. 1986. "Negativity in Evaluations." In *Attribution: Perceiving the Causes of Behavior*, edited by Edward Jones et al. Hillsdale, N.J.: Erlbaum.

Kazin, Michael. 1995. *The Populist Persuasion: An American History*. New York: Basic.

Kehler, David, and Robert M. Stern. 1995. "Initiatives in the 1980s and 1990s." *The Book of States: 1994–95*, 279–308. Lexington, Ky.: Council of State Governments.

Kelley, Stanley. 1956. *Professional Public Relations and Political Power*. Baltimore: Johns Hopkins University Press.

Key, V. O. 1936. "Publicity of Campaign Expenditures on Issues in California." *American Political Science Review* 4: 713–723.

———. 1966. *The Responsible Electorate*. Cambridge, Mass.: Harvard University Press.

Key, V. O., Jr., and Winston Crouch. 1939. *The Initiative and Referendum in California*. Berkeley: University of California Press.

Kiewiet, D. Roderick. 1999. "Proposition 13, Serrano, and Public School Finance in California." Paper presented at the American Political Science Association meeting, Atlanta.

Kimball, Kelly. 1997. "Initiative Wars: An Assessment of Direct Democracy in California." Audio recording of a workshop and panel discussion. Center for Social and Behavioral Science Research, University of California, Riverside.

Lagasse, David R. 1995. "Undue Influence: Corporate Political Speech, Power and the Initiative Process." *Brooklyn Law Review* 61: 1347–1397.

Lascher, Edward L., Michael G. Hagen, and Steven A. Rochlin. 1996. "Gun Behind the Door: Ballot Initiatives, State Policies, and Public Opinion." *Journal of Politics* 58: 332–349.

Lau, Richard. 1985. "Two Explanations for Negativity Effects in Political Behavior." *American Journal of Political Science* 29: 119–138.

Lawrence, David. 1995. *California: The Politics of Diversity*. Minneapolis: West.

Lee, Eugene. 1978. "California." In *Referendums: A Comparative Study of Practice and Theory*, edited by David Butler and Austin Ranney. Washington, D.C.: American Enterprise Institute for Public Policy Research.

Linde, Hans. 1993. "When Initiative Lawmaking Is Not Representative Government: The Campaign against Homosexuality." *Oregon Law Review* 72: 20.

———. 1994. "On Reconstructing 'Republican Government.'" *Oklahoma City University Law Review* 19: 193.

Locke, Laura. 1993. "Choice in Schools." *California Journal* 24(6): 13–15.

Lodge, Milton, Kathleen McGraw, and Patrick Stroh. 1989. "An Impression-Driven Model of Candidate Evaluation." *American Political Science Review* 87: 399–419.

Lodge, Milton, Marco Steenbergen, and Shawn Brau. 1995. "The Responsive Voter: Campaign Information and the Dynamics of Candidate Evaluation." *American Political Science Review* 89 (June): 309–325.

Los Angeles Times. 1998. "In Horowitz They No Longer Trust." October 31.

Lowenstein, Daniel H., 1982. "Campaign Spending and Ballot Propositions: Recent Experience, Public Choice Theory, and the First Amendment." *UCLA Law Review* 29 (March): 505–641.

———. 1992. "A Patternless Mosaic: Campaign Finance and the First Amendment after Austin." *Capital University Law Review* 21: 381–427.

Lowenstein, Daniel H., and R. Stern. 1989. "The First Amendment and Paid Initiative Petition Circulators: A Dissenting View and a Proposal." *Hastings Constitutional Law Quarterly* 17: 175–224.

Lowery, David, and Virginia Gray. 1993. "The Density of State Interest Group Systems." *Journal of Politics* 55: 191.

Lowi, Theodore. 1979. *The End of Liberalism*. 2d ed. New York: Norton.

Luntz, Frank. 1988. *Candidates, Consultants, and Campaigns: The Style and Substance of American Electioneering*. New York: Basil Blackwell.

Lupia, Arthur. 1992. "Busy Voters, Agenda Control, and the Power of Information." *American Political Science Review* 86: 390–403.

———. 1994. "Shortcuts versus Encyclopedias: Information and Voting Behavior in California Insurance Reform Elections." *American Political Science Review* 88: 63–76.

———. 1997. " 'Who Can Persuade Whom?' How Simple Cues Affect Political Attitudes." Working paper, University of California, San Diego.

Lupia, Arthur, and Mathew McCubbins. 1998. *The Democratic Dilemma: Can Citizens Learn What They Need to Know?* New York: Cambridge University Press.

Lyndenberg, Steven D. 1981. *Bankrolling Ballots, Update 1980: The Role of Business in Financing Ballot Question Campaigns*. New York: Council on Economic Priorities.

Madison, James. 1973. *The Mind of the Founder: Sources of the Political Thought of James Madison*. Edited by Marvin Meyers. Indianapolis: Bobbs-Merrill.

Magleby, David. 1984. *Direct Legislation: Voting on Ballot Propositions in the United States*. Baltimore: Johns Hopkins University Press.

———. 1989. "Opinion Formation and Opinion Change in Ballot Proposition Campaigns." In *Manipulating Public Opinion*, edited by Michael Margolis and Gary A. Mauser. Pacific Grove, Calif.: Brooks/Cole.

———. 1994. "Direct Legislation in the American States." In *Referendums around the World: The Growing Use of Direct Democracy*, edited by David Butler and Austin Ranney. Washington, D.C.: American Enterprise Institute for Public Policy Research.

Magleby, David B., and Kelly D. Patterson. 1998. "Consultants and Direct Democracy." *PS: Political Science and Politics* 31: 160–169.

———. 2000. "Campaign Consultants and Direct Democracy: The Politics of Citizen Control." In *Campaign Warriors: Political Consultants in Elections*, edited by James Thurber and Candice Nelson. Washington, D.C.: Brookings.

Mapes, Jeff. 1994. "One Stop Petition Sign-up Shop Provides Gauge of Public Mood." *The Oregonian*, June 19, p. G4.

———. 1999. "Initiative Reform Plan Nears Ballot." *The Oregonian*, July 2.

Marcus, George E., W. Russell Neuman, and Michael MacKuen. 2000. *Affective Intelligence and Political Judgment*. Chicago: University of Chicago Press.

Marcus, Gregory B. 1988. "The Impact of Personal and National Economic Conditions on the Presidential Vote: A Pooled Cross-Sectional Analysis." *American Journal of Political Science* 34: 373–399.

Margolis, Michael, and Gary A. Mauser, eds. 1989. *Manipulating Public Opinion: Essays on Public Opinion as a Dependent Variable*. Pacific Grove, Calif.: Brooks/Cole.

Martin, William L. 1997. "Florida's Citizen Constitutional Ballot Initiatives." *Florida State University Law Review* 25: 57.

Massachusetts Secretary of State. 1998. "Massachusetts Secretary of State Elections Web Page" <http://www.state.ma.us/sec/ele>.

Matsusaka, John G. 1995. "Fiscal Effects of the Voter Initiative: Evidence from the Last 30 Years." *Journal of Political Economy* 103: 587–623.

McCuan, David, Shaun Bowler, Todd Donovan, and Ken Fernandez. 1998. "California's Political Warriors: Campaign Professionals and the Initiative Process." In *Citizens as Legislators: Direct Democracy in the United States*, edited by S. Bowler, T. Donovan, and C. Tolbert. Columbus: Ohio State University Press.

McGinnis, Joe. 1969. *The Selling of the President*. New York: Simon and Schuster.

McGuigan, Patrick B. 1985. *The Politics of Direct Democracy in the 1980s: Case Studies in Popular Decision Making*. Washington, D.C.: Free Congress Research and Education Foundation.

McKenna, George, ed. 1974. *American Populism*. New York: G. P. Putnam's Sons.

McWilliams, Carey. 1951. "Government by Whitaker and Baxter." *The Nation*, April 14, April 21, and May 5.

Medvic, Stephen K. 1998. "The Effectiveness of Political Consultants as a Campaign Resource." *PS: Political Science and Politics* 31: 150–153.

Meier, Kenneth, and David Morgan. 1980. "Politics and Morality: The Effect of Religion on Referenda Voting." *Social Science Quarterly* 61: 144–148.

Merritt, Sharyne. 1984. "Negative Political Advertising: Some Empirical Findings." *Journal of Advertising* 13: 27–38.

Michael, Douglas C. 1983. "Preelection Judicial Review: Taking the Initiative in Voter Protection." *California Law Review* 71: 1216.

Miller, Kenneth P. 1999. "The Role of Courts in the Initiative Process." Paper presented at the American Political Science Association meeting, Atlanta.

Miller, Warren, and J. Merrill Shanks. 1996. *The New American Voter*. Cambridge, Mass.: Harvard University Press.

Moore, David W. 1992: *The Superpollsters: How They Measure and Manipulate Public Opinion in America*. New York: Four Walls Eight Windows Press.

Morain, Dan. 1999a. "Governor Race Set Spending Record." *Los Angeles Times*, February 4.

———. 1999b. "Handful of Tribes Broke Initiative Spending Record." *Los Angeles Times*, February 6.

———. 1999c. "Wealth Buys Access to State Politics." *Los Angeles Times*, April 18.

Moser, Peter. 1996. "Why Is Swiss Politics So Stable?" *Zeitschrift für Volkswirtschaft und Statistik* 132: 31–60.

Mueller, John, and James Parrinello. 1981. "The Constitutionality of Limits on Ballot Measures Contributions." *North Dakota Law Review* 57: 391–426.

Mulligan, Kenneth. 1997. "The Effects of Campaign Spending on Voting in Ballot Initiative Elections." Master's thesis, George Washington University.

National Journal. 1999. Cloakroom website video archive. <www.nationaljournal.com/pubs/hotline>.

Neiman, Max, and M. Gottdiener. 1985. "Qualifying Initiatives: A Heuristic use of Data to Command an Unexplored Stage of Direct Democracy." *Social Science Journal* 22: 100–109.

Nie, Norman, Sidney Verba, and John Petrocik. 1976. *The Changing American Voter*. Cambridge, Mass.: Harvard University Press.

Oberholtzer, Ellis Paxson. 1900. *The Referendum in America*. New York: Charles Scribner's Sons.

Olson, David. J. 1992. "Term Limits Fail in Washington: The 1991 Battleground." In *Limiting Legislative Terms*, edited by G. Benjamin and M. Malbin. Washington, D.C.: Congressional Quarterly Press.

Olson, Mancur. 1965. *The Logic of Collective Action: Public Goods and the Theory of Groups*. Cambridge, Mass.: Harvard University Press.

Owens, John R., and Larry L. Wade. 1986. "Campaign Spending on California Ballot Propositions, 1924–1984: Trends and Voting Effects." *Western Political Quarterly* 39: 675–689.

Peterson, L. 1986. "Call These Political Persuaders: The Wizards of Cause." *Golden State Report* (July): 16–23.

Peterson, Merril D., ed. 1984. *Thomas Jefferson: Writings*. New York: Literary Classics of the United States. Philadelphia: Temple University Press.

Polashuk, Robyn R. 1993. "Protecting the Public Debate: The Validity of the Fairness Doctrine in Ballot Initiative Elections." *UCLA Law Review* 41: 391–442.

Polsby, Nelson. 1983. *The Consequences of Party Reform*. New York: Oxford University Press.

Popkin, Samuel. 1981. *The Reasoning Voter*. Chicago: University of Chicago Press.

———. 1991. *The Reasoning Voter: Communication and Persuasion in Presidential Campaigns*. Chicago: Chicago University Press.

———. 1997. "Who Can Persuade Whom? How Simple Cues Affect Political Attitudes." Working paper, University of California, San Diego.

Price, Charles M. 1975. "The Initiative: A Comparative State Analysis and Reassessment of a Western Phenomenon." *Western Political Quarterly* 28: 243–262.

———. 1988. "Big Money Initiatives." *California Journal* 19(Nov): 481–486.

———. 1992. "Signing for Fun and Profit." *California Journal* 23 (August): 545–548.

Pritchell, R. 1959. "The Influence of Professional Campaign Management Firms in Partisan Elections in California." *Western Political Quarterly* 8: 278–300.

Public Affairs Research Institute of New Jersey. 1992. *Analysis: Initiative and Referendum 1–4* (January–July). Public Affairs Research Institute of New Jersey.

———. 1996. "Citizen Initiative Ballot Question Survey, 1994–1995" (unpublished).

Quattrone, George, and Amos Tversky. 1988. "Contrasting Rational and Psychological Analyses of Political Choice." *American Political Science Review* 82: 719–739.

Ranney, Austin, ed. 1981. *The Referendum Device*. Washington, D.C.: American Enterprise Institute for Public Policy Research.

Rapaport, R. 1989. "In the Beginning . . . A History of California Political Consulting." *California Journal* 20 (July): 418–424.

Rausch, David. 1996. "The Politics of Term Limits." In Alan Tarr, *Constitutional Politics in the States*. Westport, CT: Greenwood Press.

Redlinger, Paul. 1987. "The Politics of Judging." *American Bar Association Journal* 52 (April).

Remer, Larry. 1997. Interview by Todd Donovan.

Richter, Paul. 1984. *California and the American Tax Revolt: Proposition 13 Five Years Later*. Berkeley: University of California Press.

Romer, Thomas, and Howard Rosenthal. 1978. "Political Resource Allocation, Controlled Agendas, and the Status Quo." *Public Choice* 33: 27–44.

Rosenberg, Gerald R. 1991. *The Hollow Hope: Can Courts Bring about Social Change?* Chicago: University of Chicago Press.

Rosenstone, Steve, and John Mark Hansen. 1993. *Mobilization, Participation and Democracy in America*. New York: MacMillan.

Rosenthal, Alan. 1998. *The Decline of Representative Democracy*. Washington, D.C.: Congressional Quarterly.

Sabato, Larry. 1981. *The Rise of Political Consultants: New Ways of Winning Elections*. New York: Basic.

———. 1984. *PAC Power: Inside the World of Political Action Committees*. New York: Norton.

Samish, A., and B. Thomas. 1971. *The Secret Boss of California*. New York: Crown.

Schmidt, David. 1989. *Citizen Lawmakers: The Ballot Initiative Revolution*. Philadelphia: Temple University Press.

Schrag, Peter. 1994. "California's Elected Anarchy: A Government Destroyed by Popular Referendum." *Harper's* (November): 50–59.

———. 1998. *Paradise Lost: California's Experience, America's Future*. New York: New Press.

Schultz, Jim. 1996. *The Initiative Cookbook: Recipes and Stories from California's Ballot Wars*. San Francisco: Democracy Center.

Schumacher, Waldo. 1932. "Thirty Years of the People's Rule in Oregon." *Political Science Quarterly* 46: 242–259.

Scott, Steve. 1996. "Initiative Wars." *California Journal* 27 (July): 12–19.

Sears, David O., and Jack Citrin. 1982. *Tax Revolt: Something for Nothing in California*. Cambridge, Mass.: Harvard University Press.

Shea, Daniel. 1996. *Campaign Craft: The Strategies, Tactics and Art of Campaign Management*. Westport, Conn.: Praeger.

Shepard, Tom. 1997. Interview by Todd Donovan.

Shepsle, Kenneth A., and Barry R. Weingast. 1987. "The Institutional Foundations of Committee Power." *American Political Science Review* 81: 85–104.

Shockley, John S. 1978. Testimony before the U.S. House of Representatives. In *IRS Administration of Tax Laws Related to Lobbying: Hearings before a Subcommittee of the Committee on Government Operations*, 95th Cong., 2d sess., May and July.

———. 1980. "The Initiative Process in Colorado Politics : An Assessment." Boulder: Bureau of Governmental Research and Service, University of Colorado.

———. 1985. "Direct Democracy, Campaign Finance, and the Courts: Can Corruption, Undue Influence, and Declining Voter Confidence Be Found?" *University of Miami Law Review* 39 (May): 377–428.

Simon, Jim. 1994. "Initiatives against Gay Rights Fail." *Seattle Times*, July 9, p. A1.

Smith, Bradley. 1995. "Faulty Assumptions and Undemocratic Consequences of Campaign Finance Reform." *Yale Law Journal* 105 (4): 1049–1091.

Smith, Daniel A. 1998. *Tax Crusaders and the Politics of Direct Democracy*. New York: Routledge.

————. 1999. "Reevaluating the Causes of Proposition 13." *Social Science History* 23 (summer): 2.

Smith, Richard A. 1995. "Interest Group Influence in the U.S. Congress." *Legislative Studies Quarterly* 20: 89–140.

Sniderman, Paul, Richard A. Brody, and Philip E. Tetlock, with Henry E. Brady. 1991. *Reasoning and Choice: Explorations in Political Psychology.* New York: Cambridge University Press.

Sniderman, Paul, Edward Carmines, Geoffrey Laymna, and Michael Carter. 1996. "Beyond Race: Social Justice as a Race Neutral Ideal." *American Journal of Political Science* 40 (February): 33–55.

Sorauf, Frank J. 1992. *Inside Campaign Finance.* New Haven: Yale University Press.

Spero, David. 1997. Interview by Todd Donovan.

Spero, Robert. 1980. *The Duping of the American Voter.* New York: Lippincot and Crowell. *State University Law Review* 25: 57.

Sullivan, J. W. 1893. *Legislation by the Citizens through Initiative and Referendum.* New York: True Nationalist.

Sweeney, John P. 1998. "Death of Gaming Deal Gave Life to Initiative." *San Diego Union Tribune,* November 1, p. A-1.

Thach, Charles, Jr. 1923. *The Creation of the Presidency, 1775–1789.* New York: Da Capo.

Thayer, George. 1973. *Who Shakes the Money Tree?* New York: Simon and Schuster.

Thomas, Clive S., and Ronald J. Hrebenar. 1996. "Interest Groups in the States." In *Politics in the American States: A Comparative Analysis,* edited by Virginia Gray and Herbert Jacob. 6th ed. Boston: Little, Brown.

Thomas, Tom. 1991. "Campaign Spending and Corporate Involvement in the California Initiative Process, 1976–1988." In *Research in Corporate Social Performance and Policy,* vol. 12, edited by James E. Post, 37–61. Greenwich, Conn.: JAI Press.

Thurber, James, and Candice Nelson. 1995. *Campaigns and Elections: American Style.* Boulder: Westview.

Tobin, Mitchell. 1997. *Campaign Spending and California Ballot Measures, 1924–1994.* Master's thesis, Department of Political Science, University of California, Berkeley.

Tolbert, Caroline. 1998. "Changing Rules for State Legislatures: Direct Democracy and Governance Politics." In *Citizens as Legislators: Direct Democracy in the United States,* edited by Bowler, Donovan, and Tolbert. Columbus: Ohio State University Press.

Tolbert, Caroline, Daniel H. Lowenstein, and Todd Donovan. 1998. "Election Law and Rules for Using Initiatives." In *Citizens as Legislators: Direct Democracy in the United States,* edited by S. Bowler, T. Donovan, and C. Tolbert. Columbus: Ohio State University Press.

Tornquist, Leroy J. 1998. "Democracy in Oregon: Some Suggestions for Change." *Wilamette Law Review* 34: 675.

Uelmen, Gerald F. 1997. "The Future of State Supreme Courts as Institutions in the Law. Crocodiles in the Bathtub: Maintaining the Independence of State Supreme Courts in an Era of Judicial Politicization." *Notre Dame Law Review* 72: 1133.

U.S. Senate Committee on the Judiciary. 1977. *Hearings before the Subcommittee on the Constitution*, 95th Cong., 1st sess., 13–14 December.

Warner, Daniel M. 1995. "Direct Democracy: The Right of the People to Make Fools of Themselves." *Seattle University Law Review* 19: 47–100.

Washington Secretary of State. 1998. "Washington Secretary of State Initiative Elections Web Page" <http://www.secstate.wa.gov/inits/text/i688.htm>.

Washington State Public Disclosure Commission. 1999a. "Statewide Initiative Spending Totals" <http://washington.edu/pdc>.

———. 1999b. "1998 Ballot Measures—Contribution and Expenditure Totals." Available at <pdc.wa.gov/>.

Weber, Tracy. 1996. "Making Politics Pay: Cashing in on Causes." *Los Angeles Times*, March 3.

West, Darrell M. 1996. *Air Wars: Television Advertising in Election Campaigns, 1952–1996*. Washington, D.C.: Congressional Quarterly Press.

Wicks, Robert H., and Dan Drew. 1991. "Learning from News: Effects of Message Consistency and Medium on Recall and Inference Making." *Journalism Quarterly* 68: 1155–1164.

Wilcox, Delos. 1912. *Government by All the People; or, the Initiative, the Referendum, and the Recall as Instruments of Democracy*. New York: Macmillan.

Williams, Liv. 1994. "The June Ballot Propositions." *California Journal* 35: 43–47.

Winkler, Adam. 1998. "Beyond Bellotti." *Loyola of Los Angeles Law Review* 32: 133–220.

Wolfinger, Raymond. 1978. "Discussion." In *The Referendum Device*, edited by Austin Ranney. Washington, D.C.: American Enterprise Institute for Public Policy Research.

Wright, James E. 1974. *The Politics of Populism: Dissent in Colorado*. New Haven: Yale University Press.

Zaller, John R. 1992. *The Nature and Origins of Mass Opinion*. Cambridge: Cambridge University Press.

Zimmerman, Bill. 1997. Interview by Todd Donovan.

Zisk, Betty H. 1987. *Money, Media, and the Grassroots: State Ballot Issues and the Electoral Process*. Newbury Park, Calif.: Sage.

Index

AARP. *See* American Association of Retired Persons

access, buying, 155

accountability, 33, 45–46, 53, 56; of consultants, 47; of government, 176; of mediators, 70; of voters, 66

Advanced Voter Communications (AVC), 104, 115, 116

Advantage Consulting, 118

advertisements and advertising: broadcast, 114; as information source, 81; misleading, xiii, 82; sponsors of, 159. *See also* media coverage; misrepresentations

advocacy organizations, 34

affirmative action, 55, 57, 80. *See also* issues

Alaska, 15

Allen, Paul, 27

amendment/refinement of initiatives, 27, 33, 38, 41–42; lack of opportunity for, 44, 56; by legislature, 61, 151, 155–56, 163–64, 172; postelection, 164–65; preelection review for, 163, 165, 169, 174; reforms regarding, 60, 163

American Association of Retired Persons (AARP), 110, 113

American Petition Consultants, 115, 121

antidiscrimination measures, 22–23

Arizona, 79, 128

Arkansas, 17, 18

Arno, Mike, 115

Arnold, Rick, 115, 117, 119

Atkinson, Katy, 79

attorneys, 102; as initiative drafters, 135–36; political law specialists, 106, 108–9, 110–11. *See also* drafting

Austin v. Michigan Chamber of Commerce, 87, 88, 198n14

AVC. *See* Advanced Voter Communications

Bagatelos and Faten, 109

ballot access, 117, 134

ballot handbooks. *See* voter guides

ballot initiative campaigns. *See* campaigns

ballot initiative drafting. *See* drafting

ballot initiative power, 15; restriction of, 173; revocation of, 5, 16

ballot initiative process. *See* initiative process

ballot initiative proposals. *See* initiative proposals

ballot initiative types, 8–10, 41, 195n1; in early period, 13–15; in middle period, 17–20; in recent period, 22–25; variation in, 23, 24; "yes" and "no" sides, 8, 14, 20. *See also* issues

ballot initiative usage, 5–6, 8; frequency (early period), 10–13; frequency (middle period), 15–17;

frequency (recent period), 20–22; growth in, 20–21; high-use states, 52; reasons for, 79; spending levels and, 78–81

ballot initiatives, ix–x; antiminority, 167, 168, 172; as checks on government, 61, 97; citizen measures, 178; complexity of, 147, 157, 160; compromise bills, 164; history of, 64–65; legislative alternatives to, 170; national, 5; number limitations, xiv, 192; number of on ballot, 79, 123, 157, 171, 189; partisan objectives in, 50; policy areas affected, x, 6–7; purposes of, 72; similar issues in, 189; subject matter of, 85; testing, 108; unconstitutional, 42, 50. *See also* amendment/refinement of initiatives; consequences; constitutional initiatives; courts; drafting; initiative proposals; issues; minorities; qualification for ballot; statutory initiatives; success rates

ballot pamphlets. *See* voter guides

ballots, improving, 189

Banducci, Susan, 122

Baxter, Leone, 75

Beard, Charles, 74

Bellotti. See First National Bank v. Bellotti

Benjamin, Gerald, 158

bias, 40; creation by initiative, 42; in legislature, 50; for moneyed interests, 183; in public policy, 48

Biddulph, David, 80

Bird, Rose, 56, 58

Black, Hugo, 54

Bockwinkel, Shirley, 116

Bockwinkle, Sherry, 80

Bourne, Jonathan, 180

Bowler, Shaun, xii, xiii, 8, 52, 138; on initiative spending, 81; on minority interests, 167; on special interests, 174; on voter information, 154, 160

Braunstein, Richard, 84

Broder, David, 116

Broussard, Justice, 56

Brown, Willie, 96, 113

Bryan, William Jennings, 35, 172

Buckley v. American Constitutional Law Foundation, 182

Buckley v. Valeo, 86, 87, 146, 149, 177, 182, 184, 198n4

budget balancing, 28

Burkett, Rosemary, 58

Butcher, William, 80, 115, 116

Butler, David, 41

Cain, Bruce, xi, xii, 64, 66, 70

California, 52; campaign contribution records, 74; campaign spending in, 75, 76, 77, 82, 129; effect of initiative process, 176; elective offices, 40; initiative industrial complex in, 101; initiative issues, 95; initiative qualification in, 105; initiative usage, 10; judge removal, 58; number of initiatives, 79; Proposition 5, 77; Proposition 8, 56, 58; Proposition 9, 77; Proposition 10, 77; Proposition 13, x, 42, 80, 106–7, 137, 176; Proposition 22, 177; Proposition 25, 136; Proposition 37, 80, 127–28; Proposition 98, 176; Proposition 99, 176; Proposition 105, 150; Proposition 140, 50, 96, 106; Proposition 174, 121; Proposition 187, 177; Proposition 209, 55, 57, 59, 177; Proposition 226, 137, 140, 141; Proposition 227, 136; racial demographics, 51; voter guide, 111, 188

California Planning and Conservation League (PCL), 109, 132

California Political Attorneys Association, 102

California State Employees Association, 113

California Taxpayers Association, 110

California Teachers Association, 113

campaign committees, 186

campaign contributions: effect on success, 84; limitations on, 146, 150, 170; sources of, 145, 150. *See also* campaign spending campaign finance laws, xii, 86–88, 91, 146; for candidate elections, 156; campaign finance reform, x, xiv, 7, 98, 169–70. *See also* campaign spending

campaign professionals, xii–xiii, 75, 101. *See also* consultants

campaigns, xi, 132, 158; competing initiatives in, 109, 161, 170; consultants' role in, 139–41; financing of, 71–72; lying in, 131–33; narrow-material, 8 regulation of, 108–9; revenue from, xii, 128–29; sequence of, 105–23. *See also* campaign professionals; campaign spending; consultants; misrepresentations

campaign spending, 88–89, 128–29; aggregate figures, 83; big money in, 94–95; broadcast ads, 114; in candidate elections, 97, 145; critiques of, 144–56, 171; floor for, 133; for grassroots efforts, 137–38; information and, 161; initiative usage and, 78–81; as intensity measure, 161; by interest groups, xii, 73–79 lopsided, 1–2; need for, 101; negative, 82, 83; petition costs, 117–19; purposes of, 95; records and research regarding, 73–78; regulation/limitation of, 86–88, 93–94, 98, 146, 182–83, 192; review standards regarding, xii; timing of, 83; variation among states, 85. *See also* narrow-material interests; reform; subsidies; success rates

candidate elections, 124, 125, 139; campaign spending, 97, 145; contribution limits, 156; interest groups in, 130

Candidate Strategies, 102

Carlson, John, 28

celebrities, 113. *See also* endorsements

checks and balances, 49, 64, 91; bypassing, 42, 43, 53

circulators. *See* petition circulation

citizen initiatives. *See* ballot initiatives

citizen lawmaking. *See* ballot initiatives; initiative politics

Citizens against Rent Control v. City of Berkeley, 87, 146, 182

City Club of Denver, 74–75

city managers, 37

civil rights laws, 52, 57

civil service, 37

coalitions, 37, 109–10; single-campaign groups, 113–14

Colorado, 52; 1912 ballot, 13, 14; Amendment 2, 55; campaign contribution records, 73, 74–75; initiative spending in, 78; initiative usage, 10, 79; judicial invalidation of initiatives, 196n3(ch. 2); lottery in, 128; mandatory deposit initiative, 82; petition circulation laws, 116

Common Cause, 36, 110, 113, 132; paid circulator use, 152

competence, 33, 46–47, 53; of legislators, 55–56. *See also* voter competence

complexity, 67

compromise, 43, 56

conflicts of interest, 46, 60

consensus building, 33, 43, 44, 56

consequences, 28–29, 163, 168–69; cumulative, 176; indirect, 169; for minority rights, 167; recognition of, 157, 165; unintended, 162, 178

constitutional amendments, ix, 2, 41–42

constitutional initiatives, 2, 3, 11, 41, 61

constitutions, approval of, 2

constitutions, state, 39–40

consultants, 31, 47, 133–34, 135–38; areas of expertise, 101–2, 103; attorneys as, 102; availability of, 128; for candidate elections, 124, 125; clients, 105, 130; demand for services, 126, 134; employees, 119; ideology of, 116, 123, 124–26; initiative drafting by, 106; as manipulators, 139; as mercenaries, 123–26, 134; misrepresentations and lies by, 131, 132, 134; money earned by, 80, 101, 116, 120, 125–27; motives, 101; as proposal

initiators, 126–28; role of, 139–41, 148; services provided, 104–7, 115–20, 151; subcontractors, 119; survey of, 102–4; time of hiring, 106, 129; types of, 102, 103; use of, 80, 105
corporations, campaign contributions/ expenditures by, 87, 146
corruption, 36, 37; eliminating, 71; of legislators, 98, 99, 146, 198n15; by money, 87, 89, 94–95; potential for in initiative process, 97–98, 146–47; quid pro quo, 86, 87, 88
countercampaigns, 121–22, 131
counterinitiatives, 122–23
courts, 34; backlash against, 34, 57–59, 60; constitutional rights protection by, xiii; countermajoritarian difficulty with, 53–54, 58; deference to initiatives, 54–55; federal, 107, 197n20; independence of, 59; as institutional check, xii, 34, 39, 53–59, 60; invalidation ability, 196n3(ch. 2) invalidation of initiatives, 34, 52, 54, 107, 136, 164, 197n20; review role, 178; sentencing flexibility, 28. *See also* judicial review
Cranston, Alan, 64
Cronin, Thomas, 51, 85, 180
Crouch, Winston, 74, 76

decision making, collective, 68
deliberation, informed, 33, 37, 159–60; opportunities for, 43, 56, 184, 185
democracy, direct, ix, 65–66, 134; adoption of, xi, 25; failure of, 33, 48; importance of, 172; limitations on, 31–32, 92; mechanisms of, 36, 181; motives for supporting, 37–38; movement toward, 180; Populist view of, xii, 33, 35, 37, 38, 62; professionalization of, 133; Progressive view of, xii, 33, 37–38, 48, 59; as reflection of public will, 26, 185; right to, 2; voter confidence in, 176
democracy, representative, ix, 29, 62, 92; advantages of, 43; checks and balances in, 42; interest-group con-

trol of, 180–81; minority rights protection by, 165, 168; problems in, 97; reform of, 36; relationship to direct democracy, 175, 179–80; supremacy of, 65; undermining, 43, 53, 59, 199n1(ch. 5)
democratic norms, 43, 45, 55–56
disclosures, 174–75; access to, 161, 186; conflicts of interest, 60 finances/ contributions, xiv, 74, 150, 191; reform and, xiv, 158–59, 177, 186; proponents/opponents, 84, 160, 191; voter competence and, 70, 161
District of Columbia, 5
Donovan, Todd, xii, xiii, 8, 52, 137, 138; on ballot handbooks, 136 on initiative spending, 81; on minority interests, 167; on special interests, 174; on voter information, 154, 160
drafting, 44, 102, 105–7, 109, 135–36; bad, 107, 144, 161–65; as campaign stage, 148; by interest groups, x, 80; legislature's participation in, 169; minority participation in, 166; state assistance in, 162–63, 175; voter comprehension and, 144, 157–59, 192; writers' qualification for, 137, 162
Draper, Tim, 136

elections: reform of, 37–38; timing of, 114–15
electoral factors, 1
elitism, 36, 38
endorsements, 111–14, 141, 154, 160
Ernst, Howard, xi, 96, 174, 185, 190
Eule, Julian, 55
Europe, 41
expertise, 37, 46–47. *See also* consultants

fairness, 33, 47–48, 53, 56
Fairness Act, 184
Faucheux, Ron, 139
Federal Election Commission v. Massachusetts Citizens for Life, 87, 88, 182
feedback, 70

Feld, Scott, 68
Fenn & King Communications, 102
Fiorina, Morris, 159
First Amendment, xiii, 91; application
 to initiative process, 91, 92–93; campaign contribution/expenditure
 limits and, 86–88, 98, 146, 182; free
 speech rights, 92, 149, 182–83
First National Bank v. Bellotti, 86, 87, 88,
 98, 146, 183
Florida, 5, 15; ballot initiatives, 30–31;
 disclosure process, 186; initiative review, 178; judge removal, 58; number of initiatives, 79
focus groups, 107, 135, 136
Forde, Arnold, 80, 115, 116
fraud, 37–38
Frey, Bruno, 167
fund raising, 111, 116

Gais, Thomas, 158
Gamble, Barbara, 52, 167
gambling and gaming, 13, 17, 30, 77, 80,
 128, 177
Garrett, Elizabeth, 73, 152
Generalized Condorcet Jury Theorem,
 68–69, 70
Gerber, Elisabeth, xiii, 48, 84, 175; on
 funding sources, 96; on minority interests, 167, 168; on money's influence, 153, 155, 174; on spending limits, 182; on subsidies, 187; on voter
 information, 161
Goddard Clausen/1st Tuesday, 102,
 105
Goette, Lorenz, 167
governance, popular, 2–5
government: desires for, 190; "First
 Principles" of, 64–65; mistrust of,
 37, 62, 181; money's role in, 71; professionalism in, 38; public's control
 over, 13, 35, 46, 49–50; reform of, 34,
 36, 48–49; role of, 13, 35. *See also* legislatures
government institutions, 36
Grant, Paul, 90
Gravel, Mike, 62

Grodin, Joseph, 54, 58, 59
Grofman, Bernard, 68
group names, 113–14

hearings, 169, 174, 187–89, 192. *See also*
 disclosures; voter information
 sources
Hein, John, 88
Henderson, Thomas, 56, 59
Holman, Craig, 107, 151, 167, 178
homosexual rights, 52, 55, 121–22, 167
Horowitz, David, 114
Hug, Simon, 167, 168

ideology, role in campaigns, xiii. *See
 also* consultants
Illinois, 5, 15, 49
immigration, 108
incumbents, 97, 98
individualism, 35
influence, 153–55, 156
information sources, 111–12. *See also*
 voter information sources
infrastructure, 28
initiative campaigns. *See* campaigns
initiative industrial complex, 101,
 126–31
initiative politics, 10–13; citizen
 involvement in, 27; dangers of, 62;
 importance of, 91; periods of, 8; as
 reflection of public will, 185. *See also*
 ballot initiatives; consultants
initiative process, x–xi; accessibility of,
 185; accountability in, 46; big-
 money influence in, xii, 89; binary
 nature of, 44–45, 67, 139, 162; campaign finance laws in, 86–88; as
 complement to representative democracy, 39–40, 175; complexity of,
 140–41; consensus building in, 44,
 56; constitutional protection of, 92;
 defects in, 56, 126, 169, 171, 173–74;
 democratic norms in, 44–45, 53, 55–
 56, 66; fairness in, 48, 60; importance
 of, 172; as industry, 79–80; money
 entry points, 147–48; money's role
 in, 27, 62–63, 71, 81–86, 88–89, 136,

174; openness in, 45, 60; Populist orientation of, 59–60; regulatory compliance, 102; restriction/regulation of, 61, 91–94, 173; use by special interests, 72–73; voter support of, 135–36, 181. *See also* ballot initiatives; campaigns; campaign spending; democracy, direct; reform; success rates

initiative proposals: backer shopping, 126, 129; coalitions behind, 109–10; cost projections, 110, 136; funding sources, 31, 84, 89; negotiations over, 110; rival, 109, 161, 170; sponsors, x, 126–28, 130, 135–37, 160; support base for, 152–53; viability testing, 108. *See also* qualification for ballot

initiatives, indirect, 163–64, 175

interest groups, 131–32; citizen, 154–55, 163, 200n8; credibility with voters, 132; domination of initiative process by, 90, 126, 145–46; economic, 130, 154–55, 171, 192, 200n8, 200n12; educational groups, 80; enduring, 134; financial resources of, 73; grassroots movements, 130, 145; influence in initiative process, 1, 157, 171; as initiative drafters, x, 80; in legislative politics, 93; manipulation of public by, 26; mass-membership, 145; monopoly agenda power, 163–64; postelection influence, 151; reducing power of, 36–37, 60–61; reliance on, 151–52; resource mobilization by, 145–46, 152; use of initiative process, 72–73, 89; view of ballot initiatives, 79. *See also* campaign spending; issue-advocacy groups; narrow-material interests; success rates

Internet, 149; for disclosures, 150, 159; voter guides on, 188

issue-advocacy groups, 30, 130–31; one-shot, 132, 133

issue elections. *See* initiative process

issues, 6–7, 27; antiminority, 166; awareness of, 188; controversial, 6, 79, 85; in early initiatives, 13–15; legislative involvement in, 169; in midperiod initiatives, 17–18; progressive, 13; in recent initiatives, 22–23, 25, 85, 95, 172

Jacob, Paul, 94
Jarvis, Howard, 80, 107, 116
Jefferson, Thomas, 165–66, 190
Ji, Chang-Ho, 83
Johnson, Hiram, 36
Jones, Bill, 159
judges: coercion by voters, 58–59; initiative watchdogs, 56–57; juris-populists, 54–55; number of, 151, 167; state court, 58, 107, 178, 197n20
judicial activism, 56–57, 167
judicial review, 53–57; minority rights protection by, 166–67; postelection influence on, 151, 155–56; preelection, 166. *See also* courts
judiciary. *See* courts; judges

Kaufman, Gail, 135
Kaus, Otto, 58, 59, 178
Key, V. O., 159
Kimball, Fred, 105
Kimball, Kelly, 80, 101; as petition initiator, 127–28, 130
Kimball Petition Management, Inc., 104, 105, 115
Klein Communications, 116
Kuzins, Matt, 108

labor groups, 113, 137
Lanphier, David, 58
Larson, Bruce, 190
LCA (legislative constitutional amendment), 41
League of Women Voters, 36, 108, 110, 113, 132
legislation, 162; prompting, 154; refinement of, 43–44
legislative constitutional amendment (LCA), 41

legislative initiative. *See* referendum
legislative process, xii
legislatures: amendment/refinement
of initiative legislation, 61, 151, 155–
56, 163–64, 172; bypassing, 41, 42,
61, 62, 164, 180; dominance of, 40;
gridlock in, 42; influence over, 151,
180–81; initiative power restriction
by, 173; responsiveness of, 93, 167,
169; self-interest of, 48–49; signals
to, 154
liquor, 13
litigation: avoiding, 166; and initiative
language, 107; and initiative process
reforms, 175 money's role in, 150–
51, 155; need for, 44–45
lobbying, 78, 130
logrolling, 109
lotteries, state, 128
Louisiana, 49
Lowenstein, Daniel, 82, 96, 153
Lupia, Arthur, 39, 46, 66, 154; on voter
knowledge, 160, 161
lying. *See* misrepresentations

Madison, James, 63, 64, 65, 165
Magleby, David, 51, 76; on campaign
management firms, 101; on campaign spending, 82, 96; on consultants' role, 126, 129–30; on voter
knowledge, 81
majoritarianism, ix, 56, 59, 165, 177;
constraining, 50; diluting, 179; majority preferences, 171–72; subordi-
nation of minorities, 29
Massachusetts, 2; campaign spending,
86, 129; disclosure rules, 186; Proposition 2 1/2, 42; Question 2, 78
Masterton and Wright, 115, 116
Masterton, Ken, 118
McCuan, David, xii, xiii, 8, 138
McHenry, Dean, 74
media coverage, 138, 183, 184; hearings
and debates, 187, 188–89
Meiklejohn, Alexander, 65
Meyer v. Grant, 92, 117, 148, 173, 182
Michigan, 87, 150

Miller, Kenneth, xi, xii, 52, 64; on voter
competence, 66, 70
minorities: promoting interests of,
50–51; protecting rights of, ix, 51–
52, 53, 165, 171–72, 192; racial, 51;
rights of, 34, 50–51; violation of
rights, 55, 144, 165–69, 177
misrepresentations, 131–33: by consultants, 131, 132, 134; deliberate, 160;
exposure of, 161
Mississippi, 5, 20, 49
Missouri, 128
money. *See* campaign contributions;
campaign spending
Montana, 78, 88
moralism, 36
Mosk, Justice, 56

Nader, Ralph, 46, 112
narrow-material interests, 30; control
of legislatures by, 180–81; electoral
disadvantage, xi, 26, 192; influence
in initiative process, 1–2, 26, 27–28;
in initiative coalitions, 109; initiative
usage rates, 19 protection against,
185. *See also* interest groups; success
rates
National Rifle Association, 113
National Voter Outreach, 115, 117
Native American tribes, 77
Nebraska, 58, 59, 78; petition circulation reform, 149
neutrality, 113
Nevada, 79; disclosure requirements,
158; judicial invalidation of initiatives, 196n3(ch. 2)
Nixon v. Shrink Missouri Government, 91
norms. *See* democratic norms
Norquist, Grover, 137, 138
North Dakota, 49

Oklahoma, 141, 150
openness, 33, 45, 53, 56
opinion research, 107–8
opponents: endorsements by, 112;
identifying, 178, 186; legal counsel
needs, 111; non-narrow-material in-

terest groups as, 185; organization of, 137; success rates, 82, 89, 96, 124, 133, 140, 153, 192
Oregon, 2, 52; 1994 ballot, 22–23; initiative usage, 10, 79; lottery in, 128; petition consultants in, 116; special interest activity in, 74; voter guides, 111
O'Scannlain, Diarmuid, 55
Owens, John, 76, 83, 96, 153

pamphlets, official information. *See* voter guides
Paparella, Angelo, 115, 116
Parent Teacher Association (PTA), 113
partisanship, 147
Patterson, Kelly, 126, 129–30
PCL (California Planning and Conservation League), 109, 132
People's Party, 35, 180. *See also* Populism
personnel resources, 154
petition circulation, 75; limitations on, 92; paid, 116–17, 148, 151, 174; professionals in, 75, 92, 104; time for, xiii, 149, 171, 174
petition management, 104; for ballot qualification, 115; subcontractors, 115–20
petition, right to, 91, 92
politics, importance of, 93
polling, 107–8, 140
Popkin, Samuel, 159
popular governance, 2–5
Populism, 33, 34–35, 180
populist paradox, 73, 84
power, concentration of, 35, 40; avoiding, 72; entrenched, 93; through lack of financing restrictions, 73
Price, Charles, 119
prison reform, 22
process, 48
Progressive Campaigns, 115, 116
Progressive Party, 36
Progressivism, 33, 35–36
proponents: endorsements by, 112;

identifying, 160, 178, 186; success rates, 82, 98
PTA, Parent Teacher Association, 113
public: manipulation of, 26; wisdom of, 37–38. *See also* voters
public policy, 30; as discipline, 37; effect of initiatives on, 33–34, 48–53, 72. *See also* issues
public relations firms, 102. *See also* consultants

qualification for ballot, 105, 116, 120–22, 151; benefits of, 152–53; cost of, 117–20, 122, 123, 151–52; hearings before, 166; interest groups' support in, 171; methods of, 149, 156; money's role in, 177. *See also* initiative process

Ranney, Austin, 41
recall measures, 2, 5, 40–41
referendum, ix–x, 2, 4, 41; adoption of, 10, 11, 15. *See also* ballot initiatives; initiative process
reform, xiii, 34, 50, 60–62, 172; 1900–1920, 36; ballot format, 189; campaign financing, x, xiv, 7, 98, 169–70; difficulty of, 175; disclosure requirements, xiv, 158–59, 177, 186; drafting deficiencies, 161–65; effects of, 169–71; elections, 37–38; empirical basis for, 144; excessive spending, 144–56; of government, 34, 36, 48–49; increasing legislative involvement, 172; information flows, 181–82, 187–88, 190; and information levels, 185; initiative amendment/refinement, 60, 163; initiative comprehensibility, 157–59; interactions in, 170; of interest group domination, 144–56; minority rights protection, 165–69; petition circulation time, 149; political, 17; prison, 22; proposals for, 143; qualification for ballot, 149, 156; reducing money's influence, 150; signature collection process, 148–49; social,

36; unnecessary, 175; voter informa-
tion, 156–61
Reform Party, 5
Reiner, Rob, 137
reputation, 131–32
responsiveness, 40, 41; of initiatives, 43;
of legislatures, 93, 167, 169; speed of,
42
reverse discrimination, 57
Reynoso, Cruz, 58
Riley, Clint, 132
Robinson and Co., 104
Rooney, J. Patrick, 137, 138
Roosevelt, Theodore, 35, 36
Rosenthal, Alan, 90

Sabato, Larry, 190
Scalia, Antonin, 55
Schafer, Trudy, 108
Schmidt, David, 72
school choice, 121
Schrag, Peter, 126, 166
Schultz, Jim, 108, 110, 112, 117, 118
Scientific Games, 128
self-government, 65–66
self-interest of legislators, 48–49
separation of powers, 91
Shaw, Leander, Jr., 58
Shockley, John, 71, 81–82, 89, 96–97
signature collection, 115–20; critiques
of, 148; methods for, 149; public financing of, 150; requirements, 149,
171, 178; valid signatures, 118, 119–
20. *See also* petition circulation
single-subject laws, 158, 178, 189
Sizemore, Bill, 116
Smith, Daniel, xii, 90, 94, 97; on courts,
98; on spending limits, 182; on tax
campaign backing, 152
Smith, Linda, 28
social problems, 36. *See also* issues
social reform, 36
soft money, 63, 77, 93
South Dakota, 2, 74
special interests. *See* interest groups
speech. *See* First Amendment
sponsors, x, 126–28, 130, 135–37, 160;

of ads, 159 legislatures as, 170. *See
also* proponents
state spending limits, 28
states, variation among, 85
statutory initiatives, 2, 3, 41; legislative
amendment of, 61
Stern, Robert, 107, 151, 167, 178
Stimson, Henry, 35
Storris, Zeeger and Mesker, 102
Strubble Opel Donovan, 102
subsidies, xiv, 182, 183–85, 187, 191,
192–94; of signature collection, 150
success rates, 10, 42; antiminority initiatives, 167, 168; campaign contributions' effect on, 84; citizen-sup-
ported initiatives, 155; economic
interest groups, 95–96; funding and,
63, 75–76, 96, 174, 192; interest
groups, 174; judging beforehand,
140; money's role in, 1, 81–86, 89, 96,
133, 153, 174, 193; narrow-material
interests, 10, 14–15, 18–19, 23–25,
63, 183; opponents, 82, 89, 96, 124,
133, 140, 153, 192; proponents, 82,
89; recent period, 23–25; "yes" and
"no" sides, 14
summaries, 110–11, 136, 189, 192
supermajority vote, 50
Switzerland, 164, 167, 170

tax limitations/reductions, 13, 29, 152;
California, 42, 176; Florida, 31; Massachusetts, 42
technology, 62, 65
Tennessee, 58
term limits, x, 7, 25; adoption of, 49; appearance on ballot, 23; California
initiative, 96; control of government
by, 49–50; misuse of, 49–50; opposition to, 37; as Populist movement, 38
three-strikes measures, 28
titles, 110–11, 136, 189, 192
Tornquist, Leroy, 158
transparency, 70
Trippi McMahon Squier, 102
Tupper, Sue, 26

Uelmen, Gerald F., 58
unions, 137
United We Stand America party, 110
Unruh, Jesse "Big Daddy," 88
Unz, Ron, 136

validators, 119–20
volunteers, 110, 111; for cost reduction, 152; costs associated with, 117–18; as petition circulators, 117; professionals' use of, 116
voter competence, 38, 63, 66–70, 156–61, 169, 171 disclosure as aid to, 70, 161; initiative drafting and, 144, 157–59, 192
voter cues, 139, 147, 157, 159; campaign spending as, 187; endorsements as, 160; limiting, 170; proponent/opponent identities as, 178. *See also* voter information sources
voter guides, xiv, 111–12, 136, 158, 161, 187; formats for, 188; improvement of, 188–89, 191–92
voter information sources, xiii, 63–64, 111–14, 117, 134; improvement of, 158, 191; information dissemination by, 159; and initiative consequences, 168–69; interest groups, 147; limiting, 170; preelection hearings, 174; types of, 154, 160. *See also* voter guides
voters: accountability of, 66; control over elected officials, 40; deception of, 131–33; decision-making shortcuts, 69–70, 81, 84, 147; informational demands on, xiii, 159–60, 171;

information available to, xiv, 81, 156–57; information needs, 39, 47, 67; issue assessment by, 29; lobbying of, 130–31, 134; "no" votes, 123, 177, 192–93; preferences, 167–68; rationality of, 159; risk aversion, 154, 192; turnout, 115; view of initiative process, 135–36, 181. *See also* voter competence; voter cues; voter information sources

Wade, Larry, 76, 83, 96, 153
Walker, Jimmy, 63
Walters, David, 141
Washington (state), 27, 28–29, 78; anti-qualification campaigns, 122; campaign spending, 129; Initiative 200, 80; lottery in, 128; petition circulation, 116, 117; views of initiative campaigns, 127; voter pamphlets, 111
Waters, M. Dane, 172
welfare, 108
Whitaker, Clem, 75
White, Joe Slade, 102
White, Penny, 58
Wilcox, Delos, 72–73, 181
Wilke, Fleury, 109
Wilson, James, 65
Wilson, Pete, 108, 113, 141
Wilson, Woodrow, 35, 36
women's suffrage, 6, 7, 51
worker's compensation, 17
Wyoming, 5, 15

Zimmerman, Bill, 108
Zisk, Betty, 82

About the Contributors

Shaun Bowler is a professor of political science at the University of California, Riverside, and has focused his research and analysis in the area of direct democracy. With Todd Donovan he published *Demanding Choices: Opinion Voting and Direct Democracy* (1998). He coedited, with Todd Donovan and Caroline Tolbert, *Citizens as Legislators: Direct Democracy in the United States* (1998) and, with D. M. Farrell, *Electoral Strategies and Political Marketing* (1992). He has also published several articles in academic journals on direct democracy, and on patterns and the nature of voting.

Bruce E. Cain is director of the Institute for Governmental Studies at the University of California, Berkeley. Professor Cain has held his current position since 1999, but has been with the Institute for Governmental Studies for the past ten years. He has been a professor of political science at the University of California, Berkeley, since 1989 and the Robson Professor of Political Science since 1995. His areas of interest include democratic theory, state and local government, representation in Anglo-American systems, electoral institutions, legislatures, parties, and normative issues related to representation, political reform, and regulation.

Todd Donovan is a professor of political science at Western Washington University and was recently a visiting lecturer at the University of Melbourne. His research interests include direct democracy, electoral systems and representation, voting behavior, subnational politics, and the political economy of local development. Together with Shaun Bowler and Caroline Tolbert, he published *Citizens as Legislators: Direct Democracy in the United States* (1998). He has also coauthored with Shaun Bowler numerous journal articles on direct democracy, and he and Bowler have recently published reports on the same topic for the Southwest Social Science Association and the Pacific Northwest Political Science Association.

Howard R. Ernst is assistant professor of political science at the U.S. Naval Academy in Annapolis Maryland. He received his Ph.D. from the Univer-

229

sity of Virginia's Woodrow Wilson School of Government and Foreign Affairs in 2000. He is the recipient of several academic fellowships, including the Governor's Fellowship, Bradley Fellowship, and the University of Virginia's Graduate School of Arts and Sciences Dissertation Fellowship. His dissertation work analyzed the effects of campaign expenditures on the initiative process in the United States.

Ron Faucheux is editor of *Campaigns and Elections,* a monthly magazine founded in 1980 that covers the nuts and bolts of political campaigning, and is a former political official, political candidate, campaign consultant, and analyst. He received a Ph.D. in political science from the University of New Orleans, where he founded and directed its nonprofit, nonpartisan Government Leadership Institute. He teaches at George Washington University and American University. Elected three times to the Louisiana House of Representatives, Faucheux also served as the state's secretary of commerce. As a former political media consultant, he handled 116 campaigns in 11 states.

Elisabeth R. Gerber is associate professor of political science at the University of California, San Diego. She gained her Ph.D. at the University of Michigan in 1991. Gerber's research is concerned with the policy consequences of electoral laws and other political institutions. She has written numerous papers on the use of initiatives and referendums in California and other states, and recently completed two books on the subject, *The Populist Paradox* (1999) and *Stealing the Initiative* (2001), the latter with Arthur Lupia, Matthew McCubbins, and D. Roderick Kiewiet.

Paul Grant entered the legal profession after working as an army interrogator-linguist, a chemical engineer, and, intermittently, a political activist. In 1984, while working on a nonpartisan statewide initiative effort to repeal monopoly restrictions in Colorado's transportation industry, he brought a First Amendment challenge to a Colorado statute that made it a felony to pay initiative petition circulators. This challenge resulted in the 1988 Supreme Court decision in *Meyer v. Grant* (486 U.S. 414), which struck down Colorado's law and established First Amendment protection of petitioning as core political speech. Grant also served as cocounsel on another First Amendment challenge, *Buckley v. American Constitutional Law Foundation,* 119 S. Ct. 636 (1999), of state regulations of the initiative and referendum process.

Mike Gravel served in the Alaska House of Representatives in 1963–1966, before being elected to serve in the U.S. Senate in 1968. During his twelve years in the Senate, Gravel was a staunch opponent of the use of nuclear power, and of nuclear testing under the seabed of the North Pacific. Among the many pieces of legislation he authored or coauthored was the Alaska Native Claims Settlement Act. Gravel also facilitated the publication of the Pentagon Papers in the *Senator Gravel Edition,* by Beacon Press, which occasioned litigation resulting in a landmark Supreme Court decision on the speech and debate clause of the U.S. Constitution. He served in the U.S. Army in 1951–1954 and later received a B.S. in economics at Columbia University. His business career has encompassed real estate, finance, and energy. He is president of Philadelphia II and Direct Democracy, nonprofit corporations dedicated to the establishment of direct democracy in the United States and worldwide (http://philadelphiatwo .org).

Douglas M. Guetzloe is president of Advantage Consultants, a research firm specializing in political consulting in the areas of public relations, governmental relations, and public opinion. He has taken to the airwaves in this field, hosting the "Guetzloe Report" on 740 WWNZ News in Orlando, Florida. In the past he has been a public relations representative for the Florida Fruit and Vegetable Association; the Florida Medical Association; the Watson Group; the National Mortgage Investors Institute; the Florida Veterinary Medical Association; Organized Fishermen of Florida; the Attorney's Bar Association; Save Our State; The Open University; and most recently, Motorola.

Paul Jacob is the national director of U.S. Term Limits, the largest and most active term-limits advocacy group in the nation. Under Jacob's leadership, U.S. Term Limits has been involved in more than fifty state initiative campaigns as well as numerous local initiatives. Jacob is a frequent guest on talk radio and television and has written numerous articles on term limits, the initiative process, and issues relating to citizen control of government. "Common Sense," a weekly radio commentary series written and produced by Jacob, is heard on 267 stations in 48 states. His weekly column, "No Uncertain Terms," runs in over one hundred daily and weekly newspapers.

Gale Kaufman has a well-earned reputation as one of the leading Democratic campaign consultants in California and is known for her expertise in the strategy and structure of political campaigns. In 1987, after gaining extensive experience in grassroots organizing and the day-to-day operations of political campaigns, Kaufman went full time with her passion and opened Kaufman Campaign Consultants, a full-service Democratic campaign management firm. She has made frequent guest appearances on CNN's "Inside Politics," CNBC's "Hardball with Chris Matthews," and KVIE's "California Capitol Week" in Sacramento, California, and is a guest lecturer for numerous California associations and college government and political science classes.

Bruce A. Larson is assistant professor of political science at Fairleigh Dickinson University in Madison, New Jersey. He received his Ph.D. from the University of Virginia in 1998. Professor Larson has conducted extensive research on congressional campaign finance, and he is presently engaged in research on campaign finance ballot initiatives at the state level. Larson's latest work, coauthored with Larry Sabato, *The Party Has Just Begun* (2001), explores the dynamic role of political parties in American politics.

Arthur Lupia is professor of political science at the University of California, San Diego, and a member of the National Election Studies' Board of Overseers. He conducts research on how information and institutions affect policy and politics. He is coauthor of two books, *The Democratic Dilemma: Can Citizens Learn What They Need to Know?* (1998) and *Stealing the Initiative: How State Government Reacts to Direct Democracy* (2000), and was coeditor of *Elements of Reason: Cognition, Choice, and the Bounds of Rationality* (2000).

David McCuan was a visiting scholar at the University of California, Berkeley, in 1997–1998 and is presently a member of the adjunct faculty at the University of California, Riverside; he received his Ph.D. in 2000. He has published "Return to Oz: Campaign Spending, Political Consultants, and Direct Democracy," in *The Role of Political Consultants in Elections*, and he coauthored, with Shaun Bowler, Todd Donovan, and Ken Fernandez, "Grass Roots Democracy and California's Political Warriors: Campaign Professionals and the Initiative Process," in *Citizens as Legislators: Direct Democracy in the United States*, edited by Bowler, Donovan, and Caroline Tolbert.

Kenneth P. Miller is soon to receive his Ph.D. in political science from the University of California, Berkeley. He has authored numerous papers on the initiative process, such as "Judging Ballot Initiatives: A Unique Role for Courts," which was presented at the 2000 annual meeting of the Western Political Science Association. In the fall 2000 he lectured at the University of California, Berkeley, on American constitutional law. In addition to his academic study, Miller presently works for the law firm of Attorney, Morrison & Foerster, focusing on political regulation.

Kenneth Mulligan is a doctoral student of American politics at Ohio State University. His research on ballot propositions has been cited by national